D0286605

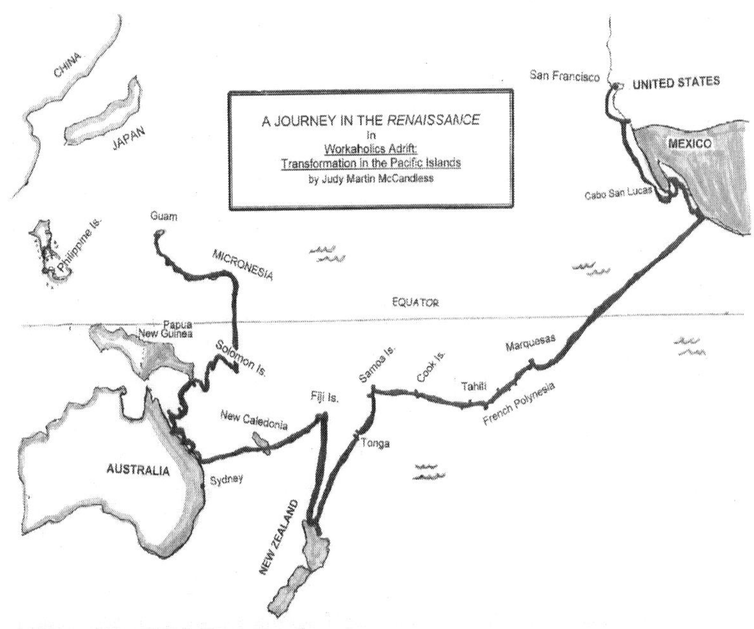

Pacific Ocean Crossing 1986-1991

WORKAHOLICS ADRIFT

TRANSFORMATION IN THE PACIFIC ISLANDS

JUDY MARTIN McCANDLESS

Copyright © by Judy Martin McCandless

All rights reserved. No part of this publication may be reproduced, distributed, or transmitted in any form or by any means, including photocopying, recording, or other electronic or mechanical methods, without the prior written permission of the author, except in the case of brief quotations embodied in critical reviews and certain other noncommercial uses permitted by copyright law. All images are the property of the author.

This is a true story conveyed to the best of my ability. To write this book I relied upon my personal journals, historical research, and called upon my own memory of events during this time of my life. I have changed the names of some individuals in this book and in some cases also modified identifying details in order to preserve anonymity. There are no composite characters or events in this book. Because the story took place over several years, I omitted people and events—but only when such omission had no impact on either the veracity or substance of the story.

Judy McCandless 2019

ISBN: 978-1-54397-228-3 (print)

ISBN: 978-1-54397-229-0 (ebook)

First Printing 2019

Printed in the United States of American

Land of the free and home of the brave

In Memoriam

JOHN P. McCANDLESS

My husband of forty years, my captain, and my best-ever friend

The purpose of life is to live it,
to taste experience to the utmost,
to reach out eagerly and without fear
for newer and richer experience. – *Eleanor Roosevelt*

One day you will wake up, and there won't be any more time to do the things you've always wanted to do. Do it now.
– *Paul Coelho*

CONTENTS

WORKAHOLICS ADRIFT

PART I

To Go or Not Go

Judy and John in San Francisco Bay

CHAPTER 1

Considering Mortality — A Trial Cruise

IT WAS THE SUDDEN DEATH OF THAT COWORKER THAT broke me away from the corporate tension in Silicon Valley.

I stood alone, a forty-year-old workaholic in the open cockpit of a thirty-three-foot sailboat. I inhaled the warm December breeze that propelled us along the west coast of Baja, Mexico, where the afternoon sun reflected diamonds across a royal-blue sea. Two white sails ran ahead, and another trailed us. The thrill of traveling again bubbled inside me like a shaken cola until an uncharacteristic, teen squeal escaped from my throat.

My husband, John, bounded up the steps from the cabin down below. Two years older and a half-foot taller than me, he wore a ball cap and a new beard. "Hey. What's up?" He scanned the horizon and squinted up at the clear sky.

"Nothing! I'm just so thrilled to be out here." I spread my arms to encompass the scene. "Travel time. This is awesome! I can't believe I scored a six-month leave of absence. Guess you don't know 'til you ask."

My smile flattened for a second with an ounce of concern about losing my paralegal job while away. The position represented years of night school and hard work for this over-achiever.

"I'm glad you did it." John gave me a quick hug and turned to check the electric autopilot. Two months before our departure, he had quit his job as manufacturer's rep to escape the stress of straight-commission sales. "With this nice breeze we should make our goal of Christmas in Cabo."

I circled his neck with my arms. "Well, your passion for this trip is what got us out here, together. I love it."

We had both grown up sailing open boats but recently upgraded to this spacious yacht for an extended work-break in the tropics. This trip constituted our first full foray into the open ocean, and during the past six weeks, we had gained confidence sailing this boat on overnight hops down the coast from San Francisco Bay.

An hour later, a voice called our boat name on the VHF marine radio: "*Renaissance, Renaissance*. Come in."

Inside the cabin, I keyed the mic and acknowledged the woman in the boat behind us. We chatted, and I ended with, "...this cruise is more comfortable than I expected."

My new friend began a reply, but a sharp voice intruded from the lead boat. "Break! Break! Bad squall. Just hit us. Watch out!"

With a blunt, "Standing by," I jammed the mic into its cradle and hurried to the cockpit where John was lounging. "There's a squall ahead," I said. I turned forward and stood tall. "Wow! Look at that!" He rose and stood beside me.

A dirty-green curtain obscured part of the horizon a short distance away. We stared in wonder until a fist of wind hit the side of our eight-ton boat and slapped her over like a toy. Her fifty-foot mast almost smacked the water. Unable to check my fall, I crashed down onto the cockpit bench. Now above me, John stood on the other bench with legs braced, clutching the heavy, brass, cabin-top winch. I stretched to release the mainsail, and the boat veered into the wind to right herself. John held his pose and stared ahead.

I yelled at him, “Let’s get some canvas down!” Both the mainsail and the massive genoa jib thrashed in the wind. The steel rigging that supported the mast shook at the outrage. John still didn’t move. “Hey!” I yelled at him. “Hey!

After a long minute, he scrambled on deck to lash the bottom of the mainsail to the boom as I lowered it. Diagonal rain pelted us. The shortened sail filled, and we set off into the rising wind.

Inside the cabin, we replaced wet clothes and pulled on safety harnesses over foul-weather gear. “Nothing in any forecast. Where did this come from?” I asked and shook my head in dismay. Back in the cockpit, I estimated that visibility had dropped to half a mile. With no way to escape or anticipate a threat, I hugged myself to suppress a whimper.

On the nautical chart, John measured from our last position and yelled up his dead reckoning, “We’re about ten miles offshore.”

I feared that the wind and growing waves would push us back toward the rocky coast, but it was impossible to judge our movement. We watched and waited. When the boat failed to make forward progress against the mounting seas, we rigged her to make short tacks back and forth across the direction of the wind. This allowed her to quarter the waves and avoid head-on smashes. Even so, she suffered many sucker punches that slammed her head aside, sea spittle flying.

By late afternoon the seas had built to about twenty feet, and the hazy light faded to black. No sight of land. The wind increased to a howling gale. Broken seas crashed under us. The belt-driven autopilot could not hold course, so John locked down the wheel.

Fear crept in, but I didn’t want to distract John with any emotion. I trusted him. I gripped the rail and searched for a horizon. I tried to think what I could do.

To further reduce our profile to the wind, John tried to drop the forty-foot-tall jib down the forestay onto the deck. But the wind blew it back up the rigging, and its control lines cracked toward us like giant white whips. He soon tamed them, but a salty gust blew the billowed sail over the rail, where it filled with water and created a dangerous drag. *Oh, shit!*

"There's too much pressure on the rudder already. I've gotta secure that jib," John yelled over the din. The boat lifted under us, and we both braced for a crashing wave nearby.

"Right," I yelled back, holding on and trying to stay focused. Strong and athletic, John could handle the task.

I scuttled down below to turn on the deck lights and rushed back to his side. He pocketed a fistful of writhing sail ties, zipped tight his slicker, and cinched its hood around his baseball cap. He clipped a nylon tether to the D-rings of his safety harness and attached the other end to a jackline affixed to the deck. He paused.

"Keep her head into the wind—at all costs!" he called out. The locked wheel still held us into the wind, and we both knew I had insufficient strength to hold the wheel by myself in the churning sea. Ahead of him, the bow rose to meet a twenty-five-foot wave. I opened my mouth, but nothing came out. I clutched the rail by the steering wheel to hold myself upright, and a gusher washed down the deck.

Crouched against the wind, John lunged from the safety of the open cockpit and dragged his tether forward on the hobby-horsing deck. He dropped to his knees and leaned his head and shoulder over the side to haul the wet sail back on deck. In slow motion, he dragged up one section, bound it to the lifeline, and then reached over for another. He crawled farther forward to begin unclipping the sail from the rigging. The boat dropped into a watery trough and he became airborne.

I drew a long breath in through my teeth. Every moment he stayed on that deck exposed him to extreme risk of injury.

Another sudden lurch knocked him on his butt. He braced his legs against the one-inch, toe rail to keep from sliding while seawater swept the deck. *Oh, God. No.* I strained toward him against my own harness. I could do nothing. The roar of the gale barred any contact between us. I growled in frustration and waited.

After resting a few beats, John rose on one knee to coil the slimy rope that held the sail. He pushed it across the deck, yanked open the forward hatch, and forced the coils through the opening. Swirling water from smashed waves followed the load into the cabin before the hatch cover slammed down on the rope still connected to the sail. He crawled back to the rail and released his slipknots. Slowly, he dragged unwieldy canvas across the deck, reopened the hatch, and stuffed it inside with the long jabs of a boxer. The hatch slammed, and he sat down hard on it. I dove inside the cabin to lock it from below.

Back in the cockpit, I watched John stagger on the swaying deck with arms forward like Frankenstein's monster. Suddenly the boat dropped like a free-falling elevator, and I lost him. *Oh my God! Is he overboard?* I stretched to peer over the cabin top but couldn't spot him. Hand over hand I pulled my way across the width of the cabin to look down the starboard deck, my heart racing. There in a shadow he lay still, curled up with safety tether in hand.

"You Ok?" I yelled into the wind. "JOHN!" *Could he hear me?* I tensed to curb a rising panic. "HEY!" I screamed. *Did he hit his head?* I glanced all around.

After two, long minutes, he lifted his right arm with an outstretched index finger to say, give me a minute. I exhaled and extended my arm. *I can't reach him!* I searched around us for other threats. I turned back, willing him to move. He began inching toward me on hands and knees. I reached to grab him, but he slid onto the cockpit seat beside me.

He slumped, trembling.

Signs of shock? "Are you hurt?"

He shook his head, no.

"You're safe now," I said and held him with both arms.

I looked back to assure myself that the wheel was still locked on course. No sign of other boats. Blackness all around us.

"You gotta rest. Let's get you below," I said.

He offered no resistance. I unclipped our tethers and guided his shaky legs down into the cabin. He gripped the overhead rail while I pulled off his rain gear and wet clothes. I wrapped him naked in a blanket and, with help of the boat's deep roll, pushed him into the sea bunk. I paused for a deep breath. Across the slanted floor, a flashlight and a loose can of peaches rolled out of reach. Ignoring them, I timed my dive across the cabin for a handhold and switched off the deck lights to conserve battery power.

Sweat trickled down my back. *What should I do—can I do?* I clung to the galley sink and looked back at him for guidance, but his eyes were closed.

I had to tend the wheel, keep us into the wind, so that we didn't get sideways and roll. I turned and struggled hand over hand back toward the doorway. I re-attached a cockpit tether to my safety vest and mounted the steps into the cockpit.

Outside in the maelstrom, I braced my body against the cabin and inserted stiff slats into a track in the threshold to keep maverick seas from bursting the entry door. It took both hands to counter the boat's irregular motion and several tugs at the heavy hatch cover to get it closed.

On my toes, I searched for a horizon, any hint of land or lights, but all was black.

Salty spray slapped the side of my face; some ran inside my jacket. Mountainous seas lifted the floor under my feet, buckling my knees. I was glad I couldn't see their size. Their foaming crests, reflected in our emergency strobe atop our mast, passed a few feet from my shoulder. The boat's hull deflected water into the cockpit, but the drains kept up.

My legs soon shook with fear and the strain of bracing my body. I sat and searched my mind for pages I had read on storm tactics. The motion grew so violent I feared my legs and clutched fingers would not hold me, so I wrapped a heavy line twice around my chest and over the stout, brass winch. This allowed me to relax most muscles and keep my seat. *How long would the locked wheel and rudder hold us into this surging flood without breaking free?* I sagged and considered—with a surprising lack of emotion—the prospect of dying in the storm. I had no friends and nothing meaningful in my life after twenty years of building a career, except a nice title, Contract Administrator, SRI International. The storm would take John too, so who would care? *Oh, well, so what.*

Down below, the marine radio squawked, but there was no time for talk. All boats must tend to themselves. In fact, having another boat nearby would be more dangerous. We could never survive a collision, which I was powerless to avoid. Ironically, the farther away from the rocky shore we stayed, the safer we were. Closed up against the ocean entering, this boat can survive, I told myself, even if the turbulent sea rolls us.

I strained to keep a lookout, trying to ignore the roar of the wind and the crashing waves. My wrist held no watch. Having begun in mid-afternoon, a simple squall should have blown itself out by now. *Damn.* I guessed it was about eight o'clock, but time dragged; I could be off by an hour or more. I doubted my strength to stand up and attend to another task, even to pull a life preserver from under the opposite bench. And reaching the life raft on deck would be like climbing Everest from where I sat. I let warm pee run down my leg. Fight or flight? *Impossible.*

The locked rudder groaned against the pressure of tons of swirling water, and the remaining handkerchief sail kept us from wallowing. My mind rejected the playing of "what-if" scenes; and once it accepted that I could do no more, it blurred with the physical fatigue of my quivering body. My adrenalin evaporated, exhaustion took hold, and I nodded off.

A massive surge jerked me awake and seemed to twist the entire boat like wringing out a towel. The storm roared like an aircraft engine, but my mind came to accept it. When my eyes registered nothing ahead or behind, my head fell to my chest, and I dozed again like a rag doll against the ropes.

Over the din, my brain stem detected a soft "clang, clap, clang," and I jerked awake imagining a nearby ship. Like trying to counteract the force of a carnival ride, I lifted my heavy head and looked up. The radio antenna atop the mast hung loose below its bracket. I watched metal hit metal and slumped to sleep.

Dragged again into consciousness by a clatter, I opened my eyelids to see John materialize from the barricaded cabin. He passed a hand over his bald crown and peered around. He was OK. The darkness blurred detail, but now I could see farther beyond the boat. The wind seemed less strong, but the seas remained immense.

I unwound the ropes that held me into the bench and staggered two steps into his arms. Relief poured out of me in runny tears.

Through a tense yawn, he said, "It's 1:00 A.M."

My long night of desolation ended. I bumped down into the cabin, shed my coat, and crawled into the sea bunk.

When I awoke at dawn, we sailed into Baja's Magdalena Bay to regroup as the storm subsided. With no sign of the boats we traveled with, we anchored near two unfamiliar ones in the remote bay. That morning we remained shaken, subdued, in awe of nature. We ate, slept, and put right our minimal damage. "This boat is a fortress," I said.

In the afternoon, we shared our experience with crews on the other boats drawing strength from their company like bruised warriors after a battle. Six of us sat together for supper around the marine radio and listened to sketchy reports that foretold the tragedy to be found at our next stop.

CHAPTER 2

A Taste of a Different Life — Tropical Mexico

FOUR DAYS AFTER THE STORM, WE ROUNDED THE TIP OF the Baja peninsula to enter the exposed bay at Cabo San Lucas. Grey clouds cast gloom upon the land and now a quiet sea. Sailboat masts lay scattered across the beach like downed pins in a bowling alley. Their owners, people like us, had saved money for years and spent months preparing these vessels for safety and comfort to carry them long distances to fulfill their dream of traveling under sail. I recalled my countless days in the dusty boatyard sanding, painting and sewing cushions; while John installed electronics, pumps, and refrigeration.

We moved closer and took turns looking through binoculars. "Those boats are a total loss," said John—his last word choked with emotion. My eyes stung, and I wept for the victims.

We anchored and tuned to the cruisers' radio network which was coordinating assistance to crews of the twenty-eight sailboats beached in the unexpected storm. The lost boats, half of them uninsured, had anchored too close to the shore; as the storm developed, the surf line widened to engulf them. Smashed together and trounced by waves, they succumbed and lay smothered in wet sand. Because most crews were ashore that afternoon enjoying the resort town, no one sustained serious injury—at least from physical wounds.

Our *Renaissance* was insured. However, our trip might also have also ended here had John not insisted before the storm that we stop to help another boat with a rudder repair—a two-day delay I had resented. That self-centered view had carried me into adulthood chasing a career. I needed a new perspective, and my re-education as a compassionate human began here.

Ashore we joined survivors and other latecomers with food to share hoping to help victims salvage their boats—or at least a few things of value. For four days, we trudged a beach scattered with soggy confetti—the contents and pieces of demolished vessels. Beside one broken hull, a shirtless man sat digging sand out of the boat's interior with his hands.

"Can I help you there?" John said to him.

The sailor looked up and blinked red eyes; he muffled a cough and turned his head, overwhelmed. While we waited for him to find words, I pulled a family photo from the sand and set it near him. He shrugged with speechless lips quivering and dismissed us with an upward wave of his arm.

We walked on. At another smashed-up boat, we found a couple we knew in California. They accepted my cheese sandwiches but lapsed into depressed silence, unable to speak about their experience.

My discomfort grew because neither John nor I brought much experience in consoling other people. Back home in business, we spent our time outmaneuvering competitors. With few local friends and our families on the east coast, we had had little need for empathy. The local situation worsened when authorities decreed that boat owners could not leave Mexico until they paid for removal of their wreckage. The oncoming tourist season forced a hasty deadline for victims to sort valuables and arrange cleanup before bulldozers arrived to bury the remains. Only four of the boats returned to the sea.

One night after supper on board, I sat with John watching the light fade on a beach that betrayed little of the storm's destruction. Threatening clouds and low barometer readings added tension to the grave mood of the place. The Cabo scene had become too sad to endure, especially with the approach of Christmas. With no further way to help, survivor's guilt arrived. I looked down at my hands and said: "This is crazy—risking career, injury and savings for a trip like this. How did I ever think we could do it?"

The travel idea had surfaced in the previous year after John dragged in from work looking despondent. He had been moody for some months since his 40th birthday and worried about developing Alzheimer's disease like his father. However, this bout appeared more serious.

At my question, he sighed and loosened his necktie. "One of the guys in Distribution dropped dead last night. Heart attack. Age 42." He shook his head and pulled off his jacket.

Too startled to respond, I waited.

He swung around to face me. "That's me next year, Judy! I can't live with this stress and competition for another twenty-five years 'til retirement. There's got to be another way, someplace where life is simpler."

That jolt caused us to take a hard look at our lives. At the time, we exhibited all the symbols of success: college degrees, lucrative careers, five years married, sports cars and a luxury townhouse. Yet it didn't feel like success. Long work hours left no time for other physical, cultural, or spiritual activities. With a lifestyle built on credit, we added payments for tax shelters and disability insurance to prevent financial collapse. A long cruise in Mexico sounded perfect.

I looked back at the beach. John took my hand. "Hey. We did do it. We are doing it. We outlasted that freak storm, and we can enjoy cruising here." I smiled at him, his enduring optimism and spontaneity. Considering all our preparations, it made no sense to return home now. I agreed to continue.

We turned and sailed south nonstop for three days across the Sea of Cortez to the mainland. Alone on the evening watch, I recalled that soon after we left San Francisco and tried overnight sailing, John realized that he had to sleep sometime and give up control of the boat. I smiled. He was learning to trust me—a significant milestone in our relationship, which also bolstered my confidence.

Offshore a day later, I challenged the course he had set for our autopilot. "You seem to assume that you are the captain of this ship," I said, hands on hips. "Since our sailing and navigating experience is about equal, I think that's just sexist. I should be the captain."

"Oh, really?" he said laughing at me. "What do you do if the engine quits? Or we need to haul down the sails?"

"Well, I'll concede your superior brawn and mechanical ability. But with the piloting course I took, I can read the intent of ships in the dark based on the lights they display." I looked away, searching for more reasons to bolster my claim. I turned back to him, my lips in a pout. "OK, you can be captain, but I'll be the admiral."

His brow wrinkled in thought, and then he put an arm around me. "You got it."

Before we sighted Puerto Vallarta, the taste of the sea and smell of fertile land merged in the wind that filled our sails. I stood at the helm and recalled how travel had exerted a magnetic attraction for me since age nine, when I pasted together a career book about becoming a flight attendant. The cultural differences we encountered in Mexico encouraged my curiosity and rekindled the fervor for travel. While single, I had traveled to Mexico and Europe, but this was John's first trip out of the U.S.

Mainland Mexico brought us the tropical beaches and relaxed living we expected and needed. The weather and our spirits improved as we walked Puerto Vallarta and connected with other "yachties" for local knowledge, gear advice, book swaps, and beach parties.

People who live aboard boats for extended periods call themselves "yachties." The benevolent way they organized help in Cabo typified them. This fellowship of sea wanderers evoked for me the pioneers of the old West, who relied on neighbors to mitigate hardships and share the simple joys of their remote lifestyle. Staying connected with them by VHS marine radio provided some security in that year (1982), when no one possessed a cellphone or GPS receiver.

We had come for some fun and found duty-free liquor a bargain. One day a group of us purchased the entire contents of a rickety beer truck that delivered to the beach. With no need to sober up for work the next day, we partied like students on spring break.

On December 24, sailboat crews gathered in a palm-bordered cove called Yelapa to share a Christmas party in the Latin tradition. Without a word, John took off in our dinghy at midday to help some guys locate an animal for the pig roast. The female half of a bickering yachtie couple swam over from their boat anchored nearby. I had been talking to her on the radio when the Cabo storm hit. I listened to her complaints about her mate and added a few about mine—while we finished off my bottle of dark rum.

After she swam away, John returned. I bitched at him for abandoning me on board. Without a response, he took the dish I made to share, some wine, and me to the beach, where other well-oiled yachties frolicked. Before the pig was cooked, I couldn't stand up. Disgusted with my drunkenness, he sent me back to the boat in a passing dinghy.

Christ's birthday brought torrential rain accompanied by hangover misery and John's disdainful silence.

We cruised further south close to the coast and reconciled. We consumed long hours exploring tropical inlets and snorkeling together in the warm, aqua sea. At each stop, my affable husband arranged outings with a diverse variety of yachties who also came for the inexpensive living in tropical Mexico. In addition to middle-aged or retired California sailors, we shared meals with young idealists who drifted hundreds of miles down the coast in kayaks and other vessels ill-equipped to challenge a rowdy sea. One lad used only an Exxon road map for navigation. Boats from the U.S. and Canada held a few children, several cats, even a golden retriever. One hand-wringing wife resented being away from her home full of conveniences and thus enjoyed little of the beauty and none of the culture. At the time, I should have checked a mirror. I was judging others harshly, and my attitude exemplified the sway-not-from-the-mission workaholism that confined me.

During our months in Mexico, we delighted in the simple lifestyle without a schedule, although the needs of our boat-home took priority. Each time we moved between anchorages, a mechanical or electrical problem arose. "I'll get it," John said and dragged out a toolbox. "It'll take me twenty minutes."

An hour later, after spurting profanity and covering himself in grease or caulking goop, he gave me the grin of a boy who had learned to tie his shoes. The new mechanical talents he demonstrated impressed me but unfortunately pressed me into the role of gopher. Our dinghy transported everything from the boat to beach and back. After completing maintenance chores, we splashed into the clear warm water. After lunch, I withdrew under our cockpit awning with a book and a beer.

I had traveled through life as a loner, then focused on building a career with no time for friends. In contrast, John needed to be with people, needed their approval, and often took the dinghy to visit nearby yachties. These contrasting traits gave us a beneficial break from too much togetherness, except when he forgot to return and stranded me. Free from buzzing phones, clocks and looming deadlines, we moved on a whim. Seagulls called. The horizon hosted brilliant sunsets and mystic displays of heat lightening after dark. We slowed further for encounters with whales, seals, and dolphin, watched pelicans dive, and snorkeled with colorful fish.

I came to enjoy interactions with Mexicans in beach towns where impromptu stick-and-thatch restaurants winked under lush foliage. On arrival in Mexico, we spoke no Spanish, but smiles and sign language sufficed while we learned local customs. Upon first encountering a *gringo* of John's sturdy, six-foot size, the Mexican men often stood with crossed arms in machismo attitude. However, they relaxed when he approached with a big smile saying, "*Hola*!" and a memorized Spanish phrase that meant "I am learning Spanish and seek your help to practice."

To become self-sufficient, we absorbed enough Spanish (John more than I) to negotiate supplies from local merchants. We walked under the hot sun with backpacks full of spare parts, food, and clothes for the local laundry ladies. We traded canned chili and beer with native fishermen who offered abalone, lobster and fish. They cleaned the catch for us with two quick swipes of a knife. The stress-free Mexicans had the right attitude with "*quizas manana*" (maybe tomorrow), but it could be frustrating for us hard-charging Americans when arranging services. We needed to practice patience and slow down even more. Often, when we walked the sandy trails, I lingered to engage nomadic pigs, braying burros, and curious kids. Feeling as fit and tan as a child of nature, I reveled in the active lifestyle with locals and yachties—far from fluorescent lights and a desk piled high with contracts to negotiate.

In February, with two-thirds of my leave time expended, I finally convinced my unemployed mate to depart Manzanillo Bay and return north.

In Mazatlán's humid open market, I stared in shock at a man who walked toward me with half of a bloody beef carcass slung over his white butcher coat. Behind his meat counter, a wall poster of the animal indicated the various cuts in Spanish. I requested a kilo of *hamburguesa*.

Back in Cabo San Lucas, with my authorized leave of absence expiring soon, I called my boss to confess a delay in my return—perhaps two months, dependent on weather. He was cordial but did not mention holding open my job—and I didn't dare ask. As I hung up the phone, guilt engulfed me at being so irresponsible. Over a four-year period, SRI had trained me as a contract administrator, paid for courses, and valued my work enough to approve this extended travel. I should have insisted we turn around sooner.

I lit a tax-free cigarette.

To reach home, we faced thirteen hundred miles of tedious sailing against contrary winds and coastal currents. Four weeks passed as we struggled north to the U.S border pounding through choppy sea swells and living for days at a thirty-degree angle. In the residual glow of our tropical interlude, we encouraged each other when we met for meals. After one stop to avoid squally weather, another month passed as we tacked nonstop up the California coast, alternating colder night watches alone on deck, while the other slept.

As we neared home, I obsessed about losing the position I worked so hard to achieve. Overdue home and boat mortgages, which we had prepaid for six months, pressured us. Our shallow bank balance necessitated a deep dip into savings, which rattled my security. Although confident, John needed time to find another professional sales job.

Nonetheless, Silicon Valley manifested a strong economy in 1983. My employer welcomed me back without fuss, and John landed another job as a manufacturers' rep within two weeks. Creditors agreed to wait for payment. The boat snuggled into a marina slip, and we spread out in our roomy townhouse. We declared the trial cruise a super success, especially since the months when we received no paycheck spanned two calendar years, so that our savings in income taxes those years covered our expenses during the eight-month trip.

CHAPTER 3

A Dream Diverted — Descent from Status Quo

OUTSIDE A WINDOWLESS, STEEL BUILDING, I CLOSED THE door on ten hours of cubicle clamor: ringing phones, pacing coworkers, proposal pricing, confrontational meetings, and rigorous recordkeeping. I drew in a breath of grey air and threw back my shoulders to shed an unwelcome weariness.

Six months after returning to my desk at SRI International, I moved for advancement to Westinghouse, a major defense contractor, also in Silicon Valley. I became the first woman and the youngest of twelve administrators assigned to monitor risk and contract compliance on federal projects. My team developed the interface for launching cruise missiles from U.S. Navy submarines. I approached the new position with excitement and pride—the career culmination of twenty years as an overachiever—primed for another steep learning curve. My peers were corporate attorneys, naval officers, and engineers like my father.

Dad expected his four kids to become college graduates. When I would ask his help with a homework problem, I fumed when he responded, "You go back there and think about it." So, I earned a B.S. degree in business, and as my career moved into management, I often heard his echo, "Hard work will bring you success." And it had.

Feeling the October chill of northern California, I shoved a briefcase under my left arm and tightened the belt of the mauve raincoat that covered my gabardine suit. A paved walkway led me alongside a twelve-foot, chain-link fence capped with rolls of barbed wire.

At the gatehouse, I presented my top-secret ID card to the uniformed guard. He nodded his acceptance. "Goodnight, Miss."

Behind the wheel of my sporty, red car, I adjusted my skirt, rotated my head to relieve neck stiffness, and settled into the seat. The paralegal, contract work suited my analytical bent, and my knowledge of military procurement regulations gave me influence in negotiations over people smarter than me. I coveted their respect, but... *how long can I keep up their pace?* I shook a cigarette from my second pack of the day, lit it, and started the engine. As I drove west, I smiled at the orange sunset and pictured sailboats gathering in Mexico for the season. I had begun to view my career not just as attaining higher positions, but as a source of money that provided independence and options.

At home, I found John, necktie askew, at the dining room table sorting through the mail. I exhaled through a smile. We had met at a ski resort over seven years ago and bonded immediately. We discovered we had grown up in the same harbor town in Massachusetts, though he attended a private prep school. He matched my delight in skiing and sailing. I still loved being the friend and partner of this charming, optimistic guy.

Soon after our "trial cruise," we decided to save for a longer cruise into the South Pacific. We would not wait twenty years for retirement but planned to get away in midlife, while physically able to gain the most from extended travel. My obsession with career had subsided, and I yearned again for the freedom of travel. I saw the trip further in the future after we compiled more savings, but he had entered an ASAP-mode.

I crossed the floor and kissed his cheek. He held up a color picture of a luxury, fifty-foot yacht. "Look at this one; she's a beauty," he said. "We need one like this—capable of sailing to Tahiti."

"Oh, just across the way to Tahiti?" I chuckled and leaned down to see it. "Hmm. Very nice!" I straightened. Can we afford it?" I opened the freezer for dinner options, heard no response, and mixed myself a tall rum and Coke.

As before, we both earned good money, but again endured lengthy workdays with little time for anything but bickering over bills. After supper each night, he stared into the blue light of the TV. I topped off my drink and edited contract proposals before weaving upstairs to bed alone, often crying myself to sleep. I loved my husband and my job. *Why these feelings of despair?*

A year after our return from Mexico, we sold that boat and ordered a new, thirty-five-foot sailboat (a full-keel, Baba 35 cutter rig) to fit our budget and long-distance needs. To participate in the launch, John's children from his previous marriage, son and daughter teens, arrived from the east coast for a week. I observed their joy as they re-connected with their dad, and he with them. I admired many women, like my mother, who excelled at raising children with love and patience. However, I knew from an early, disastrous babysitting job—where two young brats intimidated me with clamorous demands—that I wasn't able or willing to take on the long-term commitment required to grow them. Instead, I took my father's path and focused on career, hard work, and promotions.

We christened our new boat *Renaissance*, like her predecessor, to symbolize rebirth and a search for a more meaningful life. A few friends, co-workers and two cases of champagne helped us celebrate her launch. My dream of extended travel drew closer, I thought.

From age twenty-one, I relied on alcohol more and more to overcome painful shyness and inadequacies. I believe now that our Mexico cruise, which constituted one long party with no reason to control my drinking, set my condition ablaze. By age forty-two, I found it hard to deny that my excessive drinking caused problems. I drank to oblivion most nights, but somehow functioned at work. One Saturday, while we waited for a table at a popular restaurant, I passed out at the bar. John had to drag me down several stairs and dump me into his car like a sack of dirty laundry.

Our relationship broke down. During defensive tirades, I railed at him, calling him a chauvinist pig, a bastard, and worse. I attacked like a she-wolf protecting her pup (bottle). He withdrew, trying to keep the peace and avoid my verbal abuse. I insisted he was at fault. He even agreed to see a marriage counselor, where I criticized him for selfishness and not consulting me on boat expenditures (which was true). In a later session he blurted out, "The problem is, she drinks too much!" —something the counselor had apparently never considered, and I didn't want to hear.

I ended the counseling.

However, to crush any suspicion that I might be an alcoholic, I was careful never to be late for work and covered up hangover misery with raw determination. At lunch, one glass of wine with coworkers pushed my blood-alcohol level into the red zone, and I returned to work drunk. To regain control, I ate lunch at my desk with the excuse of a deadline to meet. When the team met for drinks on Friday nights, paranoia decided that others watched how fast I drank. I gave up all social contact to drink alone at my own pace. "Who needs them?" said me, the proud loner.

Soon after our boat launch, Westinghouse established an alcoholism awareness program. I snuck around the local library, which held, in the mid-1980s, few books on the subject. To dispense with this issue for good, I agreed to meet with the employee advocate. After a verbal test, she enrolled me in a company-paid, alcohol rehabilitation program before I could field a satisfactory excuse. I accepted a medical leave of absence and agreed to a twenty-eight-day hospital lockup. Back home, John looked as shocked as I felt at the sudden detour in his plans but voiced his support.

I arrived in the hospital ward drunk. I sat on the exam table with a puffy face, sweating Bacardi and knowing I was in deep trouble. *Busted! Damn, damn, damn! What a loser I am.* When the doctor probed below my ribs on the right side, I groaned with pain. "That liver is angry," he muttered.

In hopes of early escape, I tried to comply with the staff, get along with eleven other inmates, and look attentive at lectures. They explained the disease of alcoholism, which affects about ten percent of the population, and droned on about its progressive nature and its destructive impact on body, mind, work, and family. *Yeah, sure,* I thought, but an upstanding, mature, professional, woman like me did not resemble in any way, the slovenly, homeless, drunken man living under a bridge that I associated with this disgrace.

With Valium's assistance, I sweated and shook through days of detoxing, while the need for a drink screamed inside me. When I admitted this to a counselor, he gave me a small poster for my shared room that said, "ALCOHOLISM IS THE COMPULSION TO DRINK." I left his office flushed with anger and disgrace. My old insecurities—that I was never good enough, always feeling on the outside looking in—overwhelmed me. Throughout detox, I felt hopeless, helpless, and desperate to find a way out. During mandatory group therapy, I sat silent enumerating in my mind why I did not resemble those other disgusting boozers who described crashed cars, lost spouses, or jail time. The counselor said, "Focus on your similarities, not your differences!" That viewpoint made a significant difference in my future life.

In the second week, he thrust us into a public meeting of Alcoholics Anonymous at the hospital. I held my head down in shame. *Someone will recognize me.* I stole a look between my fingers. The regular members paid us little notice. Young and old, they arrived, hugged and joked with each other. *These can't be alcoholics, can they?*

On stage a man read something about AA from a ring binder. Sweat beaded on my brow. The reader sat down. A woman about my age in a silky, blue dress stepped to the podium. She looked out at fifty strangers and proclaimed, "I'm Mary, I'm an alcoholic, and this is my story."

I stifled a gasp. No way! She looks great. *She couldn't be one!* But I listened.

Back on the ward, I considered the downward spiral they said I faced. Under duress, I admitted to the group that I was powerless over alcohol. I said I'd get an AA sponsor and find a "Higher Power," which most of them called God. The latter represented another problem, because I had abandoned God twenty years previously, when prayers did not prevent my mom from dying of cancer at age fifty-two.

After four weeks of indoctrination, I returned home to John and to my job. Although glad to be back in my regular life, I stood naked and disoriented in an unstable world without the "friend" I relied on for two decades since leaving the east coast. That friend gave me courage, provided salve for lonely times and oppressive insecurities, but also celebrated good times with me.

At work, the compulsion to drink often blocked out all other thoughts. When overwhelmed, I escaped to a restroom stall and prayed for relief. Surprise—prayer seemed to help. Every night for three months, I attended AA meetings and tried to follow their program for recovery. John attended his prescribed family-support meetings. I stayed sober, even through year-end holiday celebrations.

Then I flushed it all.

One weekend in January as we worked on the boat, I discovered a stash of wine. Without hesitation, I started drinking, hiding it from John. The next day, remorse gripped me. Not perhaps by coincidence, I attended an AA meeting that night where they discussed the critical difference between admitting and accepting our powerlessness over alcohol. I had not accepted their diagnosis. That night, I drank again.

A couple of nights later, while I waited for John to return home from his meeting, I began writing in the journal they gave me in alcoholic rehab:

5:30- I'm drinking a mug-full of wine every 15 minutes. At first two sips, I felt asthma in my chest—anxiety?

6:30 John not home. I'm only drinking for myself. He may never come home — and if I keep drinking, I'll be drunk alone. How to face the challenges of work…I'm useless, hopeless now—bad news. He was so good to me this morning, and the program people so supportive with hugs. What is this need to drink?! What a waste. Where is he? Crashed on the freeway by a drunk? I'm drunk. Could I get to the hospital before he died? Noooo...

Such insanity proved, of course, what I still tried to deny. For two months, I drank, hid bottles, and suffered gut pain. Nonetheless, I continued meeting with recovering alcoholics wanting the serenity they demonstrated. Cynical but desperate, I watched and listened. Compared to me, most of them had more reasons to drink, but didn't. I was an alcoholic in denial.

Pressure at work mounted as our team entered the preproduction phase of the launch system contract. I stopped drinking for a few days and my head cleared; but on Saturday, March 12, 1985, I sat alone on the boat. Who will know? So, I drank. As I continued drinking, my journal demonstrates that I lost control, pushing toward blackout:

I hate to eat, even hungry, because it'll delay the booze effect. But damn, when you drink you pee a lot! Shit, it takes two hours to get drunk now. I've had 4 rums — shouldn't drive—so, good excuse not to go to a *meeting.*

My body shifted all systems to process the poison I downed, so I tolerated larger amounts of alcohol. However, the ability to drink more without passing out was *not* what I wanted. I only wanted to get high and happy.

As I continued writing that afternoon, I fancied I was conducting a research project to prove or disprove…something. As I drank, my hand scrawled bolder words. While cutting cheese, I sliced open my hand with the knife and watched, detached, as blood dripped on the page. What I journaled that night was a smear of self-disgust, rationalization and terrors, mixed with rehab slogans, hostility, and paranoia. My tirade progressed through dizziness, nausea, and semi-consciousness to the scarlet edge of hell before I blacked out.

I have kept that journal close for many years to remind me of the insanity I experienced. It described, I hope, my last drunk. I knew I must accept my condition and learn to live sober. I returned to daily AA meetings. I stuck close to the "winners," who took no chances with their sobriety. I began to see some hope for me.

Sober again for thirty consecutive days, but often fighting the desire to drink, I sat with John one night in a Chinese restaurant. At a table beside us, a drunken, belligerent woman swore, repeated herself, berated the waiter, and harangued her companions.

I shuddered and searched John's eyes. "Was I that bad?"

He looked down and said, "Worse." Then, he gave me a sunny smile.

"I'm sorry," I said. "What a mess I've made."

"No, hey," he said lifting my chin with a finger. "It's a disease...like diabetes. Not your fault."

Years later, John shared with me the devastation he felt when I entered rehab. His first instinct was to deny and fight it, too. It meant another failed marriage for him, and he grieved as his dream of sailing faded. Between sales calls, he sometimes pulled off the road and sobbed. While I stumbled in recovery, he told me he squirmed, but followed directions from his support group and did not upbraid me.

Our interaction remained stilted, tense, and distant. I missed our intimacy and wanted him back. Regression meant ruination, losing everything: husband, career, and the opportunity to travel.

Overriding my own pride, I accepted help from an AA sponsor and made ninety consecutive days of meetings sober (again). I prayed to my personal Higher Power to keep me sober. I often repeated the *Serenity Prayer*: "God grant me the serenity to accept the things I cannot change, the courage to change the things I can, and the wisdom to know the difference."

Self-pity receded when I began to share my roller-coaster emotions at meetings, where we all laughed through tears over our common baggage. Outside of AA meetings, I remained socially isolated, anxious about how to act around "normal" people. At work, I exhibited a strictly-business attitude with co-workers. I trembled at the thought of someone learning my awful secret, but it remained hidden. I held onto my job and six months after my last drink, participated in successful team negotiations in Washington, D.C. for full-scale production of the capsule launch system.

My sober months accumulated along with our savings. I gained more hope I could recover. My devoted husband renewed his promise of support, revived his own optimism, and moved ahead with the sailing trip preparations. Our plans relied upon my sobriety; but inside, I held little confidence that I could stay sober for an extended cruise without my sponsor and my meetings.

While planning our escape, we read articles by yachties living in exotic ports, studied seamanship, and learned celestial navigation from an often-inebriated, U.S. Navy retiree. Learning to handle the new boat with John thrilled me, even in squally weather. Our plan called for a two-year trip across the Pacific. The mortgage on the boat required that we maintain insurance, but the cost of insurance to travel offshore was prohibitive, so we had to pay off the boat loan.

After a year of sobriety, I agreed to list for sale our lovely townhouse. The remarkable real estate market in 1986 produced a full-price offer within three days, but the sudden reality of being homeless shook my fragile sense of security.

At our yard sale, I turned to watch a stranger carry away a cherished focal point from my single days—an area rug with a geometric design rendered in burgundy, brown, and gold. John had sold it for a paltry ten dollars. I ran up and raged at him. "I love that rug! It's special. How could you—?"

"Hey. You agreed," he said. "We can't keep all this junk."

"That's not junk!" I said, as the enormity of this project hit me.

With fists clenched at my sides, I stomped back into the garage, angry but conflicted. After a few deep breaths, I knew he was right. I chose travel over career and material goods in order to go now, rather than stay in place for a black-and-white future.

And I didn't drink over it.

CHAPTER 4

A New Beginning — A Different Mexico

RAYS OF SUN STREAMED THROUGH THE BRASS PORTHOLE and woke me. It was departure day. The day we had dreamed of, saved for, studied for, and changed our lives for, had finally arrived.

Over three years had passed since we returned from the trial cruise in Mexico. Excitement swelled inside me. I squealed and bounced to the edge of our double bunk. John turned over with a groan, probably regretting that last celebratory beer with a marina neighbor the prior night. At 46, he had outlived his co-worker. I was 44 and sober. Nineteen months had passed since my last drink, although I felt far from victorious over alcohol.

Our planning and preparation included many difficult decisions. An uninsured boat meant risking a $100,000 investment and necessitated a crucial reliance on each other (and upgraded gear) to keep her safe. In the prior three weeks, we had abandoned our careers, sold cars, vacated our small apartment, and closed out phone, loan, and insurance accounts.

I hit the floor and pulled on an old "Senor Frog" T-shirt and a pair of faded blue jeans. Above the navigation desk, I spied the October 1986 calendar with "25" circled in red ink. "Yahoo," I cried.

I climbed into the cockpit, closed my eyes to the new sun, spread my arms, and breathed in the warm taste of freedom. My mind ran ahead as I contemplated a life of travel with my lover, living self-contained with unlimited time to discover new places by boat.

When John joined me outside that morning, he was all business. He pointed at a tarp-covered pile on the dock. "You'd better get the rest of those canned goods put away." Then he nodded toward the marina office. "I told them we'd be out of here by noon."

"Yeah, yeah, I know," I said. "Relax. That's the last schedule we have to meet." I hugged his stiff body. This was not my ever-cheerful optimist. His attitude probably reflected the anxiety about the final break from land life. I felt it too.

While I stashed away the final load of provisions and first-aid supplies, John brought aboard boxes of tools and spare parts. We negotiated over the few remaining storage spaces down below.

Three hours later, I attempted to imitate a trumpet salute before I untied the lines that bound us to California, but he brushed me aside. "Come on, Judy. Get aboard. Let's go!"

Renaissance slipped past rows of yachts abandoned by working owners with other priorities. The mid-afternoon sun cast a golden glow on the familiar banks of the South Bay Channel. After some animated chatter about our trip expectations, we sat quietly with our own thoughts. My dominant left brain worried about what detail we might have forgotten: last paychecks deposited, power of attorney to my brother Don, credit cards paid off, instructions for our tax preparer. I looked up to see John at the wheel, relaxed now with a goofy grin on his face. A salt-and-pepper stubble, begun the day he quit work, made him look quite rakish.

I stepped behind him and rubbed his Buddha belly. "That's for luck and a *bon voyage*."

After an over-night stop inside San Francisco Bay, we set off early. We sailed in silent awe under the Golden Gate Bridge, an impressive symbol of a journey initiated. Our course lead south between the shore and the main shipping lane from the busy port of San Francisco. In the ship's log, I began recording the data vital to our safe navigation: compass heading, speed, distance run and weather conditions. Along the coast, fog lay in patches, allowing occasional glimpses of grand estates high on the cliffs. I pictured the townhouse we had exchanged for a vessel smaller than a school bus; but now I wasn't fighting six lanes of traffic on Highway 101. To accomplish a good shakedown cruise, we had decided to sail about 500 miles nonstop to San Diego. One could drive there in seven hours but sailing at our average speed of five knots (5.75 miles per hour), it could take us four days.

Soon the sun's light dimmed, the fog closed in, and the coast disappeared. Where any danger of collision lurks, that particular F-word arouses fear. Radar equipment had exceeded our budget.

After I cleared away supper, John identified a navigational buoy by the number of its flashes and updated our position on the maritime chart. "Let's start the watch schedule now," he said, setting the autopilot. "I'll take the first four hours and wake you at midnight."

"I hate this fog," I said. "Shouldn't we both keep a watch for other boats?"

"Don't worry, we are well inside of the shipping lanes."

"But we can't see the shore either. Maybe the current will sweep us in and —"

"No. I know right where we are. Get some sleep so you can relieve me later."

With a last look around, I relented, glad for a break, climbed below, and crawled under the comforter in the sea berth. I stared up at the Plexiglas hatch. I couldn't sleep, although I knew I must. I closed my eyes and imagined a huge container ship appearing silently out of the fog to ram us. Our satellite navigator ("Sat Nav"), a precursor to GPS, might find our position; but it was accurate only to within five miles—an error that could put us on the rocks. I turned over but pictured the California Current pushing us off course. *He seems confident, but how could we know…?*

A shaking on my shoulder switched on the metabolism to my stiff muscles. "It's midnight. Your watch," John said, his smiling face red with the evening chill.

"Hmm. Ooooh kay." I sat on the edge of the bunk and bit my lip. "What's happening?"

"Nice sailing, but I'd like some more wind. Sea is calm." He looked back at me. "No ships around." He peeled off his watch cap and safety harness. After our trial cruise experience, we always wore a harness while standing watch alone, choosing to remain attached to the boat instead of floating away in a bulky life jacket with no one aware you are missing.

"I just got a Sat Nav fix and adjusted course to compensate for our drift." He bent over the chart and marked our position with a pencil. "Looks like we've made good about seventy miles from San Fran. We're actually being pushed out a bit… but the fog's still with us."

Damn. "OK. I got this," I said, resigned to follow through and needing to qualify as an equal partner. When I was a kid, I learned to take my lumps without complaint, so I could play baseball with the boys, instead of spending hours in prissy fantasies with other girls and their dolls.

I pulled on my ski parka and harness, retrieved my hat, and stepped into the open cockpit behind the wheel. The air smelled of seaweed. The hazy charcoal grey of both sea and sky allowed little hint of where they joined. The only sound came from the grinding of the cog and belt of the autopilot as it moved the wheel to maintain course. Ahead, behind, I strained to pick out a shape, a reflection, or even a shadow. The only rest for my eyes (or my soul) came from the dim glow of the compass light, tinted red to preserve night vision.

Oh, crap, I don't like this situation. I clenched my teeth, lit a cigarette, and ducked below to mix a tall mug of instant coffee.

The dark hours of standing watch dragged along in this uncomfortable state of being, neither able to control my environment, nor escape it. The fog settled close. If I spotted a ship approaching, I doubted I'd have the time or speed to evade it.

Perhaps unable to relax either, John surprised me on deck at 3:30 A.M., thirty minutes early. I hugged him with relief, so grateful for his company and his self-assurance. During his watch, I slept better, even with the drone of the engine. By 8:00 A.M., the fearsome fog departed, leaving an overcast sky.

During our second night at sea, a fresh wind banished the clouds uncovering a brilliant ceiling of stars. Our speed increased to an impressive six knots. At dawn, I looked toward the coast and smiled, picturing my former colleagues arriving at their desks stacked with green project files awaiting negotiation. I imagined the din of tense, one-sided phone conversations echoing across two dozen cubicles. I did not miss that stress but hoped I had made a good trade putting my life in the hands of my captain, a small boat, and the whims of nature.

At dawn after the third night, we entered San Diego Bay, anchored, and slept entwined until noon. That afternoon a couple from a nearby boat came by to welcome us. With mutual interests and safety concerns, yachties were keen to meet and share information in this popular jumping-off spot. Later, at a beach party, we met others, traded paperbacks, and found a solution to a problem with our depth sounder.

Like before, John spent hours visiting other yachtie boats; but I hung back, this time ashamed to recall my previous drunkenness here yet uncomfortable socializing without alcohol. Mexico would be very different for me this time. I hoped I could manage it.

In San Diego, I attended many AA meetings, where I shared my story and members allayed my concerns about staying sober in isolated areas ahead. One meeting discussion centered on fear. "Fear and worry arise from trying to control things we can't," said one member. "Don't forget, 'Let go and let God.'"

Three weeks flew by while I obsessed about provisions that I thought we could never live without or find outside the country—like diet root beer. On the day before departure from the USA, we celebrated our tenth wedding anniversary with brunch in the gilded ballroom of the Hotel Del Coronado. Later, I placed phone calls to my family. I left unsaid my thought that we could sink somewhere in the vast Pacific and be lost without a whimper.

The next day, *Renaissance* crossed into Mexico propelled by a warm breeze. We rolled downwind on a soft sea swell for three sunny days. With the comfort of occasional lights on shore and a warm breeze, my night watches were enchanting. Stars popped out of a black velvet sky, plankton fluoresced in our wake, and, at dawn, dolphins clicked alongside our hull.

In Turtle Bay, we walked the dusty town together and John (who had studied Spanish at home) befriended a ten-year-old boy named Jesus, who said he could get us lobster. He waived us to *mi casa*, where his parents and two sisters welcomed us into their house like royalty. The rough cinder-block construction of the two-room home belied the tidy interior furnished with an overstuffed couch and a broad TV screen. Pictures of the Madonna and the crucified Christ hung on the wall above red, glass-enclosed candles. The women busied themselves preparing us instant coffee. The family spoke no English, but with halting Spanish and sign language, we experienced a warm and unhurried visit.

I expected to find fresh or frozen lobster but saw no refrigerator. Instead, after preliminaries, Jesus brought forth lobster tails he prepared by pounding and salting—the traditional method used by ancient mariners. He indicated they would keep for one or two years without refrigeration.

"*Dos anos*?" I said, looking over at mama. She nodded with a proud smile. When John asked the price, Papa indicated that young Jesus was "The Man." John bargained the boy down from US $4.00 each until they settled at $2 for four tails. Before we departed, *mamasita* slipped us four more tails. Our cultural exchange that day left me with more delight than the seafood bargain.

Although the calendar affirmed December, the sun in the lower latitudes saw us shedding clothes as we traveled alongside the arid Baja Peninsula. At high noon one day some sixty miles off shore, we shut down the engine and drifted. We took turns swimming naked in royal-blue water that was 660 feet deep, splashing like naughty kids free from supervision. An adult contact sport followed before we moved on.

After lunch, John called up from the chart table, "We're coming up on Cabo Lazaras." I shuddered to recall the frightful night we spent near that rocky point four years earlier. For me, surviving that storm made life's other challenges minor-league.

We approached the beach at Cabo San Lucas in the gray of dawn and confronted more ghosts: the buried remains of twenty-eight boats that perished in the unseasonal storm. Skittish about anchoring in that unsheltered bay, we crowded into the inner harbor beside other transient vessels.

Dawn jolted me awake with a cacophony of crowing roosters, a Marine bugle, and the revving of a dozen charter-boat engines. I woke laughing at our new alarm clocks—a sign that our transition from corporate life was complete. I hoped to enjoy the resort this time, but my discomfort increased with each booze-soaked event that unfolded. A chili cook-off became a wild beer-drinking contest sponsored by hovering time-share hustlers. A boat with a drunken sailor barged into the quay hitting two boats and starting a bloody fight.

John often attended yachtie parties alone, because I feared that such situations might re-ignite my compulsion to drink. I walked to biweekly AA meetings in Cabo town to gain solace. One night, John invited "a couple of people" over to our boat, and nine showed up in our cockpit with bottles. He regaled them with an exaggerated story of our experience in the '82 Cabo storm. The noise and idiocy of the drinkers increased, as did my anxiety. I doubted I would drink again, but I experienced alarm like that of a beached fish. *What? I'm supposed to entertain these boozers in my home?* On the verge of panic, I crawled into the forepeak with my AA book. The visitors departed well after dinnertime. I tried to explain my discomfort to John and remind him of his promise to support my sobriety.

"I do, I do, but…" His arms fell in frustration. "These folks are fun and interesting. What's wrong with a little socializing?"

I mumbled something vague and turned away. Unable to fit in again, I became a new kind of outcast: a non-drinker.

I endured ten days of tension and intoned many serenity prayers there before John agreed to leave his comrades in Cabo. We motored eastward and anchored in a small bay bordered with palm trees and patch-work shacks. We arrived ashore to watch fishermen drag a ten-foot-long hammerhead shark onto the sand from their open boat. A group of villagers joined us to watch them butcher the terrifying monster and parcel out pieces to all of us. Their generosity delighted and surprised me. They accepted us, though we communicated with little more than a smile and a *gracias*. The experience oddly unsettled me. I could not remember conveying such generosity toward anyone with my time or resources.

Unlike my last (drunken) Mexican Christmas, I joined holiday festivities with John and the locals during a week in La Paz. Roaming Mariachi musicians played, costumed dancers whirled around the plaza, and wide-eyed children raced among extravagant decorations. With his improving Spanish, my sociable spouse helped draw me into the culture. I noted the love and joy displayed by the natives, and it inspired me to investigate their world in more depth.

Due to our struggle in the past storm, we had talked about taking crew on our planned Pacific Ocean crossing. This would allow us each eight hours' rest between watches around the clock and contribute an extra set of hands for an emergency in remote areas.

After the holiday, a prospective crewman named Dan swung his duffle bag aboard for a tryout with us. A shock of dark hair lifted the brim of a green baseball cap over his cherubic face. Of medium height, the thirty-year-old appeared strong, mild-mannered, even shy, and described backpacking in Baja after a seasonal layoff in the oil fields up north.

After two days of living together in La Paz, we set out with him across the Sea of Cortez to the mainland. John worked with Dan, who seemed willing and adept on board. On the first night of our three-day passage, I became seasick—a rare occurrence for me, probably due to a resolving ear infection. Nausea drained me; but instead of feeling grateful when Dan took over my watch duties, I felt like excess baggage, jealous of his time with John. However, on arrival in Puerto Vallarta, I had to agree that the trial was a success. We set a date to meet again further south, and Dan departed to continue his land travels. I celebrated regaining my privacy in our confined living space.

Our mode of travel allowed us the freedom to move when and where we chose, limited only by weather. During February and March, we wandered southeast among tropical beaches, bays and villages snorkeling daily in aqua waters. John attended to the greasy mechanical systems: engine, rigging, toilet, and propane stove; he enjoyed cursing at all of them. My chores involved laundry, defeating mildew, provisioning, and preparing meals. In Mexico, I never became accustomed to unwrapping a plucked chicken to find the bird's head and its feet complete with long toenails.

During these weeks, I became more comfortable as I interacted with the Mexican people, but I sensed a sadness about the place compared with our prior visit. Perhaps my sobriety and heightened sensitivity highlighted the change, but devaluation of the peso and an invasion of developers prompted some of the gloom in Puerto Vallarta. We benefited from a new marina, but a rare bank robbery unsettled everyone. I decided that progress seemed always to involve trade-offs. The uncrowded paradise of modest living had diminished with the "improvements." Restrictions abounded. Lovely coves we previously shared with a couple of boats now bristled with fifteen; LaPaz had 80. We found charming Chemela Bay forsaken, Yalapa polluted. A luxury resort hotel engulfed Tenacatita's bluff , and guards patrolled the beach below to keep out riff-raff like us. I missed the free and simple life we found here on our last trip. If we had not traveled here before and waited for retirement, we would have missed the best features of coastal Mexico.

One warm day as *Renaissance* trolled south of Banderas Bay, I brought out my little tackle box. My earlier attempts at fishing produced little more than seaweed. Worse, John stormed at me a time or two when I left the line unattended, and it became wrapped in the propeller.

Tan and shirtless he watched me sort through the box and chided me. "Ha. You don't know what you're doing with that stuff."

I ignored his taunt. "The local fishermen recommended this." I held up a pink and white feathered lure. "I know you like to eat fish. So, I'll get us a nice fresh one for dinner."

He checked the autopilot's course, shook his head, and returned to his spy novel.

Yachties call my fishing rig a "meat line." It is all business and no sport, requiring no pole. I attached a weight to the lure and clipped it to a thick fishing line connected to a heavy bungee cord. I tied the bungee end to a cleat and lowered the lure and its line over the side careful to avoid tangles. I attached an empty soda can with a string to the middle of the bungee. "Tell those fishies to wait until I get back," I said, and went below to make lemonade.

Three minutes later, I heard the tinny clank of the aluminum can and John's yell, "Fish! Fish!" Translation: Help! Get up here. Do something! The prospect of cleaning or even touching a fish made him queasy.

I leaped up the stairs and back to the cleat to find the line taut and jerky. "Yahoo. I got a fish." John put the engine in neutral to stop the prop. I grabbed a work glove and hand over hand wound in the line over a chunk of wood to keep it taut. The fish lurched left, right, then under the rubber dinghy we towed.

"Get the net. No, no, the gaff," I said, clutching the wood with both hands. "Aah ooh. Wow. He's big!"

When I worked him closer to the boat, we bent over the side as he splashed his resistance. I stared in awe of the iridescent shades of blue, green, and yellow along the flank of a three-foot mahi mahi. John conquered his fear enough to impale the young mahi with the gaff hook—without putting a hole in the boat. Then he left me hanging over the side with the fishing line in one hand and forty pounds of wriggling mass on the gaff in the other. Finally, he located a rubber mallet and delivered a messy *coup d'grace*.

The handsome fish turned dark green, then dusky grey and died in our blood-soaked cockpit. When I returned with a cutting board and fillet knife, John looked away. With no experience in cleaning fish either, I approached hesitantly. Believing I must first gut the fish, I slit the belly, coaxed the slimy entrails into a too-small bowl and flung most of them overboard. Next, I cut and tossed the head and tail. The fish slid in slime as my knife bumped along the backbone, cutting ragged fillets.

Feeling vindicated, I faced John. "Here we have all the ingredients of a B-grade movie: action, suspense, blood, and guts. And maybe even sex, after a gluttonous dinner."

He looked back at me with a pirate's leer and said, "I love to eat fish."

In March we celebrated my forty-fifth birthday in romantic style among the white turrets of the five-star Las Hadas Hotel in Manzanillo Bay—also a cruising crossroads. From there most boats returned north for the summer, one headed south for Panama, but only two of twenty boats shared our goal of Polynesia. We could still have abandoned the three-thousand-mile Pacific crossing, but by that time our desire to go on remained strong.

Throughout Mexico, I obsessed about planning provisions for our journey. I kept an inventory and logged usage of all supplies from toilet paper to bran flakes. Our nonstop crossing to the Marquesas Islands could take up to two months. We had no information about what food or fuel might be available on our arrival. With the usage data I collected since departure from San Francisco, I calculated the mix of supplies needed to sustain three people at sea for eight weeks.

Further south among white beaches and rocky cliffs, we entered a pear-shaped bay and headed for a bouquet of multicolored, seaside shacks at Zihuatanejo. There I found a good variety of supplies to supplement those I procured in Puerto Vallarta. But, best of all, I found an AA meeting where expats and locals helped me celebrate two years of living sober. Upon learning of my coming months of isolation on our Pacific transit, members contributed AA periodicals and a cassette tape to my sobriety-support collection.

We had expected our crewman to meet us there; but a friend of his arrived to tell us Dan lost his passport, had flown home, and would return within a week. We continued preparations for departure and resolved to go without him if necessary.

Two days before our D-day, he showed up. When I saw him standing on the pier, I sagged with misgivings about taking him. *Damn, we really don't know the guy, and he shows up now after we completed most of the heavy work.*

Once aboard, however, he agreed to the duties I listed for him, so John put him to work, which included winching John's 190 pounds up the mast to inspect the rigging. They also hauled water and fuel jugs from the shore by dinghy, hoisted them aboard, and topped our tanks.

On April 4, 1987, I awoke beside John in the forward V-berth as the warm Mexican sun reclaimed the sky. We both loved the cruising lifestyle, the freedom, and a rebirth from our stressful work life. I snuggled against John's back waking him. "This is the final exam," I said.

"Yup. We're ready." With a quick hug, he slid off the bunk, padded across the floor and stepped into the cockpit to greet the day, as usual, with a pee over the side. This ritual seemed to epitomize his liberation from the social confines of his past life.

As I emerged from the head, Dan appeared from behind the privacy curtain I had fashioned around his bunk in the salon area. "Good morning," I said brimming with cheer. "Departure day—finally."

He responded with a flat "OK" and gave me his back to pass between me and the table to join John in the cockpit. I shook my head, determined his grumpiness would not get me down. The gas stove flared, and I assembled coffee and cereal, listening to their talk.

"We need one more run ashore to fill the water jugs on deck," said John.

"I still have 2,000 pesos to spend on bread and stuff," I yelled up to him.

That was it. No more stores, service technicians, telephone contact, or local weather forecasts. We traveled without GPS, cell phone, internet or email—none of which were commercially available at the time.

In "Ziwah" I had reorganized our limited storage space and on every trip ashore, had filled my backpack with non-perishables. Nonetheless, I needed three strong backs for the final haul of frozen chicken, ground beef, and fresh produce.

On our return from town, I stuffed our freezer—the size of a shoe box—and the small refrigerator. I paused before I put away the last load of groceries to watch the guys haul aboard our dinghy. Streaks of sweat marked their T-shirts. They scraped grass and barnacles from the eight-foot rubber boat, deflated it, and strapped it on deck in front of our life-raft canister.

A few minutes later, John handed down to me the three-foot-long blades from the wind generator for storage. Then, as he removed its heavy steel body from the line that held it aloft, it slipped from his hands. I gasped. It crashed to the cockpit floor, and the motor separated from the housing, rendering the appliance inoperable. His face turned red, and he boiled over: stomping mad and slamming furious. Dan and I sat down on opposite sides of the cockpit and waited about five minutes for his tantrum to subside—and a decision on our fate.

Should we wait and try to find someone to repair it or go on without the extra source of power and try to find a fix later?

PART II

In an Unfamiliar World

Renaissance heads into the unknown

This boat is a Baba 35—a "double ender" designed by Robert Perry with a swept-back, full keel and a cutter rig (mainsail plus two forward jibs) with bowsprit. She was built in Taiwan with fiberglass hull: length 34.83 ft., beam (width) of 11.17 ft. Her ballast is 8,000 lb. and displacement 21,140 lb. Her mast is 47.8 feet tall stepped at the keel and the mainsail size is 337 sq. ft. Her internal tanks carried 100 gallons of water and 75 gallons of fuel.

CHAPTER 5

Crossing the Pacific — A Month in a Capsule

A WARM TRADE WIND DREW *RENAISSANCE* AWAY FROM THE continent of North America. Twenty miles from shore, the three of us sat subdued in the cockpit drinking cold soda and perhaps contemplating the enormity of our undertaking. Ahead, there was nothing: no trees, no structure, no land, only a dim line where different hues of blue separated sea and sky. As the sun declined, each of us glanced back often to watch distant hills dissolve into a mist. Fifty or more days might pass before we sighted land again.

The Pacific Ocean overlays a third of the earth's surface with 63 million square miles of water. The large-scale ocean chart that covered our salon table put into perspective the isolation of the 3,000 miles we meant to cross. Islands like the ones we sought, looked like grains of sand strewn across its surface, and a half-inch pencil line would represent our average run of a hundred miles per day. Our celestial navigation instructor had compared our journey to crossing the sea in a peapod.

After breaking the wind generator that morning, Captain John chose to proceed with the trip even though this left us reliant on our engine for electricity. This unsettled me. We needed to power the Sat Nav for navigation and the ham radio for weather and emergency contacts; but the boat had limited storage for fuel, and the availability of diesel in Polynesia was uncertain. With our supply, John estimated that we could run the engine no more than three hours a day to charge the house batteries. Thus, we had to rely on the wind for 98% of our propulsion. I understood and accepted the need to conserve.

As our first evening at sea approached, John spelled out the trip routine. "We could be out here six weeks or more. Few vessels of any size transit this area of the Pacific, so we expect no company during this crossing. However, we will maintain a watch around the clock. Every evening, each of us will stand a three-hour watch in safety harnesses, responsible during that time to detect and report anything that might endanger us—like floating hazards, threatening weather, gear failure, or another vessel."

"Then call you," I said to clarify for Dan.

"Right. And, during daylight hours, Judy prepares meals, and I do navigation and maintenance. Dan, you will assist me and wash dishes using only the salt-water foot pump." Also, to conserve our limited, fresh-water supply, he prescribed bucket baths on the foredeck. Dan nodded agreement.

On my solo watch that night, the boat sailed a calm sea as directed by the wind-driven autopilot. Silence prevailed. I was amazed at how, without the glare of shore lights, even the smallest stars flashed through the moonless sky to display the Milky Way. However, ahead of the boat, I saw only black water. I felt a chill knowing I would have no time to evade anything in our path. I had read of obstacle encounters at sea and imagined I saw deadhead logs, dozing whales, or lost shipping containers. Over the next few nights, I considered all possible calamities, prayed for our safety, and turned it all over to my personal Higher Power. With acceptance of things I could not change, I began to enjoy the cool serenity of my nights alone on the vast sea. My senses sharpened. The wind fluffed my short hair. The rigging pinged and groaned.

During the first week, we maintained a constant southwesterly course to the Equator; and with warm breezes, fair winds and calm seas, we settled into life that revolved around the watch schedule. Having Dan aboard allowed each of us a full six hours off duty at night for a deeper sleep cycle. The sailing thrilled me. At dawn with the cool breeze in my face and soft swish of the sea parting, I felt the quiet freedom of a soaring bird, my wings the stark whiteness of the curved sail against the bluest sky. We were living a dream, on our way to paradise, seeking a more meaningful life.

At dusk, glorious orange sunsets engulfed us while we dined *el fresco*. During shared meals, we tried to draw out Dan, but he volunteered little more about his background or opinions. I began to wonder what he might be hiding. John seemed able to interact with him; but whenever I tried, I got no more than a glare or a grunt. It became obvious that he had no use for me—or perhaps any woman. Without alcohol or a corporate structure to guide my personal interactions, his dismissal grated and unbalanced me over time. We lived in a hot, enclosed capsule, thirty-five-feet long and ten-feet wide, which offered little opportunity to get away from interpersonal irritations. Due to Dan's presence, John and I talked less. When rattled, I retreated with AA materials for hope and solace.

One morning, I was in the cockpit facing aft, bending to adjust the wind vane, when I felt a smart slap on my butt. My head snapped around to see Dan standing in the cabin doorway.

I wailed at him, "What the hell are you …"

But when I turned to confront him, my bare foot encountered the villain—a granddaddy flying fish. We often found these misdirected gliders on the deck. "Oh! Ugg," I said. Dan snorted a sneer at me and withdrew below. I felt my face flush with embarrassment, and a low growl escaped my clenched jaw. *Damn, this guy is really beginning to bug me.*

On the seventh day of the passage, torrential rain pounded us. John screwed a hose into our awning drain to refill the water tanks. He and I enjoyed the opportunity to soap up our sweaty bodies and lay on deck for a natural rinse. Without Dan there, I could have enjoyed the interlude without a bathing suit. I had noticed body odor from the crew berth beside the cabin table where we ate, so when I returned to the cabin to change clothes, I suggested he also wash up in the fresh rain. His response: "Frequent bathing is unhealthy."

I stepped back. *Wow…this guy is unstable.*

Periodic rain marked our entry to the Intertropical Convergent Zone, better known as the doldrums. This band of hot, erratic weather stretches for about six hundred miles on each side of the Equator and separates the opposing trade winds of the north and south hemispheres. For many long days without wind, we wallowed in long sea swells under a searing sun, teased by a few short-lived squalls. The humid conditions intensified my itchy heat rash. I couldn't bare the extra heat from John's body in the forepeak bed, so he moved to the bunk in the main cabin across from our crewman.

During the first two weeks of the transit, John confirmed our electronic Sat Nav's position using celestial navigation. I praised him for the practical application of our classes, grateful to confirm our location on that big ocean. Dan sneered at the use of the old-fashioned sextant and mathematical tables—even when John pointed out that the Sat Nav required electricity, which might not always be available. "The salt air contributes to electrical shorts," he said. Dan tinkered with that black box and discovered some new features he shared with John. I kept my distance from creepy Dan and resented their amity.

The sixteenth day at sea delivered the customary royal-blue water to match a crystalline sky, and lacy clouds fringed the unbroken horizon that surrounded us. Without a breeze, the hot sun's rays played on the mirrored sea. Near midday, one of the infrequent satellite fixes put our position at absolute zero latitude. We celebrated crossing the Equator by abandoning ship in turns to swim in the 85-degree sea surface. Our chart indicated a water depth over twelve thousand feet. That depth supported no food chain and thus no sharks. I dove off the boat and swam with delight. Even Dan accepted a squirt of shampoo to foam up before jumping over the side for some cooling exercise.

On the other side of the Convergent Zone, a light trade wind returned to let us sail, but ocean swells rolled us in heat that subsided little at night. Sweating in the galley to put out three meals a day involved a balancing act because the floor moved randomly beneath my feet. Even shaving a carrot presented a challenge unless I engaged a galley sling that held me hands-free. Within a few days, the commercial bread had grown mold inside plastic bags; in ten days we consumed all the fresh meat I had stuffed into our tiny freezer. Out there, I couldn't nip out to the convenience store for fresh food. For inspiration with our remaining rice and canned goods, I opened a paperback cookbook and found it fascinating reading.

One night, beyond the middle of our transit, I awoke to find Dan on watch sitting below with earphones on, listening to a program on the ham radio. I watched for over a half hour, but he never went on deck to search the horizon for hazards. Afraid he might become dangerous if I confronted him, I turned over and tried to sleep.

The next morning, at my insistence, John called a meeting to reiterate watch responsibilities and the need to conserve power for essential boat systems. "The ham radio will be operated only by me for weather and ham networks." Dan just nodded. Inside I fumed; I wanted him punished.

After dinner, while Dan slept, I told John in a terse whisper, "He won't listen to you. And he shows me nothing but disdain." My fists clenched. "He just glares at me like a psycho. He reminds me of that murderer, Charles Manson."

"Easy, now." He laid a hand on my shoulder. "Remember, with him here to help, there's less strain on us." I doubted that. "This is still our trip to share." He hugged me close. He was right. No way to dump the guy now. But oh, how I missed the comfort of John's arms. "You OK, Babe?"

"Umm." I straightened up. "Well, it's too damn hot out here. Look at this heat rash," I said, extending my arms. He responded with a sympathetic smile. I realized I was whining. I knew I had to get along with Dan for another couple of weeks. Still, there remained something menacing about that guy. I didn't know what might set him off.

Inside the Southern Hemisphere, we celebrated the return of the wind, which brought some relief from the heat and allowed us to sail more. Each time I came on deck in daylight, I marveled at the infinite ocean stretching three miles to a soft horizon in all directions. We were entirely alone in perfect silence. At night, I was the first to locate the stars of the Southern Cross. Days later at dawn, the sun and the moon occupied the sky on opposite sides of the horizon. Contemplating such scenes amounted to a spiritual experience, as if witnessing the glory of creation. Out there, we were so small, so powerless. The majesty and variations of nature had to be created and managed by some higher power.

One moonless night, I stood alone in the cockpit two-thousand miles southwest of Mexico. I had been on watch for an hour when I sensed a prick of light on the sea behind us. When trying to focus hard in the dark, I sometimes saw white specks and knew my eyes could deceive me. It could be a rising star.

For the past two days, a steady breeze had pushed our little boat along with all sails set. All portholes and deck hatches stood open to pull steamy air from the cabin. We had been in great spirits at sunset after John connected with a San Francisco ham radio operator, who passed a message to my brother, Don: "Excellent voyage. ETA Hiva Oa ten days."

Again, I scanned a full circle around the boat. I peered into blackness with no hint of a horizon anywhere, except…? I blinked, trying to focus my night vision. Turning back aft, I strained to look again for that dot of light. *Yes, it's still there, maybe brighter.* I crouched behind the red glow of the ship's compass and lined up the center of the dial with the distant spark. I checked my watch. Over time, the object—another vessel faster and probably larger than ours—maintained the same compass bearing to us, which meant a collision course.

With all the space out there and no regular shipping lanes, I wanted to deny the inevitable, but I began to feel threatened. After days of tortuous drifting in the doldrums, *Renaissance* was now making great progress with her three sails drawing us forward. Even in my safety harness, I hesitated to change course and trim sails without help.

I stepped down into the cabin, turned and unclipped my safety harness from its tether. To my right, Dan lay immobile in his bunk, and I hoped he'd stay out of our way. Propping my body against the boat's tilted angle, I moved from the ladder to the bunk where my husband lay almost still against the motion of the sea, his body wedged into the narrow bunk with four pillows, his legs tangled in a blue sheet. I looked at my watch again. He had slept only two hours since I took over the watch, and he would be angry if awakened for a false alarm. However, my discomfort at the perceived danger grew. I wanted, I needed his support.

I shook his shoulder roughly, and said, "John, wake up…wake up." He turned his head and mumbled something. With his slow response, my anxiety increased, along with the volume and bark of my voice. "John, I need you to wake up" (more shaking) "Get up! Come on!" He groaned and finally sat up. I backed off toward the navigation desk, one eye on him and one on the instrument panel. I scanned the instruments and ship's log, waiting for him to come alive.

"There's a light off our stern. It's been on the same compass bearing for over an hour and getting closer." I paused to see if he understood what I said. My gut churned with impatience. He raised his head toward me, but only grunted again. "There's a ship," I said. "We have to change course."

That moved him. Pulling on his shorts, he leaned over the galley sink, dashed some water over his face and slung on his safety harness.

"Well, let's take a look" he said. His bare feet trudged up the steps into the cockpit. I followed.

"It's there!" I pointed at the intruding light and sat down. I stood up and picked at the lines restraining the two forward sails. He hunched over the compass and waited for his eyes to adjust to the darkness, as more blood flowed to his brain.

Come on, come on. When will he ever see? "It's staying on the same course. We have to get away!"

Repeating my horizon scan, he returned below without a word. He picked up the mike on the VHF radio, already set to the international emergency/hailing channel. "This is sailing vessel, *Renaissance*, calling the vessel steaming west at about four degrees South Latitude… Do you read?"

No response.

I knew he hoped to contact the motor vessel to alter course, instead of our having to reset sails in a fair wind. However, insisting on a sailboat's right of way could be our last decision.

John repeated the call on other channels—again with no response. That light was definitely brighter and closing. I could now make out a substantial ship, painted all grey. John handed up a searchlight, saying, "Here, try to get his attention." I stood up and waived the light across the bridge of the ship. I heard John transmit again: "Sailing vessel *Renaissance*, calling the motor vessel on collision course."

No response. The well-lit ship, clearly on auto-pilot, charged toward us out of the night, seeming to gather speed as it came on.

John returned to my side. "We have to tack," he said. "Get ready to release the sails."

Jam cleats held the lines that controlled the two forward sails. I uncoiled the rope ends to allow them to run free upon release. I grabbed a winch handle and yelled, "Ready." Too many seconds passed, and we didn't turn away. I looked back at John. He was struggling to disconnect the self-steering yoke from the wheel. *What the hell?!*

After days on the same course, the salt air had caused the dissimilar metals of these parts on the wheel to fuse.

To separate them, he pounded the wheel with his fist, swore, and pulled harder. The throbbing noise of the approaching engine entered my consciousness. Electric shocks of rising danger coursed through my nerves. I ventured a quick look to the right and shuddered at the image of the oncoming ship.

Hurry!" I said and braced my legs for strength.

He threw his full weight into the wheel, broke the seal, and forced the rudder to turn. "Go!" he yelled.

I turned forward and pried up the jam cleats, throwing my hands clear as the lines flew out. Our boat heeled over, propelled downward by the increased pressure on her bound-up mainsail. Sea and spray hurled over the deck and through the open hatches and portholes. John held the resistant wheel with one hand and stretched to release and reset the mainsail. Suddenly the boat righted herself and ran from danger. I hauled in the forward sails to add speed. Reflexively I began to sort out the lines in case of further action.

"Whoa!" exploded from John.

I looked over the side, then up, and then higher to gape at the sheer sides and bridge of a massive grey ship. Over 100 feet long, awash in sidelights, it rushed by our right flank pushing up the sea. I gasped in terror, screamed, and reached out to hold on for impact. *It's so close!* I blinked in the glare as we bobbed in its bow wave. Recovering a slack jaw, John hurled his entire library of profanity toward the ship, which never slowed. Diesel fumes beset me. Speechless with shock, I turned to watch it pass.

The grey ghost with no markings disappeared through a curtain of black, leaving us staring across at each other in the dark. *Did that really happen?* A thousand miles from land? John shook off more tension and looked around.

Filled with adrenalin, I stood up furious, self-righteous and yelled at John. "And you guys wonder why we need to keep a watch out here?

We could have been crushed. And driven deep into the water without a trace."

How ironic: we had left successful careers to avoid premature death like that of John's co-worker.

Dan must have awakened during the commotion but never appeared. Maybe he did have some sense—to let us handle it.

During the fourth week at sea, under light winds, we made minimal progress, subdued by the heat and humidity. Inside the cabin, decaying onions and carrots mixed with spreading mildew and the body odor from Dan's bunk, conspired to make the stench down below repulsive. Sleep deprivation and the discomfort of confinement in the cramped space (especially with our bizarre crewman) niggled us all. After our near collision, the increased tension on board spread my itchy eczema rash. Even with antihistamines, sleep eluded me. When I discovered swollen glands under my jaw, I said nothing and started on antibiotics from our stash of cheap Mexican drugs. Cranky, despondent and drugged by the heat, I had lost the energy to care. John ate little and his upbeat disposition dulled. He now ignored me when I grumbled about Dan's inattention while standing watch.

Early on Day 27, I was dozing like a zombie on my mattress in the forepeak when I heard John yell, "Land Ho." He hooted with the excitement sailors have felt for centuries after an endless ocean passage. Damn Dan beat me to the ladder as we tumbled out to follow John's pointing finger. We took turns with the binoculars. I squealed with joy and hugged John, who loosened a hand to high-five Dan. "We made it!" Without modern GPS we had located the Marquesas Islands in mid-ocean, equidistant between Mexico and New Zealand.

We raced all day toward that bump on the horizon, which grew into a four-thousand-foot volcanic peak. Although keen to end this transit, we halted offshore on that last, moonless night rather than chance unknown coastal hazards. As I settled to sleep, apprehension arose about what we might face in these isolated islands on the edge of Polynesia.

CHAPTER 6

The Marquesas Islands — Far from Civilization

AFTER TWENTY-EIGHT DAYS IN TRANSIT WITH ONLY SEA and sky to ponder, we stared awestruck as we closed on the towering island of Hiva Oa. Our mouths agape emitted an occasional, "Wow." I imagined the animation of Spaniard Alvaro Mendana and his crew when he discovered these islands in 1595 after three-and-a-half months at sea. The land emitted an odor of rich soil and fragrant foliage that delighted my long-dulled senses. Giant leaves in all sizes and shades of green topped steep bluffs of basaltic rock, and volcanic plugs rose like the thumbs of Aladdin's genie.

Despite my feelings of pride and relief at completing our voyage, anxiety gripped me again as I considered our remoteness from the western world. The lack of modern facilities could put us in grave danger. My emotions lurched from wonder to fear, then joy to dread. *What were the people like, evolved and so isolated from any other cultures?*

We moved closer. Shirtless in the humid, eighty-five-degree heat, John matched the shoreline topography of Taha Uku Bay to a drawing in the pilot book he held. I steered for the anchorage closest to Atuona, the administrative center. On our left, a beach of fine black sand led up to a steep slope and a ridge of peaks, each blunted by its own cloud. On the right side of the bay, a stone breakwater shielded a sturdy pier for inter-island supply ships. *Renaissance* approached seven other cruising boats flying flags of Germany, Egypt, France, Canada, and the U.S.A.

We had arrived before noon flying the yellow Q-flag (for Quarantine)–an international signal requesting authorization to land in a foreign territory. Without clearance, according to maritime law, only the ship's captain may land, and then only to notify authorities of a ship's arrival. After we anchored, John radioed an American boat for local knowledge. Our neighbor advised that our arrival coincided with the start of a holiday weekend, meaning we were stuck on board for another three days. We all groaned.

Then the yachtie headed off my first impulse. "Don't swim in the harbor," he said. "It belongs to an extended family of hammerhead sharks. But there's a lovely, fresh water shower on the pier, the last building next to the ice house."

I looked at the deserted pier and back to our stifling boat-prison. "Let's chance it," I said. John agreed. We unpacked the dinghy and drove for the pier, ready to risk the antagonism of French officials in exchange for a touch of land and a cool bath. Dan remained onboard.

Tormented by a prickly heat rash, I claimed first dibs on the shower, while John explored the rest of the pier. Inside a privacy maze, the cinder block walls stood five-feet high with no roof to block a spectacular view of the sapphire harbor and verdant hills topped with black rock. I stripped off my sweaty shorts and halter top and pulled the lever attached to a wall-mounted pipe. A waterfall gushed over me. I gasped at the chill, stifling a scream, then stood still letting the water cool my inflamed skin. Beyond the wall, I surveyed Mt. Temetiu and the paradise we had found here.

John barged into the cubicle interrupting my reverie. I splashed him. He yelped at the cold but shed his shorts and rushed me. "Ah, ha, me pretty," he said with a dramatic sneer. He grabbed me, as if to ravish me like a pirate; but as I relaxed to accept him, he suddenly pushed me away from the water's stream, monopolizing it for himself, his face to the sky in ecstasy.

"You bastard," I said. I slapped his tight butt and pressed myself against his tanned chest to share the torrent. His deep kiss lit a fire inside to match my outside skin. I moved against him with longing, and we surrendered to the pent-up passion denied us these four long weeks in close quarters with our rancid crewman.

Back on the boat, the evening's entertainment consisted of watching the phosphorescence in the water outline creatures of all sizes darting around below us.

While we waited for local offices to open, we caught up on sleep, cleaned up the boat, and visited other boats—two of which we had followed from Mexico.

On Monday, John walked three miles with another skipper along an unpaved jeep trail to the government offices in Atuona, where he tried to communicate with officials in his frayed, prep-school French. This left Dan and I quarantined on the boat most of the day trying to avoid each other. John returned to report our situation: to obtain a ninety-day visa covering all islands of French Polynesia, Immigration law required that we post a cash bond to cover the cost of deportation should we misbehave. The size of the refundable bond—$1,200 cash per person—was a shock. The good news: we could go ashore.

The next day, the three of us walked the dirt path to town. Native huts built from thatch or corrugated iron peeked from a proliferation of bright vegetation. Slim Polynesian women wrapped in red and yellow, cotton prints walked toward us with alluring smiles.

Inside the concrete, single-story, government building, I noted with dismay that Dan spoke better French than John, who seemed flustered. I understood little as the agent recorded our information and reminded John of his responsibility for the actions of his crewmembers. After Dan and John arranged transfers of bond funds to a bank in Tahiti, the officials granted us provisional entry with visas subject to confirming receipt of funds.

With a few words to John outside the office, Dan disappeared into the jungle. *Good riddance.*

The island prices were my next shock. I had prepared eighty-five consecutive meals standing on a tilting, rolling floor, so John took me out to lunch. In a rustic café, we satisfied customary cravings with cheeseburgers, cokes and fries. He counted out several hundred Pacific Francs for the meal, which translated to four times what we paid at McDonalds. The same markup applied for groceries; but, of course, the cost of delivering produce, canned dairy products, and packaged goods 10,000 miles from France comprised a large part of the price.

On arrival we craved crunchy vegetables. I learned that only one small farm on island grew simple, hearty produce, so I gladly paid $5.00 for a small cabbage. It appeared to us that the Marquesans had lost the incentive to provide for themselves because the French government provided such generous aid. Few natives even bothered to fish these pristine waters when one need only open a can of mackerel. The French seemed to prefer giving a man a fish, rather than teaching this generation how to fish.

In ancient days, the natives carried out constant warfare and cannibalism, even though volcanic ridges protected the valley villages. European and American traders brought waves of smallpox and kidnapping that wiped out three-quarters of the Marquesan population. French rule and conversion to Catholicism controlled remaining violence. Now, the living here appeared idyllic.

Beyond the low government building, we roamed the tiny town that consisted of a few wooden buildings holding back lavish jungle and framed by overhanging palm fronds. I yearned to talk to people, to learn about their daily lives, their customs and concerns; but without a common language, a smile and sign language had to suffice for me. In the center of the town square, I noticed several natives sprawled under the craggy arms of a banyan tree. When John asked a shopkeeper if they were ill, he laughed and tilted his head back with a thumb in his mouth. The incidence of alcoholism here was four times that in Western countries. At their plight, I sensed a rare feeling for me—empathy—but also a flash of gratitude for the rehab program that had saved me.

While Dan hiked the hills, John and I joined other yachties to share exploits and gain information about the area. One couple commiserated with us about the girl they took on as crew in Mexico who refused all work during their Pacific crossing. They had just arranged to dismiss her.

"I hope we can get rid of Dan too," I said. "but we agreed to take him as far as Tahiti. He's really weird. Onboard I'm never more than twenty feet from his glaring, sneering face. It's such a relief to have him gone for a while. I'm afraid if he becomes dangerous, the French officials could refuse us entry and force us back to sea with him. Good grief."

Because severe weather or local hostilities could necessitate a fast departure; maintenance of our floating home remained top priority. Within days of our arrival, John procured fuel. He decanted diesel from rusty, 55-gallon drums through graded filters into our five-gallon jugs for transport to our boat. The enchanted setting brought tropical downpours to sustain the lush plant life and fill our water tanks but also encouraged a profusion of mildew in our living quarters. The salty air and humidity kept bedding and clothes from ever feeling dry. Any shadow of a cloud sent me racing around, clothespins flying, to rescue semi-dry laundry from a threatened shower. The drenching rains lasted fifteen minutes allowing prompt replacement of laundry on deck lines when the scorching sun reappeared. Dan returned when our boat work was done.

Two weeks passed in attempts to confirm arrival of our bond funds and visas. John had almost reached the end of his scant patience when the immigration officer authorized our travel to explore nearby islands while we waited.

We sailed fifty miles south to a smaller island (seven by four miles) called *Fatu Hiva*. Around the cozy harbor, volcanic plugs emerged from brilliant green flora, which inspired some to call this the Garden of Eden.

On the beach, we met another yachtie couple, and Dan left with them to climb to the high plateau. John and I walked up a winding path into the dense vegetation to glimpse goats grazing the terraces and compact horses tied in stands of coconut palms. John greeted a few brown-skinned natives, but they seemed to avoid us. I couldn't decide if their demeanor was shy, suspicious, or menacing. I tensed, more alert, and again contemplated our vulnerability. However, as in Mexico, the children were unable to contain their curiosity. Several skipped along beside us while we attempted to communicate with a mixture of French, Marquesan, sign language, and giggles. Although living in thatched huts of ten-foot diameter, these kids were surprisingly aware of consumer goods and pestered us for bonbons, balloons, chewing gum, perfume, even nail polish. Once she decided we had nothing of interest, one sassy girl popped into an unmarked shack (which turned out to be a shop) and returned with a strip of twelve, multicolored jaw breakers to share with her friends.

We passed into a grove of trees laden with exotic, fresh fruit: papaya, mango, oranges and *pomplemousse*—the latter, a sweet, thick-skinned, grapefruit. After many weeks of subsisting on canned food, John bartered for papaya that he loaded into his backpack. I enjoyed the interplay, happy to trade my cotton hat for eight oranges.

Further up the trail, we encountered a herd of bright yellow earth-movers which seemed so out of time and place. They had slashed a path across the hilltop. A laborer told John that the road would soon reach the village on the opposite shore of the island where the middle school was located. Only the brightest children matriculate from there to the central boarding school back on Hiva Oa.

"Let's go up to the crest of that hill to get a better view", said John, pointing.

"I'm getting overheated," I said, pushing away a leaf as long as my arm. "You go on. I'll take some pictures and meet you back at the shore."

The bright foliage, volcanic spires, and thatched huts provided scenes more spectacular than I feared my shots could convey. Soon I broke out of nature's rampage onto the beach to welcome a cool breeze off the water. My joy turned to gloom when I saw Dan sitting nearby with three, burly natives. They were drinking beer and eating small fish raw. Unable to ignore them, I approached with a smile, trying to appear cordial, and greeted them in English. Dan grunted something with a wave of dismissal and speaking in French turned back to the men. My gut cramped with fear and anger at his insolence. *Forget this.* I wandered away, trying to appear absorbed with beachcombing.

Finally, John returned. Sociable and able to struggle along in French, he joined the guys and even drank some of their beer. After a reasonable time, I caught John's eye and motioned that I wanted to return to the boat for lunch. Dan refused to leave, so we left him and took the dinghy back to the boat. Dan had apparently bragged that we had lots of wine on board; in fact, we brought three bottles for gifts or trading. John told me he had agreed to return later with a bottle, which he seemed to regret. I groaned and said, "I have a bad feeling about this situation."

In late afternoon, John returned to the beach with the wine to demonstrate goodwill, but the men were no longer there. By casting about and asking anyone he met, he pushed through the bush and finally located Dan and the locals near a shack where they had procured more drink. The men encouraged Dan's resolve to stay there and insisted that John join them to drink the wine.

Back on the boat, I alternatively watched the clock and watched the beach using the binoculars. My apprehension grew. *Where did they go? What if they fight over the wine? What if John gets lost or injured? What would I do here without him?* Dan could cause real trouble for us. I had tried to remain positive, but his arrogance threatened my world.

"Damn him! And damn the booze." I began to pace again. *What can we do with him?* I watched the sand on the beach turn to grey as the sun descended.

The alcohol and the support of his "drinking buddies," as well as his ability to communicate in French, magnified Dan's sense of superiority and defiance of John. As darkness descended, I later learned that John confronted him in English sternly warning him that he would have him arrested by the *gendarmes* if he did not return to the boat. He finally yielded. Unable to see the proper paths, they headed directly for the fading light reflected off the water and stumbled through a churchyard carrying a sack of mangos. When they arrived on board, Dan was very drunk and very loud.

With all the force of my anxiety, I yelled at him: "You're drunk! We don't know what could happen in that jungle or village or whatever!" I slapped the galley counter. "Your behavior is unacceptable. We are responsible for you. This better not happen again!"

He leaned near and taunted me, "On the Cook Islands they would take care of a stranger better than *you* would!"

Startled, I stepped back. "Well, sorry. We are a thousand miles from there—and operating under a different flag."

John moved closer and addressed him. "Well, look, Judy was concerned."

Good grief! Put it all on me? I groaned and turned my back on them. I shook with anger. *Why can't John be more assertive?* This is our home in a primitive and foreign land. He's captain and knows he's legally responsible for misdeeds of his crew. That could mean fines or even jail time. *He's got to get Dan under control! I can't take six more weeks with this jerk.*

There I was, caught in the middle, the dragon lady, just a hired cook. I wanted my home back. I wanted to run away. *Fat chance.* Retreating to the galley full of anger born of frustration and fear, I yanked a soup pot from under the sink and banged it over the stove rail. Dinner that night was burned navy beans, but I heard no complaints.

The next morning, I enjoyed our spirited sail back to Hiva Oa on a rolling sea—and felt vindicated as I watched Dan dry heaving over the side. After the officials finally stamped our visas, we sailed overnight to explore the tropical isle of Ua Pou, five miles wide.

From a seaside peninsula we walked a dirt road beside stockpiled modern materials and heavy equipment being used to construct a wharf for larger supply ships. We met an off-duty *gendarme* officer with his wife and son who invited us into their pre-fab home for lemonade. They spoke no English, so Dan took to speaking for us, translating very little into English, and ignoring us.

Within a few minutes, John cut off Dan's crowing to encourage more interaction. We learned that the family had traveled by steamship from France for a typical two-year assignment in Polynesia. These *gendarmes* were responsible not only for maintaining civil order, but also for various legal services including death notices, notary, and issuance of ammunition for hunting. Along with the couple's cordial body language and the few words I did understand, I relished their company and an hour quickly passed. We departed with gifts of *pomplemousse* and fresh bread. They sent their eight-year-old son along with us to meet a native teacher he loved.

Diverting from the main path, the boy located a man holding court in front of a three-sided shack sporting a sign that read: "Vahine Snak Bar." George, the English-speaking grandson of a Ua Pou king, taught local kids, sponsored a native dance group, and ran the snack bar. He thanked our guide and welcomed us with a broad smile. We sat on stump stools around the shady clearing to listen to his stories. George gave us a short history of the five clans of his island, three of whom lived in the hills and had spent their short lives waging war with each other. He revealed with pride that his grandmother was a Scottish lady, which explained his lighter skin color. I imagined a slim, stately woman with flowing red hair roaming these lush valleys in the 1920's beside her tattooed Polynesian king. The historical tales George told us fascinated me. With understanding came less fear and an eagerness in me to learn more. I began to relax.

After lunch on the boat, the usual afternoon tropical downpour splashed across the deck. From inside the humid cabin, I watched rain water trickle down a clear pipe from the cockpit awning into our blue, five-gallon jug. I climbed outside under the awning, lit a cigarette, and beheld the rainforest village dwarfed by balsamic columns that stood above a carpet of green like the pipe organ of a giant. I swam twice a day and often in the rain. Although paradise shimmered before me, the presence of Dan stifled my mood like a heavy wool coat. Whenever I asked him to pay me his board or wash his sheets, he only stared at me. In a hot week of hiking, he had not bathed, and his bunk corner smelled like rotten apples. That afternoon when he came aboard sweaty and grimy, I pushed a bottle of shampoo at him.

"Get in the water and wash up," I said.

Dan responded with an arrogant tone, "Up North, you don't take a bath every day because body oil keeps off the bugs." He brushed by me to recline with a book to await his supper.

"Ugh," I said. "That may be fine for you up north, but this is my home—at the Equator, and it stinks. The upholstery is being ruined!"

John stood nearby trying to ignore this interchange. Unwilling to support me, he left me powerless. When he worked with Dan on maintenance tasks, and when they used French, I felt left out, the shrew, the slave labor. I stopped speaking to both of them—and they were probably glad.

The next day John dropped Dan ashore early and tried to cajole me into contentment. He pulled off Dan's sheets, plunged them into a soap-water bucket, and listened to my tirade. I needed to vent. My anger, fear, jealousy and frustration overflowed.

"You're too passive," I said. "And compromising your own values. You can't be his buddy. My needs and concerns are dismissed around here." I filled another bucket with rinse water as he wrung out a soapy sheet. "Why do you always take his side? He's so weird. He glares at me like a seething psychopath. He's ruining our cruise."

"You're harping and nagging too much to get what you want," he said.

I turned and spoke through a clenched jaw. "I cannot live with him on this boat."

"Let me handle it," he said. "Come on. Let's hang these up to dry."

As suppertime neared, John cranked up the outboard motor to pick up Dan as agreed. I could see through binoculars that Dan was missing again, which required John to return for him later. I was sick to death of placating this jerk. By the time they returned in the dark, I was furious at them both, but bit my tongue to give John his chance to deal with the guy.

Three days later, when we arrived on Nuku Hiva, the largest island of the group and a popular rendezvous for yachties, a solution finally appeared. Apparently, Dan had tired of my complaints about his demeanor and hygiene and told John he had arranged passage to Tahiti on another cruising boat.

In a tropical downpour, we trudged up a hill to the *Gendarmarie* in Taiohae. Dan walked beside John. From behind them, I watched Dan labor under a backpack and large duffle bag, their straps creasing the back of his yellow slicker. Outside the office, I sat on a concrete bench waiting with growing delight while John completed paper work to relinquish responsibility for Dan. When we met outside, I mumbled a goodbye, but John wished him good luck. Without a word, Dan turned and strode off toward town, his head bowed against the pelting rain.

I hugged John close and said, "Thank you."

Relieved of the tension of Dan's presence, I bloomed with the excitement of a child freed to explore a new playground. I bathed in the yachtie fellowship at beach parties and book swaps. I discussed writing with noted Australian author and sailor, Alan Lucas, who arrived with his wife and son. As always, yachties gave freely of their time, skills, and spare parts to help others in such remote areas. John's earlier apprenticeship on diesel engines put him in high demand, which is how we met yachties Fred and Rita on the sailing vessel, *Oracle.*

While the men worked on Fred's engine intake valve, Rita and I sat in their cockpit with iceless iced tea and laughed as we shared disastrous experiences of cooking on a moving stove. "I sloshed orange Jello over and under the gas burners, and John took them apart to clean them," I said. "He didn't seem to mind doing that out here."

Rita laughed and slid a hand down her freckled face. "I wasn't really thrilled about doing this trip, but it's taught me that spills sure aren't important in the grand picture." The retired Seattle couple became close friends, and we crossed paths often along the routes favored by yachties.

After a month in the Marquesas, *Renaissance* coasted alone to the opposite side of this big island, Nuku Hiva. We slowed to pass a waterfall that cascaded over a thousand feet down a black cliff into the sea. At anchor in a river-cut cove for two lazy days, we snorkeled and planned our approach to "The Dangerous Archipelago."

CHAPTER 7

The Tuamotus — The Dangerous Archipelago

WITH HER ENGINE IDLING AND SAILS DOUSED, *Renaissance* paused in the deep blue water outside the oval-shaped atoll of Manihi. Ignoring two-foot seas splashing at her flank, she hesitated, her bow pointed at a blue ribbon of swirling water in the narrow entrance to the coral lagoon. At 2:30 P.M. with partial overcast, the light needed to navigate the reef passage was fading. Delay increased the danger of not spotting a jagged coral head just below the surface that could slash through our vessel's thin fiberglass skin. Go or no go? Pressure mounted to proceed.

After a tiring, four-day transit from the Marquesas, we hoped to avoid another night at sea among scattered reefs in water too deep to anchor. We had located Manihi among the seventy low-lying islands of the Tuamotus that spread across our 720-mile sea route to Tahiti. Centuries before our arrival, volcanic islands that hosted fringing coral reefs sank, leaving circles of coral skeletons called atolls. Within the lagoon, coral heads (columns) can grow up to a hundred feet from the floor of the lagoon to the surface. Because corals cannot grow above sea level, the atolls are difficult to spot when approaching from the open sea, even after they pick up sand and palm trees to become motus (keys). As a result, the Tuamotus have claimed many ships and earned a reputation as the Dangerous Archipelago.

Now was the time to test and trust all we had read and mined from other sailors about navigating such a treacherous area. John climbed the mast steps to improve his view into the water, hoping to direct us to the deepest part of the passage as represented by the darkest water. My grip tightened on the wheel to maintain the compass course exactly at thirty degrees as prescribed in the hand-drawn chart beside me. Inside a vast atoll like Manihi, the deep lagoon contains huge volumes of water, and tides can generate furious currents through breaks in the atoll walls.

Sweat dripped from my brow. Ahead of us, the water looked choppy, but flat in spots. Further inside, whirlpools indicated a strong current. *Was the water flowing out or in? With us or against us?*

"Ready?" I yelled up the mast, afraid I might back out of this.

"OK. The water's really clear," he said. "Go ahead."

I eased the throttle forward. The depth sounder found the bottom and began flashing readings of eighty, then sixty feet. Tanned to bronze, John looked like a statue staring ahead with his left arm circling the mast. The next time I looked up, his other arm chopped the air to the right. I changed course to follow.

Our keel needed six feet of depth to pass over the coral-strewn bottom. A quick look over the side gave me flashes of white sand between purple, lime-green, and fawn-colored corals. *The bottom is so close!* But the depth gauge registered fifty feet. *That can't be right.* However, we were committed now, and my screaming would only be a distraction. I clenched my jaw and proceeded.

I looked up again. John calmly waived me to the right. I adjusted course, then leaned left to snatch a look over the side again. The water was so clear there was no way to judge the depth by sight.

Suddenly I heard, "Neutral!" I yanked back the shift lever to stop the prop. A neural shock crossed my chest as I noted the speed gauge and realized an incoming current had hold of the boat. *Is she out of control?* The narrowness of the pass left no room to turn; in fact, getting crosswise to that current could press our keel and capsize us. I looked from the compass to the water with a third eye focused above, trusting guidance from John, as he trusted me to maneuver. As we accelerated, the depth sounder reading bounced from fifty to forty feet, down to twenty, back up to fifty, then volleyed between fifteen and twenty feet. Abruptly the dark water widened, confirming we were inside the lagoon. As the boat slowed, the depth sounder began flashing, indicating a depth greater than its sonic reach.

Before I could relax, John yelled, "Starboard! Starboard!" chopping his arm hard to the right. "Coral head." I put the engine in gear and flung the wheel aside, then back toward the sparkling beach where he pointed. Tethered there sat two sailboats with homeports in Australia and Spain, and beyond them, village huts peered from foliage near the swirling pass.

Anchor down, we jumped into the cool water. I surfaced bursting with laughter born of relief and delight. Together we had accomplished a 520-mile voyage and entered our first coral lagoon without help. No longer a danger, the spiny reef wall became our protector from the open ocean.

As John swam out to check our anchor, I climbed back aboard to stare in awe at nature's glory. Coconut palms arched over a sparkling white beach that stretched to the horizon on each side. This was like the sparkling aqua water in a swimming pool. *But wait—That's backwards. This is the original.* I saw what the western world attempts to copy. Living in such a scene washed away any of our hardships. I splashed back into the lagoon and floated in ecstasy, until John pinched my bum and popped up beside me. We tucked in early to catch up on our sleep.

The next morning, we stood together marveling at the fine sand that separated lime-green flora from blues and greens of the water. My ears detected only the rustling of coconut palm fronds and the thrum of ocean surf across the motu. The jade lagoon measured six-miles wide and double that in length. Between the boat and beach, we snorkeled amidst an array of dazzling tropical fish: zebras, angels, rainbow darters, and blue-green parrot fish that flowed in and around craggy brain coral, green cabbage corals, twirling ship worms, pointy staghorn coral, and soft corals waving lacey fans of purple or green.

Nature also provided this lagoon with the rare combination of salinity, temperature and nutrients necessary to cultivate rare black pearls. Natives imbed a tiny plastic pip inside black-lip oyster shells and bundle them in chicken wire for three years before harvesting. Through my swim mask, I watched the anchored traps rise and fall with the currents.

When we visited the small village next to the pass, I realized how dependent the natives were on their colossal cement cisterns, which collected vital rainwater, and imported food delivered by a supply ship twice a week.

The next day a sailboat with crew we met in Mexico entered the lagoon. John agreed to help the yachtie take his scuba gear to a resort across the lagoon for repair. I watched with some trepidation as their dinghy disappeared from my sight. They remained out of communication for hours. As shadows of the palm trees grew, so did my sense of vulnerability in this remote location. I conjured up several disaster scenarios that I might be left to deal with alone.

John returned after 6:00 P.M. to face the brunt of my growing anxiety. He tried to laugh off my worries about his welfare and admitted staying for "a couple of beers" at the pool bar overlooking some topless French sunbathers.

"That's not funny," I said. "You should be more considerate of me."

My worry and anger soon disbursed while we enjoyed exploring, snorkeling, trading, and sharing pot-luck meals with a dozen other yachties who came and went during our week in Manihi. The candor, curiosity and empathy of these ocean vagabonds filled me with joy.

On the day we planned to depart the atoll with three "buddy boats," we found that a coral head had entangled our anchor chain fifty feet below the surface. By freediving, John tried and tried to release us.

"Damn. I just can't reach it!" he said as he climbed back aboard. "We'll be too late entering the next lagoon. Shit! Shit! Shit!" He pounded his fist on the rail and looked around. "Take the wheel. Maybe we can unwind it."

With him on the bow, I circled the coral head in each direction, but the bow dipped as we tightened the noose. John's anger (or fear) turned into a rage that disturbed me. Hearing the commotion, a Frenchman from a nearby boat helped free us using his scuba gear. After he offered the man profuse thanks and needlessly explained to me the seriousness of being trapped like that, John recovered some calm.

We escaped the lagoon in mid-afternoon through a quiescent pass. In the open sea, a warm wind filled the sails drawing us overnight through the archipelago. With little light from the heavens, I tensed to imagine uncharted reefs in our path.

By noon the next day, *Renaissance* stood outside Rangiroa, the largest atoll in the archipelago. This ring of coral lies on the sea like a discarded necklace, one hundred miles in circumference studded with 240 pearl motus. Using our nautical chart, we lined up a course through the narrow reef pass. Although a rip current churned the water in places and caused low waves to break to our right, the route through the coral appeared clear. This time John took the wheel, and I kept watch near the bow. As we started into the pass, I stood gripping the lifeline and strained to look into the water for hazards ahead of us.

Suddenly, a huge gray shape loomed high to my right. I screamed and fell to my knees. An enormous dolphin had leaped completely out of a wave only six feet from the boat. It turned in the air and dove back to sea. I gulped a breath and forced myself back into position to look ahead. Once in the current, the coral on the sea floor flashed by so fast that we would have hit any obstruction before I could warn John. Inside the lagoon, he steered around a tiny islet and halted behind a large motu. He released the anchor and returned to the cockpit.

"Did you see that big dolphin?" I said.

"Where?" he said, looking around the anchorage.

"No, no. In the pass!" I recounted to him the acrobatics I witnessed.

Rangiroa is apparently the only atoll where dolphins play like that at the deep-water passes. With seas breaking over the windward reef and incoming tides twice daily, massive amounts of water, fish and nutrients from the deep lagoon gush out these passes attracting dolphin, shark and other pelagic fish. I yearned to try the popular local sport of drift-diving the pass with snorkel gear, but our dinghy motor was no match for currents up to six mph. Oceanographer William Van Dorn wrote, "The risk of a fatality from a shark attack is about one-fifth that of driving your car to the corner drugstore." That assumes you don't increase your odds by spear fishing in the pass, like some Tuamotuans who bore scars of attacks from sharks attracted to fish blood.

In order to check in with authorities, we crossed the lagoon by dinghy to government offices at Tiputa. The tidy tropical village on the sandy shore displayed crushed coral paths bordered with whitewashed chain-link fences. In a modern one-story office, John charmed Madame Mayor with his smile and some earnest French. Nearby an impressive little *boulangerie* (bakery) with stainless steel ovens supplied us with fresh baguettes. A humble, wood-framed store operated by a Chinese family held frozen vegetables and chicken parts, which we took for granted in the States, but would trade gold for after eight months of far-flung adventures.

Rain gushed onto the cockpit awning that night, and by morning we had collected fifteen gallons of water. I washed out cotton briefs and T-shirts for my sensitive skin and hung them on the lifelines. Unwanted in the intense heat, a bra never left my drawer. John lived shirtless in swim trunks and ball cap, which minimized his laundry. I smiled recalling the mountains of clothes I had laundered, ironed, and hauled to the dry cleaners in my past life to maintain the corporate image.

The yachtie John helped in Manihi mentioned being low on cash and food. In the past I would have shrugged and thought, tough luck, you should have prepared better. When I invited the couple over for dinner, John's head swiveled to stare at me in surprise. As a loner, after marriage and especially in sobriety, I avoided entertaining at home. I expected guests to judge me harshly. This time I reasoned that this couple were not big drinkers; and that if we were needy, they would help us. I decided to share some of my hoarded food.

John made things easy for me by kettle-grilling chicken we purchased there, and I added a marinated, canned-vegetable salad. I thought we all enjoyed the evening together. When they climbed back into their dinghy, I handed down a bag of canned goods to sustain them for their transit to Tahiti. Their heart-felt thanks embarrassed me, but helping them produced in me an unfamiliar feeling, something like gratification.

After two days of play in our private paradise under a deep blue sky, we returned to the edge of the atoll where we had entered. On a breezy morning, I took my position behind the wheel, and John assumed the lookout position on the foredeck. We edged toward the reef pass, and he began directing me across the colorful corals beneath us. Close inside the lagoon, the tide created back-waves, which I could not see on approach. Suddenly the stern lifted, bending my knees, and I clutched the wheel. The boat picked up speed and surfed toward the cut in the reef. We slid down a wave, and I caught a glimpse of a depth reading that put our keel two feet from the seabed. "Hold on!" I screamed and held my breath waiting for the keel to hit bottom. The jolt never came. "Yikes," I exhaled.

All at once outside of the atoll, we entered the deep blue ocean. We paused to set all sails for a "downhill run" with no time to reflect on my brief terror. Free in her element again, *Renaissance* bore off at hull speed in a strong trade wind toward Tahiti.

CHAPTER 8

The Society Islands — More than Tahiti

CRYSTAL WHITE WATER SPLASHED ALONG THE HULL OF our sturdy ship as she surged toward a 7,300-foot extinct volcano that rose out of ocean ahead of us. I stared in awe and tingled with anticipation. The circular island of Tahiti, portrayed as the world's ultimate paradise, represented a goal we had held for four years of planning and voyaging.

Wide-eyed, we entered a broad pass into the blue lagoon at Papeete, the administrative center for the Society Islands. Two French naval frigates parked just inside the reef signified ownership. The smell of diesel fuel and the drone of truck traffic assailed us. Although a bit noxious, the place seemed novel after ten weeks of isolation. We drank in the scene like newly arrived Martians. I was excited to return to a modicum of western civilization and to experience the lore of this special island. Beyond the commercial pier bordered with warehouses and stacks of multi-colored shipping containers, we found anchorage in front of a white church with twin steeples.

While I tidied up the boat, John spoke via VHF radio with yachtie friends who had arrived earlier. They confirmed that the inter-island *Heiva I Tahiti,* an annual celebration of Polynesian culture, would begin in two days and continue for three weeks.

"Terrific!" I said after he signed off. "I really want to see the dancing and singing groups from all the islands. And outrigger canoe races. We need to get a schedule of events—"

"Hold on, Judy, we're not on a vacation tour here. We have chores to attend to first," said John picking up the maintenance log. "For one, I need to find a machine shop to repair the wind generator motor (the one he dropped just before we left Mexico)…Also, repair the sail, replace the fire extinguisher, paint the…"

"I know, I know. The boat comes first." I resigned myself to days of delay before we could play. "First, let's launch the dinghy and look the place over."

I took a sponge bath and wrapped a cotton skirt over a clean tee shirt but couldn't locate a lipstick. We rode ashore to check in with Immigration officials. A bank furnished us Pacific Francs, the post office supplied letters from home, and I enjoyed the great luxury of dinner at a modest restaurant. On the way home, I sang like a joyful child: "We made it, we made it, we sailed to Tahiti."

On subsequent days, John dropped off our propane tank for filling and searched for various hardware items, while I roamed the *super-marche*, astounded at the range of imported goods. As expected, prices were steep; but with time and a pocket dictionary, I fulfilled our basic needs. We rode the bright-colored, open-air, public transport vehicles called *Le Truck,* and John's improving French permitted more meaningful interaction with the islanders and expats. I stood beside him watching facial expressions and now caught more than what John could translate for me.

Three days after arrival, we cruised along the island's verdant coastal plain to join fifty other yachts anchored along Maeva Beach. The featured view across the channel encompassed the black peak of Moorea Island.

After reunions with friends, snorkeling and more boat work, I again became impatient. "*Renaissance* is back in good shape now. I want to explore the island more," I told John at breakfast one morning.

He exhaled and slumped. "Well, the cabin floor needs to be varnished. And I wanted to work with Dave on the *Pursuit.* He's installing a new alternator."

"Well, big whoop! I'm tired of talking about boat gear," I said, "And evenings trapped on other boats, especially with heavy drinkers. Once you get a buzz on, I can't get you to leave 'til forever."

"Hey, these are great folks, and I learn a lot from them to keep us safe." he said. "I thought you liked them, too."

"I do. Of course. And I do appreciate your keeping things ship-shape. But there'll always be yachties around." I stood, faced the shore, and spread my arms. "And, hey, we're in Tahiti—the long-time object of our desire! And we'll miss the Polynesian cultural festival."

He sat down. "OK. What if we paint this morning and spend the rest of the day ashore?"

"Great. And you can help me locate an AA meeting," I said before I turned back to him to share a kiss to seal the deal.

Our first attempt to locate recovering alcoholics was unsuccessful, but, while exploring, we blundered into a torchlight demonstration in Faaa town to commemorate the 1844 massacre of Tahitians who stood firm against French domination. Speakers addressed the animated crowd using the Tahitian language. It was like stepping from a time machine. The mob of natives chanted and carried signs to promote Polynesian independence and decry continued nuclear testing by the French on mid-Pacific atolls. Considering their irate mood, we tried to make it clear that we were Americans.

The next day we boarded *Le Truck* for the Pirae district and located an AA meeting place where four members welcomed us. Within the past year, a priest had started this group, but I was shocked to learn that local Catholics denounced AA as a sect (or a competing religion) due to its spiritual content. My new comrades struggled to counter this misunderstanding while guarding their members' anonymity. No one spoke English, but the universal format gave me great comfort. With over two years of sobriety, some might consider me a group elder, but I was quick to express humility in the face of alcoholism, a disease that waits patiently to reclaim us. The group discussed staying sober just "one day at a time," and John translated as I shared my reliance on a personal Higher Power. One attendee, a respected member of the native community, drove us back to Maeva Beach.

As we crossed the hotel grounds to reach our dinghy, we came upon a dance troop in costumes woven from fronds and flowers performing for the guests. We sat on the lawn and watched twelve rhythm-makers and thirty dancers portray the emotions of lovers and warriors. I sat close to John with my head on his shoulder and glowed with gratitude for a full and ideal day.

We attended several events of the *Heiva I Tahiti* festival. The inter-island competitions covered every aspect of Polynesian life including tattoo art, weaving, spear throwing, agriculture, canoe and foot races. One evening in an open amphitheater, we watched finalists in various dance and choral competitions perform under the stars. Powerful Polynesian voices joined in close harmony that rose to convey universal yearnings and raise goosebumps. I gripped John's arm with a mixture of joy and awe at the primal display of exultation.

Three weeks after our arrival, John tested the repaired wind generator and declared our to-do list complete. We motored a few miles across the channel to explore Moorea. That afternoon, I sat in the cockpit cleaning the teakwood trim and waiting for John to finish an oil change. My mind wandered. After years of anticipating Tahiti, a sadness seemed to settle in my core. Was it just an anticlimax or a yearning for the life I left behind in California? I looked back across the aqua waters to Tahiti's towering peak and felt again the allure of Polynesia. Only one couple we knew had flown here to visit us. Why wouldn't family join us here? Any opportunity to travel had always excited me.

Why don't people travel more? Travel is only one of many options that compete for our money and the meager vacation days allowed by U.S. employers, but few workaholics, even use the time they earn. I used to feel guilty spending a day off work accomplishing nothing and afraid I might be replaced while away. Americans may relocate for a couple of weeks to unwind, but they resist exploring outside their known world. Most isolate themselves inside a resort compound with others of similar taste and views of life to "hurry up and have fun."

It is natural to feel uncomfortable around strangers and diverse customs, but extended travel allowed us the time to reconsider priorities and pursue curiosities. Without email or a cell phone to distract us, we learned to interact with strangers to obtain supplies, considered alternate viewpoints, and discovered a world beyond what we had known. In breaking free from my career climb and the wallop of alcoholism, I began to open myself to change by taking small risks. For me that entailed caring to know yachties in a personal way and developing friendships. John showed me how to reach out to people. Not only had I gained back some social confidence, but I recognized I had options. Staying home was an option. I chuckled and turned back to my chores with renewed contentment to our adventure together.

We departed Moorea to venture deeper into the French Society Islands, an archipelago about 220 miles long. In late July, winter in the Southern Hemisphere moderated the tropic heat we had endured for months. Although our Fahrenheit wall gauge showed seventy degrees, John recorded "cold and windy" in the ships log.

The next morning, he spotted the volcanic peak of Huahine Island. Sailing with a brisk wind in an agitated sea, *Renaissance* entered the narrow lagoon. Measuring about eight miles across, Huahine could be a one-third scale model of Tahiti; but in 1987, the haze of "progress" endured by her big sister had not reached her. Behind the inter-island shipping wharf, the village of Fare (home) lined the waterfront with square, two-story buildings containing a few shops. Inside a general store the size of a barn, a Chinese proprietor scurried among a jumble of merchandise from screwdrivers to stew pots, flip-flops to fresh pastries. To support the island population of three thousand, the sleepy outpost also boasted a post office, a church-school, a gas station and two small banks—all with limited hours.

Having read that the island's north side was one of five major archeological sites of Oceania, I was eager to explore it. We peddled our folding bikes along a dirt road from Fare and turned off at the Bali Hai Hotel, the island's largest employer. The lobby displayed artifacts recovered during the hotel's excavation twelve years past: a carved paddle, personal ornaments, fishhooks and an adz tool for shaping canoes. Adjacent panels indicated that Hawaiian archeologist, Dr. Yosihiko Sinoto, supervised the dig and had carbon-dated some of the pieces back to 850 A.D. We stood near the source of major Polynesian migrations, much of which remains a mystery.

Back on the road, we coasted alongside Lake Fauna and stopped to examine numerous stone *marae*—sacred platforms outlined in basalt blocks, which the ancients built to honor ancient gods. Hoping for some answers about their origin and not wanting to encroach on any taboos, I suggested we approach two men who sat talking together twenty yards away. One was a sturdy Asian in his early sixties; white hair flowed two inches below a brimmed cap that shielded his eyeglasses from the intense sun. He was dressed in khaki walking shorts and a safari vest. The dark-haired Caucasian, taller and half the age of his companion, was speaking rapidly in English.

They turned when I hailed them. "Do you know about these platforms?"

The men laughed. "Yes," said the younger, "Yosh has studied them for twenty years." He indicated the older man.

"Yosh? The archeologist? Are you Dr. Sinoto?" I gushed like a groupie. "The expert on the Polynesian migrations?" Our book on Polynesia credited him with most of what is known on the subject. "

That is I," said Yosh, with a soft smile, "but many fine assistants like this one have done all the work."

"We saw *marae* like these in Moorea," I said.

"Yes," said the younger man, "They are found all over the Pacific, but Huahine has the most concentrations of sites."

With humility and patience, Dr. Sinoto answered my many questions about his research—with embellishments from his assistant. The sixty *marae* sites, and their unique placement side by side here, provided evidence that the chiefs of eight districts met and lived peacefully in this sacred village called Maeva, which hosted significant religious ceremonies and constituted a staging area for major migrations since the first century. The scientist studied the developmental sequence of Polynesian artifacts such as tools and fishhooks.

In 1972, while evaluating a structure where we stood, a runner called him to the site being prepared for the Bali Hai Hotel. "The construction manager approached me and said, 'I saved this one piece for you because it looks like something man-made.' As soon as he showed it to me," said Yosh, "I jumped up and got very excited because it was a *patu*, a kind of flat club that had never been found outside of New Zealand."

His comparison of it with pieces from other Pacific islands provided vital evidence of native migration routes. In fact, it was the first hard evidence of a cultural link with the Maori people of New Zealand, whose origin had long remained a mystery. Yosh explained that the hotel site, with layers of sediment to preserve its contents, yielded unique artifacts, including a voyaging canoe of over 65 feet—the only material evidence of the long-distance canoes of the great Polynesian navigators. It remains interred on site.

"In a few days," said Yosh, "I will travel west to study the *marae* on the islands of Tonga, which appear to have characteristics like those in Huahine." He stood and pointed in the distance toward a substantial thatched building held aloft by stilts. "Would you like to see the traditional meeting house? It's a replica built in 1974."

"Oh, yes!" I said without hesitation. While in school, I had always considered history a boring pursuit because it focused on ancient events, memorizing dates, and scratchy photos of bearded men. Here, a human expert had popped out of a textbook to show me the cultural life of ancient Polynesians. I wanted to learn more.

I crawled up a rough-hewn ladder behind the scientist to enter the house, which stood about twelve feet above the ground. Massive sculpted beams framed the structure; thatched palm fronds secured with natural woven twine covered the walls. The roof rose to a peak about thirty feet high. Inside on a woven mat sat a withered black man whose smile revealed few teeth; but his bright eyes and open arms conveyed his welcome. I smiled and bowed to him. As Yosh spoke about the dwelling, I could imagine the chiefs assembling here, making critical decisions for their people, and calling on their gods for favor.

The scientists did not rush us, but I felt we must leave them to their studies. We wished them well and pedaled to the end of the peninsula where older huts still perched on stilts over the water. Across a bridge on the outer reef motu where watermelons grew, a monument commemorated the 1846 battle when the Maeva natives, resisting French rule, killed twenty-four crewmen from the naval vessel *Uranie*. Such conflicts began with the arrival of Europeans a hundred years before that.

Back on our boat, we explored more of Huahine's lagoon and left the protection of the reef at Avapeihi Pass. Back in her realm, *Renaissance* lifted on a six-foot sea swell, and a brisk wind inspired her acceleration. We sat together in the cockpit with our legs braced to counter the boat's heeling angle and reveled in the exhilaration of sailing free on the open sea. John set course for the mountain ridge on Raiatea Island, twenty-five miles away.

A few hours later, we passed through the barrier reef at the spot where early Polynesians launched migrations throughout the Pacific navigating only by observation of the stars, seabirds, and the wind and wave patterns. We followed channel buoys through a wonderland of limeade water and sugar-cookie sand bars into a vast lagoon which enclosed the islands of Raiatea and Tahaa. A week passed there with new friends on another yacht while we explored and waited out tropical rains.

Finally, we succumbed to the lure of mystical Bora Bora, her black peak splitting the sunny sky twenty miles away. As we approached the island from the sea, I gulped several breaths to help my middle-aged brain record this astonishing beauty, perhaps sensing how important my recall would be when future life was not so bright.

"Look at this place!" I said, as John piloted us through the wide reef passage. Beside us, ocean swells tumbled over the wide reef surface like a waterfall, separating clear water into shimmering shades of green and blue inside the lagoon. Ahead of us, the volcanic cone burst from the emerald jungle island. Cotton-ball clouds dotted the horizon below a rich blue sky.

Inside the lagoon, we anchored near the Oa Oa Hotel, known as a rallying spot for cruisers from around the world who bond over our lifestyle. When we entered the spartan hotel bar, John grabbed a beer and set off across the room, hungry for the attention and social interaction to offset periods of isolation aboard. His fingers pulled at the graying beard on his chin as he engaged another captain. I wondered what tall tales he would spin again, especially without a witness. As a rule, I preferred the solitude on board, but that afternoon I sought the camaraderie of the plucky women from several boats we had encountered along the way. I cradled a Coke and joined the reunion with much less anxiety among drinkers than I had experienced in Mexico.

"Yachties are great, especially the women," I said from our dinghy as we headed home for supper. "There's no competition, no agenda, just a great sense of adventure, and the ability to roll with what life brings."

"Yeah, it's good to see some of that motley crowd again," said John with a chuckle. "Oh, and we're invited over to *Oracle* for dinner tomorrow night."

"Great, but I can't wait to explore the island and meet more Polynesians."

By ham radio, we had kept in touch with Fred and Rita on *Oracle* since John helped Fred in the Marquesas. Redheaded Rita matched John's personality: outgoing, optimistic, and spontaneous; and Fred matched mine: reserved and analytical, yet he possessed a comic wit. They joined us on their folding bikes one day to circumnavigate the island, where we uncovered WWII cannons in jungle overgrowth and stopped to cheer a ukulele jam session.

To capture a sense of local culture and enjoy again the choral music, John and I attended a whitewashed church with twin steeples. My cotton gauze peasant dress, its hem dark from the wet dinghy floor, seemed paltry compared with the bright, polyester dresses and broad brimmed hats of women who entered ahead of us. The native men arrived in rather formal garb: dark pants and starched white shirts, in sharp contrast with John's crumpled sport shirt and draw-string pants. Yet enthusiastic was our welcome. The native women sat across the front of the church, the men in rows behind them. As in Tahiti and Moorea, the harmony of their hymns of praise covered my arms with goosebumps and afforded me a natural high.

"No." I said, "It's too expensive. We are spending too much on all this yachtie partying. Running a tab at the Oa Oa is bad enough; then the outrageous prices at resorts like Club Med." I sat at our salon table, working on my provisioning inventory. My alley cat had returned in the dinghy from his regular round of yachtie visits in the anchorage as a light rain began to fall.

"Oh, come on." said John, "The paella at the BB Yacht Club they say is fantastic, and we have to reserve in advance. Fred and Rita are going."

"Do we have to please them?"

He turned back to me. "I thought you liked them."

"I do, sure. But you and I should decide things together. If we're going to splurge, I'd rather go to the Bora Bora Hotel."

"Oh, crap!" He turned away.

John, the product of a more affluent family than me, was always up for spending on spontaneous outings, especially those suggested by others; yet he complained if I bought a T-shirt. Why did I feel I begged him for things I wanted—and from money I earned too?

"Why don't we agree on a weekly allowance for extras like eating out, souvenirs, and your beer?" I said.

He groaned. Then he turned on me. "Yeah, what about your cigarettes?"

Ah ha. A constant point of irritation. I tried to hide the high cost of imported smokes within my grocery purchases. Sure, cigarettes remained an addiction I could not shed, but my fear of being without money, which I equated with loss of independence, was almost as bad. John and I were living on an average of $800/month, but this did not account for any major services or equipment replacement we might require in remote areas. Without a way to anticipate how much money we needed or how long it would last, I feared overspending. I also hoped we stayed healthy and would be back at work long before our allotted savings ran out.

Still, I hated to see him unhappy. "OK," I said. "We'll go with them tonight, but only if we order from the cheaper menu items. We have to save for unexpected needs."

John complied, we enjoyed the evening, and I agreed that the paella Rita shared with me tasted delicious. I decided to try to loosen up.

On the beach one day, I found John and Fred getting a lesson on how to open a fallen coconut. "These have great status with islanders," said Mike, a compact New Zealander, "and many a shipwrecked sailor has been saved by the lowly coconut."

"It looks like a dried-up, factory reject," said Fred, a retired systems engineer.

As we knelt before him, Mike grasped the grey sphere in the palm of his left hand and swung his machete. He tugged apart the fibrous outer husk to reveal the greenish nut. "After you uncover this, you line up the three eyes and…(whack)." He struck the nut, breaking it cleanly in half. He turned the pieces in his calloused hand, spilling little of the milk inside, and passed the halves around for us to drink. The liquid was thin, warm, and not as sweet as I expected; but quite welcome under a burning sun.

When the other wives joined us from down the beach, he cut the nut into small pieces, and we gnawed out the coconut meat. Rita stood up and brushed the sand from her bathing suit. "We found a gorgeous patch of coral down there past the arching palm," she said and moved to follow her pointing finger. "Bring your snorkels!"

I stood and took in the endless scene of sand and sea and palms and felt flooding joy for having made the time to learn about the natural world while immersed in it, as well as having adventurous friends with which to share it.

"I'm coming," I yelled after her.

We moved the boat several times to explore Bora, and each time John manually winched up the heavy anchor and chain. He had complained of low back pain several times since Moorea, but always bounced back with ibuprofen and overnight rest. One day as he sought to haul a heavy toolbox out of deep storage, I heard a strangled "Aaaaarg" and a crashing thud on the cabin floor. I found him beside the toolbox, bent and immobilized with muscle spasms. I helped him to the settee. This time the pain disabled him for several days. With him out of commission, my awareness of our vulnerability surfaced again.

Three days after his injury, the weather turned cold and stormy making our anchorage in front of the hotel dangerous. Since John could not move without painful spasms, I called on yachtie friends to help raise our anchor for a move to a more protected bay. There I picked up a mooring to insure we could escape quickly if necessary. However, I stayed awake all night worrying about the condition of the mooring line. If it parted, we might end up on the reef before I could start the engine. With no insurance on the boat, we would lose our greatest asset.

Back at the Oa Oa Hotel the next day, the wind kicked up waves in the anchorage enough to cause the mooring line of a small sailboat to part and drive her onto the reef with a dog aboard. From the shore, I watched dinghies launch from three vessels and converge on the foundering boat. After several lasso attempts, one yachtie jumped aboard it, slung a line around the boat's mast, and drove the bitter end back to *Cool Change*, a 50-foot sailboat.

Gary, her captain, agreed without hesitation to attempt the rescue. First, he ordered his two children to stay below in the cabin. Then, securing the towline to his boat's stern, he motored into the wind to slacken his own mooring line. As his wife, Karen, released their mooring, a gust caught their dinghy and blew it out of reach. The heavy yacht heeled sharply as the wind dashed it broadside and pushed it toward the reef. Gary jammed the throttle forward, and the big diesel roared out gray smoke as he struggled for control.

This represented a very tenuous position for him, especially with a slack towline over the stern, which could wrap his spinning prop and render him helpless. Ignoring her lost dinghy, Karen ran aft to tend the stern line. Gary gained control of his boat and bore away, taking up the slack, and then slowed to turn the bow of the distressed vessel and gently dislodge it from the reef. Other yachties tied the wayward boat to a mooring then rescued the dog and Karen's dinghy. Instead of becoming a total loss, the little boat sustained minor damage to the rudder because of caring strangers.

Gary was heroic to risk his boat and family in this endeavor, but I believed that we and other yachties would have come to his rescue were the tables turned. In Mexico, in Huahine, and later in Tonga we witnessed similar rescues by yachties and natives, which characterized the cruising lifestyle. Such benevolence was fast disappearing in America, where we retreat behind our iPhones, tablets, and laptops, such that we don't know or care about our neighbors. In adulthood, I ignored others and strove to attain status and money for myself, but my heart grew cold and my life flat. I was awakening to a different kind of world where people cared about each other, and it started with AA.

A few days later, when the sun returned to highlight our paradise, and John's back recovered, he steered *Renaissance* across the lagoon to a secluded coral cove for a break from the non-stop social life. I thrilled to find his optimism returning with his strength. For two days away from the Bora scene, we chased manta rays and rainbow fish in warm water as clear as gin. No phone or alarm clock interrupted, no schedule pressed. Tan and fit, we laughed and splashed, swam *sans* suits, and made love on the beach. We recalled tales of other cruisers and their vagabond lives and chuckled at how they (and we) bounced back from various calamities. We had gained confidence in adapting to the unexpected.

"Our lives have sure changed since I chose to travel—and you ran away from home," I said, looking across the lagoon. "Such an awakening since we left California...only nine months ago." I turned to him. "We face real risks living out here contending with the many moods of nature. But the freedom is invigorating. We're more self-sufficient. Life is much simpler—and it's become more wonderful with you."

John propped himself up on his forearms, squinted into the sun. "Ah, paradise. It was so worth any privation to get here. What other challenges might we face?"

CHAPTER 9

The Cook Islands — The Koras of Suwarrow

DIAMONDS CUT FROM AFTERNOON SUNBEAMS SPREAD across a corrugated sea as we sailed downwind from the Society Islands, anticipating a six-day journey. A hundred miles from land, *Renaissance* maintained a steady pace via autopilot toward the Northern Cook Islands. *

Below decks on the salon table, I fanned out hundred-dollar bills like a deck of cards atop a nautical chart. "We're rich!" I cried.

John ambled down the steps from the cockpit to stand beside me. "What are you doing?" His hand shot out toward the table, but I slapped it away.

"Wait! I want to commemorate our four months in French Polynesia."

Our departure from French jurisdiction in Bora Bora required that the government return the $2,400 U.S. cash bond we surrendered in the Marquesas. I snapped a picture of the cash lying atop a chart of Bora. "I hope there's no pirates hereabouts."

He shook his head to dismiss my silliness. "Don't you worry about that, I have plans for these little babies," he said, stuffing the bills back into their envelope.

"Let me guess…more boat gear?" It shocked me how freely he spent money. However, he always bought the best quality, where I usually went for a cheaper item—not a good idea for gear that could save our lives.

Setting out on these jaunts across the ocean now seemed rather normal, compared with our first, tense overnighters. Longer voyages allowed us to adjust to the alternating watch schedule for better sleep and allowed more time together in daylight. On this passage, instead of the usual canned food mixed with rice, I baked a defrosted chicken in my swaying, gimbaled oven. That night we ate under sail and tossed bones into the sea without a care.

John monitored high-seas weathermen on the ham radio and spoke daily with Fred on *Oracle,* a day behind us. Hundreds of miles after our collision threat, the magic of the night watches returned for me. Immersed in the sky of a thousand stars, a quarter-moon seemed close enough to touch. On the dawn watch, I arrived on deck and froze, mistaking the bright light of Planet Venus rising above the horizon for the masthead light of an approaching boat.

The Cook Islands, an independent, self-governing democracy and protectorate of New Zealand, consists of fifteen islands and numerous atolls spread over 1.36 million square miles of ocean. Along our route lay Suwarrow atoll, a popular stopover for yachties, which we believed to be uninhabited. Visiting there was illegal without formal entry into the Cook Islands, but that required sailing a thousand miles out of our way to the Southern Group. We hoped to sneak into the atoll for a brief rest without any trouble.

After covering 650 miles in five days, *Renaissance* approached another area of low-lying reefs like she dodged in the Tuamotus. John rose at dawn to help me search for any break in the horizon or change in water color. We could not trust our infrequent satellite fixes when closing on such a small target. With no other landmarks, we could not confirm a relative position. My binocular search revealed an unnatural orange chunk ahead, which became the bottom of a rusty freighter atop a reef. The wreck was not marked on our old ocean chart and thus no help in fixing our exact position. It served as a warning, however, and caused all my muscles to tense.

A chart of Suwarrow, hand-drawn by a yachtie, depicted the atoll as roughly circular with a lagoon measuring eleven miles across; but from sea level, it was very difficult to imagine. Finally, a few bumps of palm trees appeared on the horizon. We doused the sails and motored toward them at trolling speed. Once we identified the reef passage, I steered through the short, coral-filled channel with John directing me from the foredeck.

When we arrived at the spot where our rough chart indicated an anchorage, I called out our depth reading. "Sixty-five feet."

"Oh, shit," said John. That would require dumping out almost all 200 feet of chain—and worse, cranking it all back up later. He looked around for options. "Without a better chart, it's too dangerous to try for a shallower spot with the sun so low."

I watched him on the foredeck struggle and curse as he wrestled with the heavy coils of chain that must have tangled in the locker during our transit. He was able to clear and feed out only a foot or two at a time. Concerned about a repeat of his back trouble, I put the engine in neutral and went forward to help. As I labored with him under the hot sun, my scalp prickled, the skin on my arms turned red, and sweat dripped beneath my T-shirt. Within a few minutes, I noticed we were moving back with an incoming current. I returned to the wheel to maintain position. Finally, the anchor buried itself in the sand, and the boat jerked forward.

I cut the engine and looked around, while John set the anchor bridle. I saw only an ancient wooden ship, apparently abandoned some distance away, and no sign of life near a small pier. My fiery rash itched all over me. I lowered the boarding ladder. "I gotta cool off! I'm going in," I said. He crossed the deck to join me. We stripped off our sweaty shorts and tees and jumped into the water together.

After a week without a proper bath, I can still feel the joy of that refreshing, clear water closing over my head. I lay floating on my back in the water luxuriating in its fluid support, squinting at the sky, feeling energy flow back into me. Hearing a splash, I turned to see John's feet as he dove toward the anchor to assure himself that it was secured.

Casually glancing again toward the tumbled-down pier, I noted with alarm, a small boat had set out in our direction. I yelled to John and pointed, then stroked quickly to our boat, pressing my naked bum against the hull, and sucking in air to make myself smaller. *Can't hide here, they'll see me.* The motor noise increased; I bounded up the swim ladder to the deck. I saw three, burly brown men in an aluminum boat propelled by a growling outboard. I ducked below. Clearly, this atoll was not uninhabited. *What could they want of us? Were they pirates or hermits?*

I yanked up clean shorts, pulled down a tee shirt, and returned to the cockpit. John zipped his muddy shorts, greeted the natives, and tied their boat alongside. Without a word, the tallest man offered up a palm-woven basket filled with four coconuts. I waved away the offering, assuming these men were some type of boat bums trying to sell us something we couldn't use. Their faces fell with disappointment, but they soon recovered their smiles. I noticed an alert boy of about six years sitting close to one of the men, and my wariness softened. Unaware of nautical etiquette that required permission to come aboard, they all began climbing our boarding ladder, handing up the child first. John and I exchanged looks. I read no concern on his face, only curiosity, so I took a deep breath.

"Do you live here?" I asked, hoping to discover their intent.

"Yes," said one of the men. A pause as they arranged themselves in the cockpit.

"Is there also a government official?"

A pause. "Ah, that is me," said the elder man, who was dressed in shorts, a pink-and-blue Hawaiian-print shirt and a red baseball cap. "I am Petuela Kora, representative for the Cook Islands, and these are my sons, Kora, Mokoha and—," he paused and searched. He found the little one snuggled behind an older brother. "And Apii. They are 18, 16, and 8."

I let out a sigh of relief and looked again. These smiling, handsome men had the slim build and brown skin of Polynesians blended with the broader nose and tight curls of Negroid ancestors. They were well-muscled and well-mannered. John introduced us, and I felt my face flush. I must have offended them by not recognizing the coconuts as a traditional gift to seafarers, and by our nakedness as an affront to modesty inculcated by English missionaries who arrived in these islands in 1821.

In perfect English, Petuela explained that the atoll was a designated national park, and his family the only occupants—his wife and another son Enoka, age 14, had remained ashore. "My wife is a qualified teacher," he added with pride. I could not resist matching the smile in his well-lined face.

"I have two more sons back in Rarotonga," he continued proudly. "They were adopted by an aunt…because she wanted them." Perhaps an infertile woman, I thought, what a remarkable custom.

Only after they learned about our home and families and heard stories of our travels, did Petuela initiate his official duties. John helped him complete a simple form listing the boat name, homeport and passport-particulars. I feared we might incur trouble for not entering the country at an official port, but he seemed unconcerned, asking to see neither boat ownership papers, nor customs information. Then, he "fumigated" our cabin for ten seconds with an aerosol spray can.

Having learned of John's sore back and our tussle with a tangled anchor chain, Petuela offered us a mooring close to the small pier. He departed, leaving the two older boys to help bring up the anchor—lucky for us, because the chain had wrapped around a coral head again. As I watched the young men labor in the heat, I regretted how quick I was to assign them ulterior motives. Instead, they showed us brotherly love.

Our old corporate lives involved manipulation of others. These folks made that world look selfish and petty.

We motored to the spot young Kora indicated. Twenty feet below the surface I could see an enormous anchor from an ancient vessel splayed on the sand. Once we secured the boat to it, the boys drank the water I offered and bid us come ashore to visit. They dove over the side and swam home.

After lunch and a proper swim-bath, we both dozed under a fan, but woke after an hour or two, curious about the family isle. John rowed us the short distance to the four-posted pier. Paths of white sand bordered with plants led to the shade of coconut palms. At the base of a sixty-foot flagpole, a simple signboard proclaimed in block letters: "Suwarrow Atoll National Heritage Park, established 1978." An attached card defined its mission as "conservation of sea birds, turtle, coconut crabs and other marine life."

A simple plaque nearby memorialized Tom Neale, a New Zealander, who lived alone on the atoll for sixteen years until his death in 1978—an authentic Robinson Crusoe. My eyes took in the striking physical beauty of this *motu*, but my mind hesitated at its isolation, even for a dedicated loner like me. After Tom died, his brother collected his personal effects, but left the logbooks of visiting vessels, which the caretakers maintained. We signed in and became part of the atoll's official history. In a clearing sat Tom's hut, built of broad, imported timber and still standing against insects and withering storms after twenty-five years. The hut was now home to the Kora family.

As we approached, the current mistress of the atoll, Jane Kora, set aside her nearly-completed woven basket and greeted us each with a hug and kiss on the cheek. Her warm, brown skin made mine seem so pale and poorly-suited to this setting.

"Welcome, welcome," she said, with a pleasant sincerity. Stout, strong and modest, Jane exuded a clear contentment for this primitive lifestyle with her family. She invited us to sit in the shade and turned around to stir up the cookhouse fire for tea. Hot tea seemed a

British anachronism not well suited to the eighty-five-degree heat, but we indulged.

"We've read about the hermit, Tom Neale, who died here, but we expected Suwarrow to be uninhabited," I said, comforted in her motherly presence.

"Oh!" She nodded. "We arrived many months ago for a five-year service to tend the park for the Ministry of Outer Island Affairs. The men use the motorboat to fish and keep watch in the lagoon, and I tend my garden there." She pointed across the swept path to a fenced area. "We are very happy here…although I know Kora, my eldest, misses his friends back in 'Ra-ro.'"

"But you are six hundred miles from Rarotonga. How do you get supplies, like your rice?" said John. He pointed to a woven, waterproofed bag leaning against the hut, "and the outboard fuel?"

Jane smiled. "The inter-island supply ship is scheduled here every four months—unless delayed by breakdowns or storms," she allowed, averting her eyes. Then she brightened and said, "The ship just came three weeks ago" As we talked, Jane poured steaming tea into tin cups.

I admired the official-looking outhouses at a distance. Jane laughed and told of the recent arrival of a great schooner with 45 passengers plus crew. To please them and avoid confusion in such a "crowd," Petuela had hurriedly painted labels on the doors: "Ladies" and "Gentlemen."

Petuela arrived and showed us the "coconut shed," a long, three-sided lean-to with a tin roof where they stored coconuts and prepared and served food. We followed him to a roofed corner to see his radios, both ham and single-sideband. "I use these to contact 'Ra-ro' (government offices) to report visitor information, park status and weather. Oh, and perhaps you know of my brother-in-law, Arnold, who transmits the Pacific area weather. He uses New Zealand Oceanic and station reports like ours."

"Of course!" said John. "Arnold's Net, on 14.317.5 megahertz, at 0400 GMT. His weather analysis and commentary are excellent…and much appreciated by yachties."

As the men launched into discussions of atmospheric spikes and ham radio quirks, I turned back to Jane in her weaving spot to learn more about her. She had recently visited a clinic in Rarotonga for an eye problem, which they did not specifically diagnose, blaming it on sun glare. (She wore no sunglasses.) This left her the only option of travel to New Zealand for treatment should it worsen. When I suggested that a modern medical center at Pago Pago was closer, she reminded me that Suwarrow had no airstrip and sat far from any regular shipping lane toward Samoa. I persisted, concerned about how the family (or we) would face a medical emergency. "Many yachts pass here in transit to Samoa and would readily agree to take you there." She demurred again, preferring to wait months for the Cook Islands ship to return her to Rarotonga should it became necessary. I sat silent, realizing too that yachts come only during a short season, and none returned here against the prevailing wind and seas. Jane clearly preferred to suffer a potentially serious ailment with her family, rather than with distant strangers. A difficult choice, but one I began to understand.

As our hosts turned to preparation for the evening transmission to HQ, I returned to the jetty with John to find Kora and Mokoha cleaning grouper and barracuda that they caught in the pass with hand lines and red-skirted lures. They assured us that these were safe to eat, as none contains the *ciguatera* poison common in fish near the Society Islands. Without prompting, Kora handed me a nice red grouper for our dinner, and Mokoha retrieved our dinghy from the beach, like a country-club valet, to put us aboard from the jetty.

We slept late the next morning repaying our sleep debt, finally rising as the heat did. Before us sat another pristine paradise; such views of which I never tired. Our friends on the good ship *Oracle* entered the lagoon and yelled a greeting as they breezed past to cast their anchor.

The captain of *Anita*, the wooden ship I had noticed in the distance upon our arrival, came alongside with an invitation for coffee and a tour of his vessel, which was half a world away from her Scandinavian homeport. Aside from the sun-wrinkled captain and first mate, the crew consisted of three men and three women in mid-twenties, blond and glowing with *joye de vivre*. With her traditional sails, wooden blocks, and rope rigging, the old sailing ship could have been a copy of Columbus' *Nina*. The ship's galley, salon and bunkrooms were sparse but personalized with small treasures from their travels. When we returned to the open deck, Petuela waved us over to join his boys, *Anita*'s crew and *Oracle*'s crew. I marveled at this international confab brought together by our shared interest in voyaging on the sea, although we all represented distant homes and different customs. Jane and Petuela invited us all for dinner the following night.

Unsure what to expect, we rowed ashore with a potluck side dish. A spectacular feast covered a rustic table about ten-feet long inside the coconut shed. After we assembled, Petuela positioned himself in the center and clapped his hands for attention. He commenced to deliver "in the mudder tongue" the traditional island welcoming speech, which Jane translated into English. The throng applauded with enthusiasm. Then, in English, our host explained that the Ministry of Outer Island Affairs had first sent him and two other men to work on the park for three months. Upon his return to Ra-ro, the Ministry designated him as administrator and employed his family to maintain this outpost.

In the fading light, Jane appeared with woven platters of fish baked in the traditional Polynesian earth oven, whose hot stones and coconut shells slow-cooked the feast wrapped in broad leaves. Sea salt and a hint of coconut flavored the warm grouper. With added side dishes prepared by yachties, we ate from plates and utensils we were asked to bring. Stuffed-full faces glowed in the light of a bonfire. We lounged on warm sand until the Norwegian captain produced a guitar, and his crew began to sing in their language.

Overnight, a typical downpour filled our water tanks and the Koras' concrete cistern ashore. On September 7, we came ashore early in swimsuits—the women wrapped respectfully in *pareos*—to allow for frequent dips in the clear lagoon when the spirit moved. John and Fred brought ashore various spare parts to help Petuela kludge together a radio antenna. As the sun rose higher and the men bent over their wires and transistors nearby, Rita and I lolled in the shade. Jane joined us with her basketry, and I asked about her early years. She and Petuela both grew up on Manihiki, a smaller atoll 150 miles north, but they didn't connect until Jane returned there after completing teachers' college in Rarotonga.

As she paused, Petuela, in earshot, told the men (again) that his wife was a qualified teacher. I admired her too. From behind Jane, little Apii said, "When can you teach me?" His English was not as good as the other boys, who had attended school on the main island. Kora, the eldest son, hoped to return there soon to complete an apprenticeship in motor mechanics and to travel with his New Zealand passport.

Life in Suwarrow atoll, as Jane described it, was not dull. During the fine weather (May-October) they logged in and entertained visitors. Their diet consisted mainly of fish, rice and coconut, supplemented with breadfruit. Despite the sandy soil, Jane pointed out sprouts of new taro plants and greens, arrowroot, and sweet potato in her garden. I asked about the few chickens I noticed ranging around the homestead.

"We do not eat the eggs, in hopes of increasing the flock, but will fatten the best chicks with coconut and food scraps for Christmas dinner.

The radio antenna was ready for a trial. Lean and handsome with thick Afro hair, Kora Kora, dressed only in shorts, stripped a fibrous palm frond, tied his ankles together with it, and scampered up a coconut tree to place the antenna on high. I admired his body as well as his climbing technique. The improved reception allowed his dad to tune the radio and talk to a passing yacht that night.

The family would soon begin preparations for the December-March cyclone season to minimize storm destruction in this area which was dangerous to mariners. "Last season, my boys crossed rough lagoon waters at dusk to investigate a "mayday" transmission, but found no trace of a ship in distress," said Petuela. As he expounded on his experiences, our host truly exemplified the generous, fun-loving nature of the Pacific Islanders of lore. He also appeared to be a conscientious administrator and had even expelled some visitors who had violated park regulations. Petuela offered his boys to take four of us fishing on the reef in their twelve-foot aluminum boat on the next afternoon, to which we all responded enthusiastically. I was anticipating some great snorkeling too.

The next morning while I was baking, John rowed our dinghy ashore to work on the radio project. Two hours later the steel utility boat drove by me carrying John, Fred, Rita, and two Kora boys. When I appeared on deck, they waved. I threw my upturned hands out to John to say, "What gives?" but they all laughed and sped past me. John had not spoken up for me, and another visitor became the sixth passenger. "What a selfish bastard! You knew I wanted to go," I wailed after him. Being left out struck a deep hurt inside me. That feeling of being on the outside looking in surfaced again, and I wallowed in pity and stomped around the boat all afternoon.

When John returned, I railed at him for not including me, "You know I love snorkeling. You are so inconsiderate and self-centered!" I couldn't leave it up to him to consider me. I had to be more assertive about my needs.

Saturday made up for my lost trip. Alf, the Norwegian first mate, John and I crossed the lagoon with the Kora boys in their boat; *Oracle*'s crew followed in their dinghy. On Bird Island, we walked with our guides in the nursery where large white birds sat in nests exhibiting no fear of us. A chick speckled with black wobbled his first steps from the nest.

The nearby reef at low tide was a moonscape: wide, brown and spiny where it rose above the water's surface. Many deep pools trapped marine life as the water receded. Ahead of me, John plodded along nervously in his reef sandals. Suddenly a living thing thrashed past me and slammed into John's ankle. Startled, he yelped and turned to behold a stranded shark, three-feet long with a gaping mouth and characteristic scythe tail.

"Aaaaah!" He wailed harder at the sight. The pelagic fish, startled from a pool and slightly more panicked than John, wriggled back into the lagoon.

"Wow," I said, trying to calm him when no blood appeared, "He must have hit you with his fat nose. But now you can spin a story for your kids about your shark attack in the wild Cook Islands!"

We caught up with Kora and Mokoha to help them catch crustaceans along the reef wall. Below the surface, the water was as clear as air. They sent us greenhorns to poke at the gray-green crayfish from behind, and the islanders deftly speared them. After stashing an abundant catch in the boat, Kora beckoned us to swim a short distance into the lagoon to admire a tower that rose twenty feet from the sea floor festooned with corals in vibrant shades of green, yellow, and purple. I felt a current of very hot water pouring up from the pinnacle, which I guessed arose from the atoll's sunken volcano.

We watched Mokoha spear a nice string of red snapper. With his guidance, John tried the spear but with no success. His jabs looked too timid, perhaps aware of the small, white-tip reef sharks that circled us. Mokoha laughed watching John, perhaps amazed that a man could grow to maturity without knowing how to handle a fishing spear. Our guides also collected an octopus and some giant clams, and Kora even trolled with a hand line as we motored back home in a boat full of fresh seafood, free for the taking—if you know how!

That night in the cookhouse, the Koras prepared and shared the catch with crews from (now) four visiting boats. After dinner, the boys stoked the fire to heat rocks for the earth oven to cook the family's Sunday dinner overnight. As the evening ended, Jane quietly explained that the family "would be occupied" with religious observances the next day, and that no work was permitted. There was no proselytizing of their religious beliefs; they just exemplified God's commandment to love one another.

On Sunday after the Norwegians departed, John and I tried to read and rest, but felt much deprived of the company of the Koras. We rowed over to *Oracle* for a potluck chicken supper, where we all tried to explain the peace that we felt in being with our island hosts. By our standards, they were poor, yet showed none of the misery that status connotes. Content with the simple life we sought, they demonstrated unconditional love toward people and gratitude for life's bounty. More than accepting their lot, they found joy in it and shared it with us.

"Think of all the stress and loss we Americans endure to amass all the stuff we think we need," I said.

Fred turned to me. "You were a contract administrator. You must be restless out here. In my experience with CA's at Boeing, they were very intense—two suffered heart attacks before I retired."

"I certainly started out that way, but I'm recovering…some balance." I said.

We spent two more days following around our native family members like curious puppies as they went about the business of living in paradise: Petuela keeping his radio schedules and logbooks, and Jane sewing a bright yellow and purple quilt, while the boys fished, tended the garden, or chased coconut crabs through the oversized flora.

One week after our tense arrival, we went ashore for a sad goodbye. John cried along with me as the family presented us with a souvenir scroll decorated with colorful Cook Island postage stamps and a note that read:

To my dear friends, John and Judith:

Thank you very much for all your help in assisting in fixing my antenna. I'll never forget you in my life. I miss you and hoping that one day we will meet again. We say goodbye: Aere ra kia manuia. *All the best pleasant sailing.*

From your friend, Petuela, wife Jane & sons Kora, Mokoha, Enoka & Apii. We love you. We hope that little gift will always remind you of us here in Suwarrow.

At noon we cast off from the antique anchor and retraced the coral-strewn channel. Once clear of obstacles, we looked back to find Jane and Kora, who had crossed the island on foot, waving palm branches from a hill.

After the island faded from sight, John contacted Petuela on a prearranged ham radio schedule. As they talked, emotion choked up the men, so I took the microphone and spoke to Jane. We all cried out our love and good wishes until we could speak no more.

* *Named for the British explorer, Captain James Cook, the island group became a British Protectorate in 1888 to thwart French designs on them. This vast area is believed to have first been settled in the sixth century by Tahitians, and the inhabitants are ethnically linked by language and custom with the Maori people of New Zealand.*

PART III

Staying Together

Jone, Vaki and their kids with John in Soso, Yasawa, Fiji

CHAPTER 10

The Islands of Samoa — A Separation

FROM TWENTY MILES AT SEA, WE DETECTED THE entrance to Pago Pago Harbor that nearly bisects the old, volcanic island of Tutuila, the largest of five islands of American Samoa. I flicked on our short-range VHF radio, and various voices shouted at us from the port.

"Pago Pilot!?" (*squawk*) "Break, Break!"

"Radio Pago, *Phuket Maru*."

"Stand clear! Docking operations in progress."

"Radio Pago to the vessel calling."

Our eyes met with concern at the commotion. The frenzied calls continued as we passed between the portal bluffs of the broad harbor entrance. The long waterway narrowed into a dogleg left that ended in a canyon of steep, green hills fifteen-hundred feet high. After the tranquility of Suwarrow Island and three calm nights of sailing, we suddenly found ourselves inside a bustling, international port. Our heads swung in all directions, startled and distracted by the echo of heavy machinery from tuna fish canneries, screeches from towering cranes unloading container ships, and the growl of monster earthmovers ashore. The hills pressed in, and the clamor of civilization made me tense. John called in and followed the Port Captain to another radio channel for clearance instructions.

Renaissance advanced like an innocent lamb into the pungent, effluent-filled waters and scraped rudely against the concrete Customs Wharf. Stern bureaucrats quickly surrounded her like a trapped prey: Port Captain and officials of U.S. Coast Guard, Customs, Immigration, Agriculture, and the Environmental Protection Agency. Because we arrived midmorning on Saturday, they demanded an overtime fee for clearance. I was out of cigarettes and John out of beer, so we agreed to pay, rather than be quarantined at anchor until Monday. After departure of brusque civil servants, we wrapped our dock lines in rags and duct tape to protect them from chaffing as they passed over the grisly pier.

At 3:30 P.M., a timid *Oracle* came in and nuzzled against *Renaissance* for comfort. On the radio, we heard the Port Captain tell Fred he must wait until Monday for clearance with a stern warning not to go ashore. When they came alongside, Rita clambered onto our boat and handed me their priority shopping list: rum and beer. John and I hopped ashore with backpacks and some of our Tahiti-bond cash to find a store.

Locals directed us to a weathered, retail warehouse, which represented heaven's big-box store for vagabonds. It was operated by The Burns Philp Company—Pacific traders since 1872. A focused shopper, John located the booze and a bag of ice and hustled me out after I grabbed some treasures. On our return to the boat, I stowed the first eggs and beef we had seen in months. The quarantined *Oracle* crew relaxed in our cockpit with cocktails. Curious expats came by to hear of our travels and answer a few questions about Pago Pago. Within two hours, John and Fred were royally drunk. As the voice volume and the idiocy increased, I withdrew to our forepeak bunk to brood and fell asleep early.

I arose at dawn on Sunday, which was observed in Samoa, like in the Cook Islands, as a serious day of rest and spiritual reflection. While John remained abed entertaining his hangover, I luxuriated in the public shower beside the pier. I walked with an unwelcome gloom along the waterfront of Pago Pago harbor, where the canyon walls minimized me. At the makeshift marina, I spied yachtie kinfolk recognizable by our usual attire: faded T-shirts from exotic ports, pull-up shorts, and flip-flops. From the head of the gangway, I was thus recognized and welcomed by Paula, a friendly woman who began my orientation to the island.

"I work at the Mental Health Clinic. There are plenty of jobs here in Pago, and a lot of cruisers have stayed two or three years—of course, everybody's off work today." She waved me down onto the floating dock to meet her mate.

A tall, tanned man with sun-bleached and tousled hair joined us. "Hi, I'm Phil. You just get in?"

"I'm Judy. Yup, via Suwarrow. Three days of great sailing," I surveyed the well-worn yachts beyond them. "Looks like you've got a nice community here."

"Sure is," he said. "Where's your crew?"

"Pretty hung over," I said with a discomforted chuckle. "John, my husband, with a buddy-boat crew, got drunk last night. Found ample supplies here!"

Phil responded with a sympathetic snicker. "Well, I don't drink any more. Can't handle it. Got sober in California."

"I did too!" I said, cheered up. "In Sunnyvale. How amazing."

"Yes!" He said, "I helped a girl get sober there."

"Pago has AA, you know, three times a week, at the hotel," Paula said. "It's easy to find." She held both my hands. Phil hugged me with compassion, and we parted.

I finished my walk along the strand in better spirits, but this over-regulated environment, along with yesterday's clash with the drinkers, brought forth dismal demons from my past. Shame about my alcoholism lay just below the surface, covered by a thin layer of delight at having a new culture to explore. I tried to buoy myself by anticipating all that Pago promised on Monday: letters from home, fresh food, Laundromats, restaurants, supermarkets, a clinic, book swaps, satellite TV, even ice cream.

After fixing lunch for John, I spent the afternoon at the coin-op under mounds of laundry, with the promise of fresh, fluffy towels—impossible to wash by hand. That night we joined local yachties for a BBQ potluck in a park adjacent to the marina. We enjoyed the company and, as usual, drifted apart to talk with different people on different topics: he on mechanics and boat gear, me on the island highlights and native culture. He drank a lot again and resisted returning to the boat. I walked back to the Wharf and slept alone again.

On Monday morning, I awoke from a dream with a start, convinced I was drinking again. It set me up to relive those wretched days of desperation. John, after an early "hair-of-the-dog" beer, landed on the pier to help Fred complete check-in procedures. The dirty harbor forbade my usual cool morning swim, so I began to attack the mildew inside lockers by applying vinegar. As I worked, the sun rose higher and the skin on my arms and legs burned with a flare-up of my eczema. I began to cry, then sob.

What is your problem? There's nothing here to cry about. I groaned in misery. I pictured John happily bullshitting with officials in an air-conditioned room and then negotiating replacement of some boat gear by waiving hundred-dollar bills from our bond refund. Considering the intensity of his drinking and the growing distance between us since arrival, I felt the hurt of rejection and gloom of grief.

I was still whimpering when he returned and said we must leave the Customs Wharf immediately. He showed me official papers that threatened, "SAILORS ARE REMINDED THAT HARBOR MOVEMENTS ARE PROHIBITED WITHOUT PRIOR WRITTEN APPROVAL FROM THE DIRECTOR OF PORT ADMINISTRATION. EACH VIOLATION IS A SUMMARY FINE OF $100."

"This is an outrage," I said. "Movement prohibited! Surrendering our freedom to those self-righteous bureaucrats?"

He started the engine. "Let's go. Get the lines."

Inside our assigned area, our anchor dug into the encrusted harbor floor only after several bounces. I sat down heavily and took a deep breath trying to clear the sorrow that flooded me. When John noticed my distress, I tried to explain it.

"I'm unhappy." I coughed to force back an oncoming flood of weeping and avoided his eyes. "You're drinking a lot. I can't be around you, then." I shook my head and stared at my hands. "I'm always itching in this heat." I began to snivel again. "Oh, I don't *know*!" I sobbed.

He moved closer. "But I was just celebrating arrival with our friends on the weekend! You're overreacting. "We can get things we need for the boat here and some necessary maintenance. And you can get some steroids for your skin."

I turned away. *I'm being irrational.* His logic made my concerns seem trivial, but a deep fog of despair closed over me. I couldn't say what I wanted or what was hurting. The drinking, the polluted harbor, the regulations, our conflicting goals all clashed violently with the love and serenity of Suwarrow atoll. All the things I thought I'd left behind fueled my distress. I felt trapped, discarded, lost.

After lunch, we rode the dinghy ashore. He sent me off on the public mini-bus to get some skin ointment and to find some solace at an AA meeting. I met with three other alcoholics in a storage room at the Rainmaker Hotel. The brief discussion group only served to recall my drunken past and left me feeling worse.

At dinner in the hotel, Rita admitted to the same sadness and sobbing, which she blamed on the unfulfilling drudgery of our role on board. That certainly contributed to my sadness. *But why am I so depressed.? What do I want? Do I need to be more assertive…?*

After a week of tending to maintenance and gathering supplies and services for the boat and ourselves, I hoped to explore the Samoan culture. Contacts with Dr. Sinoto in Huahine and many natives had piqued my interest in the history of Pacific Islanders. Their communities and customs seemed to offer qualities I might adopt to replace some destructive aspects of my former life.

A hereditary *Tui Manua* (king) had ruled a vast Pacific empire that included the Cook Islands, the Samoas, Tonga, and Fiji Islands until he ceded power to the U.S. in 1904. Forty miles from Pago lay the nine islands of Western Samoa (since 1997, called The Independent State of Samoa) which had been a possession of New Zealand for about fifty years. I wondered how different these two Samoan island groups were since a European treaty had separated them almost a century ago. With a half-fare flight and an offer to stay overnight on a friend's boat there, we decided on a quick visit.

At the Pago Pago Airport we boarded a schizophrenic 727 painted on one side with "Air Polynesia" and on the other, "Cook Islands International Air." I laughed at this, as it seemed to reflect my inconsistent moods. The plane flew low over luminous coral reefs to the big island of Upolu in the steamy shadow of six-thousand-foot Mt. Silisili.

We landed back in early Polynesia. Apia, the capital, reflected the pride of *fa'a Samoa* (the Samoan way), a traditional system of morality and responsibility that spells out Samoan relationships within extended families and with authorities. Fragrant flowering bushes, white-washed, stone markers along the roadsides, and trim *fale* (oval-shaped homes) reflected a congenial community. No trash spattered the ground; no smelly, screeching machinery to tolerate. I dragged along behind John, sweaty and forlorn, but in this sweet place, I found some hope that I could regain my equilibrium. The structures along the harbor front displayed early styles of sequential British, German and American occupiers. The friendly folks at the New Zealand embassy provided us six-month visas we would need later.

At the beat of a snare drum, I turned to witness the approach of the Western Samoa Police Band. White battle helmets covered the men's heads, though they marched in leather sandals. Their sky-blue uniform jackets matched below-the-knee skirts. In the persistent heat of the area, the wraparound skirt, *lavalava*, represented the primary article of clothing for both sexes, as it provided the best ventilation. The *lavalava* made of gabardine projected a more business-like image.

At the edge of town, the open marketplace brimmed with a colorful collection of people and produce. Wooden tables displayed mounds of coconuts, tomatoes and greens drawn from the rich volcanic soil in land owned communally by clans. I called John's attention to two men with traditional, black tattoos swirling around exposed thighs. The broad tattoo designs, which extend from waist to knee, would be painful to acquire, since custom demanded that the design be completed once begun. Beyond ubiquitous woven baskets filled with fresh fish, shy vendors carved parts of chicken and pork for villagers. The preeminent Taro root, a starchy staple food that originated in Southeast Asia, arrived here with Polynesian ancestors about 1500 BC. The efforts of these vendors satisfied their needs and maintained their culture here—without the extensive imports upon which Pago Pago and French Polynesia relied.

The next morning, we toured the area in an open-air van with a jolly Samoan guide past waterfalls and plantations with sun-absorbing rows of coffee, taro, and banana plants. My ability to use English with natives here also improved my mood.

At sunset, we joined yachties and a few tourists at historic Aggie Grey's Hotel for *fia fia*, a traditional Samoan celebration of feasting and dancing. Many a WWII serviceman enjoyed R&R at Aggie's while stationed in the Pacific Islands, in the tradition of traders, pirates and ex-pat adventurers before them. Festooned in fresh flowers, a troupe of about twenty dancers, drummers and guitar players wearing red, white and yellow *lavalava* took the stage. In short grass skirts, the women gracefully portrayed stories with their arms, but without the Hawaiian hip-swaying. Handsome young men danced to fast, drumming tempos that employed vigorous body slapping, foot stamping, and bent-knee knocking. Their happy "yip, yip" yelps echoed throughout the room. Swept up in the drama and excitement, I swayed to match their genuine joy. An extraordinary feast followed that included suckling pig, slow-cooked in the traditional *umu* underground oven.

My contentment did not last. The day after our return to Pago, I woke with a sore throat accompanied by an achy exhaustion. A doctor at the LBJ Medical Center diagnosed bronchial pneumonia and ordered two weeks of rest to insure the antibiotics took hold. John again spent long hours ashore without me, drinking with other yachties between errands. He rejected my suggestions to explore and became obsessed with departing the noisy, foul harbor. Petty theft reflected the Samoan custom of communal ownership of property, but it added another irritant. Out in the harbor, the humid heat made chores torture for me. Weak and alone, I read, dozed, and wrote letters. I resented being trapped on board while John's spent so much time socializing ashore without me. Feelings of self-pity and despair returned, and depression engulfed me.

A few days after my pneumonia diagnosis, we sat in the cockpit eating chicken and rice as the sun touched the top of our canyon. "This place is a sewer," John said. He turned away from the bay to face me. "You're sick and the boat is being eaten by putrid barnacles. We've got to get out of here."

"But I want to see more…interact with the people here. I love the simple way of life of the islanders…the close, extended families, like Petuela and Jane."

"But you are ill, you're sick." He moved closer. "Your skin is grey. You look like hell."

"Oh," I turned away defeated. A cold silence ensued.

Pushing his plate away, he tried again. "I've met a young New Zealander. He's been serving on a Christian missionary vessel across the harbor." John waved off my sullen stare. "Warrick has skipper's papers and experience in these waters. He and I can sail the boat down to Tonga. You should stay here, until you're well enough, then fly down to meet me in Vava'u."

I could see he was determined. My throat tightened, and I coughed. He was going to reject me first. We had not been apart even one day since we set off from San Francisco almost a year ago. Panic gripped me. I always assumed my new life would include him. I felt discarded, abandoned. *Leave the boat, just because I'm sick*? I lit a cigarette.

He turned on me. "How can you smoke, when you can hardly breathe?"

"I'm an addict," I said to shut him up.

I pondered his proposal. I recalled our bad experience with taking crew and the expense of the flight bothered me. "No," I said. "It's only a three-day passage. I can do it."

"You need to stay here," he retorted and rambled on, rationalizing his plan.

I could see he was excited about sailing with this guy.This had to be about more than my welfare. *He's trying to get rid of me*. Our interests had continued to diverge. Booze was more interesting to him than island culture. Hours with him discussing boat mechanics spread a glaze over my brain. I felt anger rise. *Oh, hell. Maybe we should split up for a while.*

Worn down by John's diatribe, I agreed to meet Warrick.

On the day we parted, I awoke to barking dogs. Again, *Renaissance* bumped against the coarse Customs Wharf. Warrick appeared promptly at 7:30 A.M. He and John bounded off to Immigration to replace me on the official crew list for clearance out of the country. Upon their return, John carried my duffle bag and daypack to Herb & Sia's Motel. I stood weak and shaky in the small lobby. He paced while I checked in. Looking sheepish, he gave me a hug, turned and strode away. I felt a chill as he departed, but not about concern for his safety at sea. *He's holding something back.*

I settled into my non-floating room with the big fan and shared bath. Without a need to conserve water, I could shower, sleep and enjoy my books without interruption. With all that luxury, I felt giddy. I would eat in restaurants and get to know some Samoans.

When I left my room in early evening a boy politely turned me around, saying it was the time of evening prayers. Back inside, Sia told me with regret that even with the curfew, such customs were now crumbling as many families neglected their prayers and no longer attended church.

In the coolness of early morning, I walked to town, shielded from the sun in a broad-brimmed hat, a loose cotton shirt and long gauze pants. I bought an airplane ticket to Viva'u, Tonga. At the telephone exchange, I called my brother Don, who was handling our affairs. Thrilled to find a favorite sibling at home, I updated him on our planned itinerary. He offered little family news and no problems with my credit card bills. I left the building cheered by our connection.

On the street, I smiled at women in their colorful cotton skirts. At Hillside Variety at the far end of the harbor, I visited Mr. Ah Soon—the answer to "When will my order be ready." He had the T-shirts silk-screened with a picture of our boat, which I had ordered as Christmas gifts. I returned to my room exhausted.

The next morning, I swallowed more antibiotics and ventured further from town to learn more about the place. American Samoa became a U.S. Territory in 1904, and during the Pacific War from 1942 to 1944, the Naval Station at Pago Pago Harbor became a vital supply base. At that time, the U.S. employed many natives, and our Marines outnumbered the local population. The continued presence of military personnel influenced the local culture.

On the unpaved street before me, I spied the open-air jitney bus to Tufu, the end of the line on the island's north side, according to my map. I pulled myself up four steps to a seat behind the driver. He smiled and assured me that he circled the harbor and returned "right here in a couple hours."

Off we went in a cloud of warm dust with rock-and-roll music blasting from his cassette player. The dashboard was decorated with glittering Christmas swags, tiny mirrors and cotton popcorn trim. Along the route he greeted everyone in English or Samoan in great depth. Ninety-five percent of the islanders I observed were stout, smiling Samoans; five percent were *pelangi* (Caucasian) or Chinese merchants. At a stop near a tuna cannery, I climbed down to visit the girls in their white uniforms on their mid-morning break. They smiled at my compliments, but their shyness hindered much discourse. I longed to belong.

Away from the busy harbor, we passed deserted beaches bordered by massive, tropical fern trees. Worn volcanic peaks framed the horizon. With few other riders, my open bus climbed cliffs beside the sea where aqua water stretched to meet crystal waves breaking on the reef. Further along, parts of the cliff had washed away creating a small, tall island upon which two or three palm trees clung. *Being detached is brave but lonely.*

My bus stopped at several tidy villages, giving me a closer look at rural life. Builders reproduced traditional oval-shaped *fale* in various combinations of hand-woven thatch, brick, stucco, and corrugated iron. No matter the material, the front yards of many houses displayed above-ground, concrete tombs for ancestors like those in Western Samoa. Although this practice unsettled me, I admired the love and respect they displayed toward elders and ancestors and each other.

At the end of the line, I disembarked while the driver took his break. The music stopped and silence ruled. I wandered down a path toward the secluded beach and paused at a building site. Most of the men working in the rising heat preferred colorful *lavalava* to shorts, and I struggled with the unusual sight of a muscular, tattooed Samoan in a skirt hefting a box full of bricks.

A group of children approached. In school uniforms, accompanied by their teachers, they stopped to say hello to me. Hmm. Actually, they all said, “bye” even as a first greeting. The people in Western Samoa had used opposite words as well. When asked a direct question, most natives looked tense and answered "yes," even while knowing that answer was untrue. *Why would they lie?* I learned that they considered "No" disagreeable or impolite. I mulled that idea. When I say no to someone's request for help, isn't that being unpleasant to them?

I returned to my room tired and weak again, but grateful for a day to interact with the people of Tutuila Island. John's recent disinterest in exploring together and our abrupt separation distressed me, but I swore I would not stay with him if his drinking dominated our relationship. For my own sake. Yes, I might be stranded in the middle of the Pacific Ocean, but I had had the courage to give up a secure life and cross the Pacific to find a more meaningful one. *I lived without him for thirty-three years before we met, and I can do it again if necessary.*

CHAPTER 11

The Kingdom of Tonga — Discord in the Friendly Isles

AFTER CLEARANCE FROM THE DOCTOR IN SAMOA, I FLEW about 400 miles south to the Kingdom of Tonga—the last remaining monarchy in Polynesia. As the plane descended, I strained against my seatbelt to view some of that nation's 170 sparkling islands scattered across the International Dateline. My commuter jet landed on the high plateau of Vava'u, largest of the islands in the northern group.

Still weak from pneumonia, I hefted my duffle bag down the stairs into the white heat and dropped it on the tarmac. A billboard greeted me: "Welcome to the Friendly Islands." And then, I thought I heard trumpets. A twenty-five-piece brass band, uniformed in sky blue and white with gold trim, sat on a platform in front of the terminal. I looked around for a celebrity and beheld under an awning, His Majesty King (George) Taufa'ahau Tupou IV of Tonga sitting like an apparition in formal regalia with members of his court. *What a welcome!* In truth, his party waited to take my airplane back to his palace on the southern island of Tongatapu. Never mind. I loved it. I lifted my bag and trudged up the path toward the royal entourage. I paused beside the majestic and popular king for a closer look and bowed my head toward him.

Inside the terminal I obtained an entry visa, and I introduced myself to a matronly, native woman. She directed me to the Vava'u Guest House and provided assurance I would be safe there while I waited for my husband. Located on a hill above the port of Neiafu, the lodging was inexpensive, though more reminiscent of my old Girl Scout camp than an inn. The long, wood-framed structure enclosed a shared bath and four rooms ventilated via a chicken-wire opening at the top of each wall. My tidy room contained two hard bunks and, in place of a TV or telephone, a bible that reflected the cultural connection with early Methodist missionaries. The space felt quite large after our cramped quarters on our boat—and it was all mine.

Our dismal split-up the past week still hurt. Sadness and self-pity, familiar companions always waiting to surface, dogged me after we parted in Pago. Still shaky and resenting John for the time he spent partying there, I wallowed in the ache of his rejection and departure on our boat. I strained to push aside my depression.

So, he wants a separation "to give me time to rest?" Really? I folded my arms and sat on the bed. *Well, by forcing me to choose between him and sobriety, he loses!* I reaffirmed that I would go on, if necessary, without him, to travel, to explore and learn, and to find a good life, a sober life.

My respite from the boat and its drudgeries also set me outside the shadow of John's dominant personality. I did need rest, but I could go or stay, sleep or stay up without his manipulation. I wandered the town able to speak English with shopkeepers and local women who sat in the shade weaving fine baskets. I attended a church celebration feast, petted some pet pigs in a yard and enjoyed their human family. Now I had room to breathe. I relished the freedom—rather like my uncoupling from Silicon Valley. At the Paradise Hotel, I joined happy-hour reunions with yachties from our Bora Bora days. I ordered a Coke and told my own stories without John's usual interruptions.

Two days later when the yachtie grapevine at the hotel advised me of *Renaissance's* arrival, I was glad to hear they were safe. My seven-day separation from John, the longest in over eleven years of marriage, felt sad, like a failure, but I acknowledged mixed feelings about rejoining him. *Could we travel together again without a bottle between us?* My self-pity at the time crowded any consideration of the pain I had caused him over my drinking.

I borrowed a friend's mobile VHF radio and hailed *Renaissance.* "Hi, John. I heard you made it...how was the trip from Samoa?"

"Hi, there. We got in too late to clear with Immigration, so we're stuck here 'til Monday."

"Too bad," I said, but secretly relished the extra nights alone on shore.

"Guess what?" He said. "The day after we left Pago, that bronchitis you had? It knocked me flat. But Warrick was great crew. He handled everything for the last two days, with pinpoint celestial navigation. He even baked scones!"

I recoiled at the perceived put down to my abilities. "That's sure a difference from our last crew," recalling the Dan debacle. Although he neglected to ask about my health, I added, "I'm still on antibiotics for the pneumonia, but feeling better. See ya Monday." It was the most enthusiasm I could muster for him.

"OK. *Renaissance* out," he said to terminate the contact.

Two days later, with my shore leave ended, I packed up and trudged downhill to the government wharf in Neiafu. After the last official departed, I climbed aboard and returned John's big hug. His familiar, sweaty smell and touch comforted me. I stretched to kiss his lips, which responded. Recovered from his bronchitis and back to his cheerful self, he remained unaware of my feelings of loss and sadness—feelings he could not know, since I still could not explain them. I feared that his selfishness and drinking would continue and that he preferred the company of others anyway. I mourned him.

I looked around the tidy cockpit and peeked down into the cabin below. It felt right to be back in our boat home. I couldn't leave. I loved him and this vagabond lifestyle. I wished I were more assertive, but there was that old hesitancy to complain. I needed him, but…

I turned back to make conversation. "The Tongans are very friendly—you'll love it here. I went to a feast at the church up the hill on my first day, and there's lots of —"

"That's great," he said and without pause, expanded upon how great Warrick performed as my replacement on the three-day trip.

"Well, sorry," I said with a shrug, "Now all you got is me." Tears brimmed up, stinging my eyes.

He stopped and looked at me, uncomprehending. "But— you're my baby. My love, …my all-around first mate."

I hugged him again. "Thanks, I really needed that." I pinched my nose to mask a snuffle. "Guess I've been a little blue." I turned to the dock lines. "Start her up and let's get *Rennie* over to the anchorage."

Before Warrick departed for his New Zealand home, he introduced us to an aspiring minister, Villiami Vakapuna, who invited us to spend a weekend in his village. John and I accepted without hesitation. In contrast with our Samoa experience, John now seemed eager to experience the local culture with me. Perhaps Warrick, a missionary volunteer, had piqued his interest, or, just maybe, he wanted to share my interests. Villiami became our ambassador explaining Tongan language, customs and lore. His brown skin, sturdy build, and moderate Afro hairstyle were typical; but not the trim beard that circled his chin and the thin mustache that framed his dazzling smile.

On Saturday morning, he came aboard and guided *Renaissance* around sparkling coral ridges to an empty anchorage near Okoa village on the north shore of Vava'u Island. A gaggle of curious children met us on the beach and tagged along as we walked up a path of red dirt to the village. Adults wearing *lavalava* skirts and mismatched, thrift store clothing passed us with shy smiles. Dwellings were constructed from a patchwork of woven pandanus fronds, wood panels, and squares of corrugated iron. Inside the huts, people endured dirt floors.

I caught up to the men. Villiami proudly ushered us into a new "*pelangi-*" (European) type house with a shingled roof, planked walls painted green, even glass windows. Upon entering, John whispered to me, "There's no electrical wiring or plumbing in here. No kitchen." The only furniture consisted of platform bunk beds with four-inch-thick, straw mattresses in a side room. Apparently, the village used the house only for visiting elders, nobles or missionaries.

From the rear of the house, an uncharacteristically slim woman appeared in a polyester dress that reached to her ankles. Fapuiyaki (Pui), Villiami's wife, fresh from her job in Nieafu, boldly shook our hands and welcomed us. Educated in Hawaii at Brigham Young University, Pui bustled with intelligence and the kind of social energy that had attracted me to my husband. Villiami held up the couple's children, ages six months and eighteen months, for a photo. Abruptly he handed them back to the care of his sister, and we saw them no more. These infants certainly recognized their parents, but I detected no special bonding between Pui and her children. I suspected she was under much more pressure to procreate in Tongan culture than I dealt with in mine; but for her, childbearing seemed of no more importance than passing an English exam. I admired her self-assurance.

We dropped our backpacks in the bunkroom and presented gifts of canned food, raisins, and nuts which were abruptly accepted and set aside on beams of the unfinished wall. Hustled into the backyard, we met some extended family—siblings, uncles, cousins, and a pastor—gathered near the open fire of the exterior cookhouse. Few of them spoke English, but our hosts translated for us. No fences separated the yards.

The men drew John into the bush gardens to collect coconuts, papaya and orange-flavored bananas, while I sat on a bench watching women layer the *umu*, (earth oven) for Sunday's main meal. The women's smiles were sincere and hospitable. The children made no effort to contain their curiosity, following my every move. I laughed at the antics of the runny-nosed tykes as they chased black piglets between the huts. An irresistible three-year-old twin called James shyly approached me, pointed and whispered with awe, "pork-a," to acknowledge the high status of porkers in his world. With the average temperature of eighty-five degrees, all children ran naked until the age of six (when they started school); the older ones wore only shorts until puberty.

After sunset, Pui invited us inside the house to sit on the floor on a fine mat woven by hand from the pandanus leaves. Atop a tablecloth before us lay a bountiful meal large enough for six people: rich mutton ribs and gravey called *sipi* accompanied by dishes of Ramen noodles, coconut creamed greens, baked yams (which indicated special respect) and chunks of fresh fruit. It tasted like the best of barbeque and comfort food. As in Suwarrow, our hosts insisted we eat first and deserted us. I tried to temper John's huge appetite, reminding him to leave some food for our hosts, as I suspected they awaited our leftovers.

After we finished eating, elder men arrived to include John in some serious deliberations at their meetinghouse, not so subtly indicating no women allowed. I chuckled behind my hand at this anachronism. The invitation conferred respect on John, but the men spoke only in Tongan. Young Villiami had insufficient status to interrupt for translation, so John endured an hour sitting on a floor mat with legs crossed, drinking ceremonial kava and unable to participate. Later, he described to me how they crushed dry, spindly roots of a pepper plant into a carved bowl and added water to make a grey broth, which they scooped out with coconut-shell cups.

"It tastes like dirty water and makes your lips numb," he said with a sour face.

While the men communed, I happily followed Pui down the hill to open her 5 x 9-foot village store. She swung up and latched a half-door over the counter, uncovered a scale, and pulled out a record book. Her regular job, keeping accounts at the Fisheries Department five-and-a-half days a week, paid the loan on the little store.

"Villiami is supposed to run the store during the day," she said, "but he seems to spend more time as a roaming ambassador. He's a dreamer."

I laughed. "That sounds like John. He spends hours wandering the docks talking to other boat people. It's his full-time job now."

I sat astride a tall stool and looked around. Two rows of shelves on the back wall held at least thirty cans of mackerel, eight kinds of corned beef, a few cans of fruits and vegetables, and some condiments; under the counter I saw tins and sacks of dry goods. Villagers began arriving to pay on their accounts and procure salt, lard, flour, thick soda crackers or loose tobacco, which Pui weighed and wrapped in paper.

In the cool evening people stayed to tell stories, roll smokes, sing, and practice their English. I consumed a sweet and warm orange-pineapple soda bottled in Tonga's capital city and absorbed a loving acceptance from these village people. Two young mothers brought me a tattered Family Circle Magazine and pointed with skepticism to an article about a Tongan couple in the U.S. who had quadruplets. I assured them it was even possible for women to have eight babies. When I held up that many fingers, they gasped. I resisted venturing into a discussion of fertility drugs.

When our husbands returned, John joined Pui behind the counter and played the huckster using silly expressions and sign language to exaggerate the benefits of every product at hand. We all laughed at his antics—even those who understood no English—thus attracting more neighbors. A single Coleman lantern cast a yellow glow, and Elvis Presley sang from a battered cassette player. The night ebbed and swelled with laughter as we compared dance steps and joined simple games with the children. The shack store rocked until 10 pm.

At dawn on Sunday morning, a rhythmic tat-ta-tat-tat of a drum outside our window called us to the makeshift church next door. I groaned and turned over, lofted back to sleep by hymns in a lilting Tongan tongue. When we arose, Villiami directed us to the most elegant toilet I ever experienced—an outhouse at the end of a rickety pier with a view of the aqua lagoon and a distant island headland.

When the drumming began again at 10:30 A.M., I rounded the corner of the house to find a young man beating a rhythm on the side of a hollowed-out log with a heavy rounded stick, reminiscent of the drummers in Tahiti. The adjacent "church" where Villiami proudly served was little more than a shack framed with rough-cut tree branches and a patchwork of thatch and corrugated iron. Turning our backs on the bold morning sun, we ducked under the roofline to enter. Inside the fifteen-by thirty-foot room, the atmosphere was cool and dark with a musty smell. One hatch-type window on each side of the building, held open by a tree branch, provided the only light and ventilation. Teetering in the gloom, my foot sensed a broad-planked floor with four rows of thatch mats for sitting. Aware that Tongans find it disrespectful to have the bottoms of one's feet facing another person, I tried with difficulty to sit on mine for very long.

A shriveled minister in an over-large suit officiated, and our host and three well-scrubbed lads in *lavalavas* participated in the service. Villiami read from the Book of Psalms in a Tongan-language Bible, stumbling to translate for us. During the minister's droning, four men lounging behind us punctuated key portions of the service with a deep, drawn-out, "*Maaa-low.*" *Malo* means thank you (Lord). During one solemn moment, a piece of corrugated iron slid from the roof with a loud crash. I jumped, but it seemed to distract no one else but John. Villiami closed the service with a prayer that soared into a song taken up by three women in flowered hats with the chilling harmony reminiscent of their Polynesian sisters.

After lunch of fish cooked on a stick over a bonfire, Villiami took us to visit his parents in their simple home. At age 47, Susanne, with perfect complexion and ample figure, expressed contentment with her life as mother of ten living children—Villiami being the eldest at 29. The senior Villiami, a trim and handsome fifty-something, spoke no English, yet he and John enjoyed each other from the start, using outrageous sign and pigeon language. John tried out a Tongan pillow, a tiny wooden bench that held his head level with shoulders while sleeping on his back. The senior Villiami learned to make the OK sign with thumb and index finger; then he cajoled John into a *lavalava* and *talofa* (a straw-woven cummerbund).

Was this the same man who told me in Samoa, "You'll never get me into one of those skirts"? Once ensconced, he exclaimed how much cooler he was than with trousers (Tongans found shorts for adults immodest). With his hand, John fanned a breeze between his legs and exhaled through a grin. Even the kids hooted with laughter.

Beyond the village, Villiami showed us a vanilla bean farm where wide drying racks awaited sprouts now poking through the soil. When John, always the salesman, heard he could buy the beans green and after drying them, make four times his investment, I could almost see the cartoon dollar signs in his eyes.

Near sunset as we prepared to leave, Pui and Villiami decided to sleep on our boat. As we all set out in the inflatable dinghy, I feared the antler coral, unseen in the dark, might puncture its skin. With a flashlight at the bow, Villiami directed us with confidence, helping John pilot the outboard motor through a shallow maze. I jumped as a startled manta ray flew off to the left and tensed as a striped sea snake fled before us. We bumped something, and I clutched the gunnel. Suddenly a flurry of white ruffled the water ahead, and a small fish dropped out of school into the dinghy stampeding the white-skinned occupants. Sophisticated Pui, still in her long, knit dress, immediately trapped it, disemboweled it with her right index finger, and ate it raw in two bites.

On the boat, we snacked on popcorn I popped. Villiami described a dispute between Tongan and *pelangi* partners over vanilla beans, which grow abundantly in Viva'u. John began planning a business in earnest: "We should buy a hundred kilos green. We'll do the drying when we return in June, then pack and ship to Seattle, where..."

I stared at him. "Oh, yeah? That's not on my itinerary." I wondered when he might include me in these plans. As they discussed their dream of riches as bean brokers, I handed a pillow to Pui, the other practical one, and headed for my bed in the forepeak.

Weeks flew by as we explored surrounding islands with yachtie friends. We spent two additional weekends with our Okoa friends exploring their gardens, delivering fish, and visiting more family members. I felt an uncommon delight in being part of their community. Most memorable were the uplifting days at an annual fundraiser and feast at the stately Wesleyan Church with Villiami, Sr. as master of ceremonies.

Upon our initial visit, I had judged these villagers as poor—poor, as in pitiable poverty and despair. I came to realize that definition did not fit them. Although they lacked material possessions and access to services, they beamed with pride. They didn't envy us, but instead, accepted us as equals. The Okoans placed no value on fancy homes, matching outfits, electronics or plastic toys. They expressed gratitude for God's gifts, radiated contentment, and conveyed a spiritual awe of nature. They practiced charity, enjoyed their extended families, and honored their elders. They loved the children as a commune would and taught them responsibility from an early age. The older kids watched the little ones, and I heard no whining.

Poor? No, I didn't pity them. I admired them for the generosity and serenity in their lives. I envied their happiness. I reflected on similar experiences in villages all the way back to Mexico and decided that *we* were the poor ones. While I chased promotions, possessions, and money, I lost my humanity—if I ever had any—or kept it at bay. Perhaps I could recover some sense of compassion.

Five weeks passed quickly with new friends on the islands of the Vava'u Group, but a change of seasons again pressed us to move on. On departure day, Villiami met us at the hotel dock to deliver a promised gift. A full taxi waited as he approached with a large bundle. Explaining that he was late for a funeral, he paused before us, looking torn and forlorn. Sadly, I sensed he had fought with Pui, perhaps over the gift, since she remained in the cab. John thanked him for his hospitality in the village. Looking stricken and perhaps giving up on a prepared speech, he thrust the package at John and moaned, "Goodbye." We hugged, and he ran back to the car, leaving us standing in the sun with a four-foot diameter mat, hand-woven with brown highlights in subtle shades of tan.

I turned to John. "How did we deserve the love he showed us… and a gift of such great value?

We hugged goodbyes to yachtie friends and sailed overnight to the low islands of Tonga's central Ha'apai Group, an area containing active, undersea volcanos and two hot-spot islands that periodically rise and sink beneath the sea. Among these islands, we spent four, lazy days alone wandering virgin beaches and snorkeling under a hot sun until my itchy heat rash returned. Along the archipelago, I spotted Lifuka Island visited by Captain Cook on his second voyage to the South Pacific in 1773. Because of his warm welcome there, Cook dubbed Tonga the "Friendly Islands" and the name stuck. However, Captain Bligh, who followed twelve years later, would have disagreed. When his crew, cast adrift from the *Bounty* by mutineers, approached this area in an open boat, the natives attacked and forced them back to sea.

Further south we visited Tongatapu Island, the hub of the Kingdom. No European power ever colonized Tonga, but in 1900 it accepted status as a British protectorate and in 1970 became a sovereign nation. During the Pacific War, the U.S. and New Zealand established a supply base here. To defend against a Japanese invasion, they trained two thousand natives, many of whom saw action in the Solomon Islands Campaign. I could appreciate how war devastated people in these remote areas.

In the small boat harbor of the capital city of Nuku'alofa, we joined sixteen cruising sailboats and several local fishing vessels parked parallel in shallow water. This was a major rallying point for yachties to prepare for the thousand-mile voyage to New Zealand. We talked with some of them over a shared thanksgiving feast and were surprised to learn that most had interacted little with Tongans. We described our cordial experiences with Pui and Villiami. All seemed interested in our tales, but few appeared willing to initiate such connections. This again illustrated how travelers prefer to stick with their own crowd rather than risk the unknown. I credited John's outgoing nature for introducing me to an outreach method of travel, which let me see deeper into the soul of a community.

The capital city appeared more scrubbed, orderly, and westernized than the northern port, and it offered many more services. An Australian-trained medic in a well-stocked pharmacy administered a steroid shot to me that provided great relief from my itchy eczema. We mailed our gift mat back home and picked up a much-anticipated packet of forwarded mail. Letters from my family seemed to include lots of whining that nothing new ever happened in their lives. I laughed, turned toward the northeast, and called to them, "Consider your options and make a plan to try something new!" Once considered, it is surprising how many choices we have in life. Doing nothing is a choice too. And we must prepare to live with those choices.

One morning we rode our bikes along the waterside drive past gigantic churches to the modest, gingerbread palace of King Tupou IV, who had met my plane in Vava'u. Reflecting Polynesian reverence for great physical size, the king at one time carried 440 pounds on a six-foot frame. Health conscious now at age 64, he had slimmed down to 350 by riding a bike three times a week. We saw him approach and dismounted our bikes. King George peddled past on a standard bike with extra wide seat, his chin buried in a yellow polo shirt. Palace guardsmen in uniform shirts and shorts jogged beside him. His death in 2006 represented the end of the sovereign Kingdom and a romantic era in the South Seas.

Living among a large group of yachties again, John took great pleasure in the social scene. This provided drinking buddies and an audience for exaggerated stories with which to impress other sailors. As usual, he monopolized conversations and often cut me off when I tried to participate. He didn't listen to me or show interest in other people, except where it furthered his need to impress his fellows. I hated this side of him.

One day, I left John on the main street while I shopped for provisions. When I returned two hours later, I noticed his bike tied in front of a pub. I groaned; yet happy to have procured my cigarettes duty-free at the hotel, I peddled home. As we prepared the boat for the next sea voyage, we splurged on a buffet show at the Atata Resort. The Tongan costumes and brisk dances closely mirrored those I observed in Tahiti and Samoa. I followed the performers with delight, but my mind interrupted with a jab of concern that my travels with John would end soon.

Our two-month visit in Tonga opened my eyes to amazing natural beauty and the loving people of the Friendly Isles. However, the season of cyclones approached, and pressure mounted for yachties to get south out of their paths. Conversations centered on the route to New Zealand along the Tonga Trench, a six-mile-deep gash in the sea floor along the continental shelf. This stretch of water produced perilous weather patterns. The rhumb line, which a muscular crow might fly, covered 1100 miles; but high seas, contrary winds and currents in the area could set a sailing vessel off the line by hundreds of miles.

John became anxious and irritable, like he often did when facing a long passage. I ticked through my departure checklist. He monitored the radio and picked a weather window from maritime reports. I cooked a big batch of rice and set up easy access to meal accompaniments. After most boats had departed, we cast ourselves into the deep blue sea. We anticipated a difficult, two-week transit and got it.

CHAPTER 12

New Zealand—A Reset to My Earlier Life

WE SET SAIL UNDER GLOOMY SKIES AND SOON LOST SIGHT of the low islands of Tonga. Two days of ideal sailing conditions let us settle into our watch routine. John's usual, first-day seasickness resolved in time for him to repair the autopilot—twice.

However, four hundred miles offshore, gale-force winds and ten- to fifteen-foot seas assailed us and held firm for most of the trip. Our course into the wind caused the boat to smash into waves; the mast rigging shook and jangled. The irregular motion meant walking, cooking and resting in a world with the floor and the stove tilted at 45 degrees. This required that I always hold on to something or sustain a bruise from a fall. I collected several. We found it hard to sleep off watch even wedged into the sea berth with pillows. Inside the cabin, with portholes closed against splashy seas, the humid air exceeded 82 degrees Fahrenheit. My eczema returned.

We made good progress. Our little boat skimmed southward over the Tonga Trench at 35,500 ft above the sea floor. I looked to the dull horizon and marveled at the power of nature—the changing color and texture of the sea and sky—then contemplated our Creator who put it all together to sustain life. After three long days, the wind moderated, the sky cleared, and the sun set with regal colors of red, purple and orange. A gigantic moon lit our way on the evening watch. That reverie banished the tension and discomfort.

On the tenth day of our transit, I donned a sweatshirt and took over the dawn watch at 3:00 AM, while *Renaissance* carried us at top speed through the dark toward New Zealand's North Island. Erratic currents and gusty winds made our exact location uncertain. I settled into the cockpit with a mug of coffee, hoping for a return of the dolphins we had sighted at sunset.

Three hours later, dawn's dim light divulged no land, only a cloud-bank. Then, without warning, the wind shifted and accelerated. It separated the haze like a curtain on opening night to reveal, in a tentative spotlight of sunbeams, bright green hills inside the Bay of Islands. I gasped at the glory of the sight—a joyous contrast after endless days on a grey, turbulent sea.

"Land. There's Land!" I yelled. John joined me on deck. We buzzed with anticipation as the light revealed more of the coast. Seven hundred years before us, the Maori people arrived here from the Cook Islands in ocean-going canoes. They called it *Aotearoa* (land of the long white cloud), and that was the cloud I saw.

Inside the bay, the shoreline reminded me of New England where I grew up: boxy, two-story homes, white with black shutters, on streets lined with hardwood trees and spring-green lawns. Behind them, heavily-wooded hills trailed back into the mist. Even the grey, cold (65 degrees) weather matched. I missed my mom again—her comfort and support in times of insecurity. She died much too soon.

Rumpled and salt-stained, we congratulated each other in a rush of relief and triumph. Exhausted after crossing 1250 miles of troubled seas, we tied to the Opua Customs Wharf on December 9. Overhearing our radio transmission to authorities, several yachties came by to hear details of our fast transit which averaged 140 miles per day. The group included friends Fred and Rita on *Oracle,* who we last saw in Vava'u. My heart lifted with pride to be part of this heroic, adventuresome fraternity. We chatted across the pier and watched an agriculture agent stuff red hazard bags with my eggs, popcorn kernels, even the canned Argentina beef I bought in San Diego. As soon as we earned a stamp from the Immigration Service, I bounded up the pier to the tiny post office to find our mail package from home.

Back in Tonga, we had received a letter from John's mother informing us that his father had died of complications from Alzheimer's disease. John took that news with a shrug. In Opua, he opened an attorney's letter, grunted, and passed it to me. It said that he would inherit nothing from his father's estate. He had expected this. An intense and successful businessman, John's dad apparently showed no patience with his eldest son, and, like lots of men of that time, interacted with his children only to discipline them. I never learned the source of their twenty-five-year rift.

A financial newsletter reported that the stock market had dragged down our savings in the recession of 1987. I worried this might end our travels, but John expressed confidence that the market would recover in the year ahead.

A letter from his daughter and new college graduate, Jennifer, confirmed she would arrive with a girlfriend within days to share Christmas with us. I felt uncertain about this, having spent little time with Jenn since our marriage; and yet I was glad for a touch of family for the holidays. John perked up, proud and eager to see her.

A week after arrival, we joined Fred, Rita and two others in a rented a van for a rollicking ride to Auckland, a major city on the North Island. As the others headed for the marine chandleries to find spare and repair parts, I stole away for three, consecutive meetings at a 24-hour AA club. In a women's discussion group, I was welcomed like a long-lost sister and introduced around. I described my crying and feelings of isolation and rejection during the past three months, especially when John left me so often to drink.

"That's a perfect set up for a return to drinking for many of our ilk," warned a senior member. *Bingo. That's my fear, my source of despair.* She faced me and held my eyes. "You know you can't keep him from drinking if he needs it, right?" I nodded, and she continued. "That's up to him. Your own sobriety is first priority. You just stick here with the winners!" She and others hugged me warmly and gave me AA contacts in towns we planned to visit along the coast. Much fortified, I met the yachties for the drive back to Opua.

A busy ten days passed with boat maintenance and yachtie socials before our fetching young grads arrived. At anchor on a drizzly Christmas morning, we grilled French toast and shared gifts, including a coupon from the girls for "breakfast in bunk." In preparation for Christmas dinner aboard a larger yacht, I suggested my favorite tradition: making sugar cookies. John sat on the settee with a rag and oilcan lubricating the innards of a winch, as we crowded into my tiny galley. Jenn mixed butter with sugar, while Kris prepared to measure the vanilla extract. A powerboat approached with a growl that intensified; its wake rocked us as it passed.

"Aaaak!" said Kris. With her hand, Jenn tried to catch the liquid as it sloshed off Kris's teaspoon. She juggled her mixing bowl and tried to brace herself against the counter. They looked at me expecting criticism, but I laughed their plight, which I had suffered many times.

As Jenn struggled with the thick cookie batter, the wooden spoon broke with a crack prompting, "Oh, no!"

"Sorry," I said, "there's no space for an electric mixer, or the power to run it, so it's back to grandma's manual methods. Here's another spoon."

The girls cut out festive shapes at the table, some freehand, while I baked. We sat around the table decorating with colored icing and sugar and admiring each other's artwork.

At midday the four of us climbed into the rubber dinghy, balancing plates of food and party gifts on our knees for a short trip to a larger boat. We scrambled aboard to the aroma of pumpkin-pie spices and a roasting turkey. The cruising orphans, separated from families back home, contributed voluptuous varieties of traditional dishes and wine. The crew of *Oracle* and a fourth boat joined us to make a jolly group of twelve to devour the feast.

From a pile of gifts gaily wrapped by secret Santas, I received a denim apron covered in silly puns. John netted sexy Playboy briefs with the following poem attached to underscore his notorious disdain for clothes in Polynesia:

XMAS "MOURN" ON RENAISSANCE

T'was the morn after sailing
And all through the boat
No one was stirring
It was just afloat

When all of a sudden
Panic runs rife!
The anchor is dragging
Jump for your life.

And who should appear
Just clad in his shorts
But John up on deck
All pushed out of sorts

On his face is a leer
As he looks all about,
"I don't give a damn
If it's all hanging out."

When a voice from below

'tis Judy I fear
Says, "Put on your pants,
It's embarrassing dear."

'cause we feel sorry
For all of your crew
We give you these Jockies,
The old ones for new.

Fred & Rita McGinnis
Oracle

T'was the most memorable Christmas since my childhood. The girls left us at year's end to backpack around the country picking apples for gas money to power the battered car they purchased. I missed their company and said to John, "I might have had kids if I could guarantee getting some like those two."

We moved *Renaissance* across the bay to a sheltered cove beside the town of Russell, site of the country's earliest European settlement. Arrival of the whaling ships began in the early 1800's inspiring the bars, brawls and brothels typical of any frontier town. Ancient tombstones in the churchyard and a rebuilt Duke of Marlborough pub on the waterfront helped me picture those perilous days. At the pub one night, I watched John down a few pints of ale with supper, while we tried to figure out the rules of televised rugby.

Another night at a cozy AA group, we met a local couple and spent many pleasant hours in their home. It occurred to me that being an alcoholic provided an in-depth introduction into new communities wherever I might travel. I found lemonade in my life's lemon.

Early one morning we walked into the Russell town square, where a road-rage confrontation appeared to be unfolding. As a bulky bread truck backed away from the general store, a giant tour bus coasted in behind him, slid to a stop in the gravel, and rocked into reverse. The vehicles stopped with rear bumpers inches apart. Out of the bus jumped the driver, Peter Hallowes, a trim, tanned, fifty-year-old in white uniform shirt and dark slacks. The burly truck driver stood with fist raised and growled, "Awww, ya drive like an old woman. Pull 'er up!"

Peter advanced but delivered a chum's clap on the man's shoulder. "Just wanted to see if you're awoik, mate!" They laughed together.

After they untangled their vehicles, Mack, the chunky storekeeper, appeared on the loading ramp pushing a dolly stacked to his forehead with trays of wrapped bread. "What's the bloody hold up?" he roared, though he obviously enjoyed getting into the mix. Both drivers threw sarcasm back at Mack.

Peter flung back the rear coach door and acknowledged us with "'Ow ya goin'?" Without waiting for an answer, he began loading the bread, a mail bin, boxes of groceries and cartons of all sizes into a freight area that consumed a third of the bus.

John approached closer. "We need to retrieve a freight shipment at the port of Whangarei." After introductions and Peter's "no worries, mate," we climbed aboard and took the front row seats beside our driver.

As the three of us blasted out of town, Peter asked, "Where you Yanks from?"

"Is it that obvious?" John said. We all laughed.

I sat clutching the armrests, trying to adjust to hurtling along an undulating ribbon of pavement—on the "wrong" side of the road. The swaying bus climbed rapidly through a thickly, forested area until the view opened on miles of green swells below foothills that reached to the horizon. Sheep spread themselves across lime-green grazing lands like pebbles across a billiard table. I could easily imagine how the country sustained more sheep than its three million people.

I remarked on the richness of the land, and Peter said, "Aww yeaaah. I did a bit of farming for a while…actually, came to "N-Zed" on scholarship from South Africa to study dairy farming. It's a good life here."

At a small crossroads, Peter broke off his story to help an ample, brown-skinned Maori lady haul herself into the bus. He asked about her son's dairy cows and stopped the bus again about a half mile later—without her bidding or asking for a fare—to let her climb down beside a rusted mailbox. The milk run continued with a variety of stops. The hills flattened for cattle ranches on the plains; shining beaches and resort towns appeared among coastal cliffs.

After learning our story, Peter described his early life in Africa with the Kenya Special Police at the start of the Mau Mau Uprising in that British Colony. Another piece of world history came alive as he spoke.

We flew over a rise, and the big Coachliner suddenly veered off the highway past a tilted, wooden sign announcing Jack's Bay. We helped Peter carry bread and groceries inside a rustic store and caught up on local gossip at the campground. Back on the highway, Peter navigated blind curves and gravel roads with stops to deliver milk bottles, prescription drugs, scuba tanks, newspapers, even a case of Beefeaters gin to a jolly ole Brit.

On arrival at the bus terminal near the port, he pointed us to the freight carrier's office. Only a few minutes later, he met us at Customs to make sure his "mates" attended to our clearance papers. John and I ran other errands and met Peter three hours later with our freight.

The bus retraced our route, and I began to understand what a loving lifeline he provided to people in these isolated settlements. It was more than just a job for him. Back at Russell, he even backed the lumbering bus forty yards down a muddy path to the shore and then helped us unload 120 pounds of freight.

Peter would accept no payment for its transit saying, "Nah, you're nice folks, and I enjoyed having you along."

As the bus pulled away, I turned to a stunned John and said, "What an amazing guy. He certainly went above and beyond for everyone all day long. It's like the late 50's when people in our communities used to be like that." Americans like us run around so busy, focus on strict interpretation of our job descriptions and spend waking hours maneuvering for status and wealth. And now, we barricade ourselves behind technological devices. I felt the joy of a life like Peter's but wondered if I could ever be so patient and generous with my time.

Beside the bay, we set about unpacking and assembling our new rubber dinghy where it sat, because it was too heavy to carry. Another yachtie couple came along to help us, and their two kids played in the shipping crate. The whole day of caring and cooperation reminded me of peaceful times growing up in my small seaside town—a life I left so far behind to pursue a career. Extended travel on the boat had forced us to slow down and interact with other cultures in order to meet all our needs; in the process, we learned from them and could pass on acts of kindness. This seemed like a much more civilized approach than constant striving to "get ahead." Blending our God-given abilities made more sense.

We learned the N-Zed language with a touch of hilarity. At one rare restaurant meal, my head bobbed up when a "mum" at the table beside us admonished her fussy child, "Eat your tea!" The first time a local invited us for tea, we ate supper before arrival, not realizing that she prepared a full meal for us. However, when invited for "a cuppa", we learned to expect only tea or coffee with "biscuits" (cookies). At the butcher, I bought "mince" instead of ground beef. On the waterfront one day, I overheard a native report that his mate (friend) "got into the 'turps' (hard liquor) and was mighty 'crook'" (sick) that morning. Always the optimists, Kiwi folks (nicknamed for a rare, flightless bird) used happy phrases like, "no worries," "she be right," "good as gold," and my favorite, "box of birds."

Our stalwart vessel, *Renaissance*, had carried us safely since San Francisco and was overdue for a haul-out inspection and maintenance. Because their tides drop eight feet, the Kiwis routinely lean sailboats against pilings and paint their bottoms quickly before the tide returns. We opted to give our girl a cradle and a rail ride out of the water. With a wire brush, I set to dislodging crusty critters that cling to the through-hull fittings; John attended to the electrical and mechanical challenges—and found more drinking buddies.

John needed to be the technical expert and had little patience with teaching me anything. I realized mechanical know-how could save my life, but the workings of boat gear either intimidated me or just put me to sleep. This always left me with the drudgery work, but that division of labor seemed a reasonable trade-off to live the great adventure we shared.

In late January we harbor-hopped 130 miles down the coast of the North Island and met more delightful characters before settling into a marina in the city of Auckland. With a borrowed car, we explored the area. Among acres of hot springs in Rotorua, we found a Maori cultural center. The local clan, *Ngati Whakaue*, proudly traces its origin to one of the eight women who arrived in seven grand canoes of The Great Migration. Reflecting Polynesian roots, Maori life centered about the *marae*—in this case, the word referred to a black-and-red-painted meeting house. Inside, I recognized in the women's swaying dance and men's war chants similarities to those we witnessed in central Polynesia. The Maori men's facial tattoos of broad black waves and scrolls mirrored those of Tahitian men; this confirmed the connection Captain Cook observed through their language, although those islanders lived far apart for 460 years.

In March, we left the boat in Auckland to tour the South Island's gardens, glaciers and mountains by train and bus. On our return to the boat, I appreciated the convenience of marina living in Auckland: a coin laundry, unlimited fresh water, and easy trash disposal. However, John began spending long afternoons in the pub at the Ponsonby Cruising Club. He laughed as he described to me a section of the bar they call "death row" where the leading drinkers advance to the last stool before falling over dead.

I listened deadpan. "Not funny. Your drinking threatens my sobriety and drives a wedge between us. It's been a problem since Samoa." He turned away, and I advanced to face him. "I am prepared to leave you if you cannot leave it alone." I pointed into the distance. "The International airport is just over the hill there." He brushed me off with more rationalizing.

Many mornings as John slept off hangovers, I rode my bike around the city. I investigated unfamiliar supermarket offerings and visited a dermatologist. A Chinese dentist with a charming Kiwi accent foresaw a root canal procedure in my future. I stocked up on AA support meetings and even told my recovery story on stage at a sizable AA assembly, which earned me applause and encouragement. My sobriety felt more secure. I knew it did no good to nag John about booze, especially if he had the disease. I also realized he had called my bluff. I loved him, so how could I give up my marriage or my boat? I couldn't leave. Perhaps we spent too much time together, and he needed another break. I decided to hang on and hope he'd shake off the bingeing.

Cyclone season abated in April, and we cast off the marina to explore islands in the Hauraki Gulf before returning north. When a storm threatened, we dashed fifty miles back to the mainland to seek shelter inside the soaring headlands of Tutukaka. A cyclone never materialized, but a significant encounter did.

At the town dock, John began talking with Nick, a robust retiree from the merchant marine service, a Dutchman who married his Kiwi love, Pauline. Upon discovery that Nick and I shared an intolerance to alcohol, John and I became regular guests for dinner at the couple's home atop a cliff overlooking our tiny cove. I adored spending time with peaceful Pauline. Built like Ernest Hemingway, Nick was a perfect balance of gentle and tough with a vagabond spirit. On our first evening with them, John surprised me by refusing the beer Nick offered to him. I made no comment.

Over the next six days, I watched John develop an open, honest relationship with the man. Although nearly blind, our host prepared Indonesian dishes to thrill our naïve palates and regaled us with his stories of the sea and helping other alcoholics. I shared my recovery story with them both; and, in private, told Nick about my trouble getting

John away from the Ponsonby Club. That weekend, they took us to a regional AA jamboree full of exuberant, optimistic speakers in recovery. On the day we planned to depart, Nick knocked on our boat hull at 7:00 A.M. to say goodbye, bringing gifts of rooted parsley and lemon grass air freshener. We drank instant coffee under a grey sky and then drove him in the dinghy across to the beach below his home. Leaving these new friends in Tutukaka was especially heartrending; but like the birds, nature called us to migrate north.

We arrived back with the yachtie fraternity in the Bay of Islands in time to attend a weather-forecasting class taught by a cruising veteran. Afterward, I invited friends Fred and Rita to come over for spaghetti the next night.

"Welcome Aboard," I called as they arrived alongside our boat. "What's been going on with you two?" We all hugged and sat in our cockpit.

"Well," said Fred with a grimace, "Since we last saw you in December, *Oracle* has spent all her time in the Opua boatyard. The engine's been rebuilt, but much remains to get her seaworthy. It's been a hassle-and-a-half."

"Oh, no," I said, disappointed for them. "Didn't you get to see the country?"

"Yeah, we got away some," said Rita. "We toured by car, but only a couple weeks at a time so we could supervise the boat work. The locals we did meet were delightful, though."

"Looks like other Americans got stuck up here," John said. "I spoke to one guy who was pretty bummed out about the place...said he got ripped off, and on and on. I think some yachties isolate themselves in compounds like this and interbreed negativity...like tourists do sometimes."

"That's true." I said. "But you can't label the whole country if you don't spend time with its people. I try to find common ground, listen and learn from the other viewpoints on things. Oh, yeah, the Brits and Kiwi's teased us along the way, but we gave it right back and really enjoyed each other."

"Wow, Judy," said Rita. "You sound more vivacious. This place must agree with you."

It was true. I was becoming more confident and comfortable in my alcoholic skin, which I credited to my AA mentors. However, even with two years sobriety, I remained too ashamed to share my condition with pals like these, fearing their condemnation.

"Yes, I feel good. I loved the people we met—and the sheep." I chuckled and stood up. "So, what can I get you to drink?"

Fred requested a beer, but John asked for lemonade. I took a step back. *Had Nick impacted him?* "You got it!" I said and ducked back into the galley with a hopeful smile.

In late April, excitement swelled among the fleet as yachtie crews prepared for a 1200-mile, non-stop voyage north to the Fiji Islands. We topped up fuel and provisions, said more goodbyes, and checked out with Immigration officials. While waiting for a low-pressure cell to pass, we sought updates on news that Fijian natives had overthrown their government. Although I looked forward to visiting Fiji, it was unclear exactly what situation awaited us in "The Cannibal Isles."

CHAPTER 13

The Fiji Islands — Three Cultures and a Coup

EXHAUSTED AFTER EIGHT DAYS OF ARDUOUS SAILING, WE entered the Suva channel on the main island of Viti Levu, Fiji, hoping that recent internal strife had calmed. We knew only that nine months prior to our arrival a military coup in the parliament had inflamed tensions between Melanesian natives and East Indian residents, and that stories of unrest and food shortages persisted.

After official clearance and ten hours of sleep, we sought out fellowship and local knowledge from our own tribe: the yachties. At midday, we entered the modest, wood-frame home of the Royal Suva Yacht Club. In the entry hall, I slowed to view faded photographs of sailing regattas organized by early British colonialists who governed the island nation for one hundred years before granting it independence in 1970. John rushed ahead to greet the tanned white faces at a round table. As he boasted about our fast passage to Suva, I sat down and admired the ice-filled glasses and heaping plates of chicken fried rice prepared by someone else.

"What's going on with the military coup now?" John said, after catching up with everyone's travels. "Are there still hostilities?

"No, there's no trouble. That's just rumors," said an American we had known in Mexico. "We were here when it happened," he hoisted a beer, "and it never affected yachties. The native instigator, ole Colonel Rambuka, is laying low now."

An expat Brit chimed in. "He just wanted to evict the Indians from control. They outnumber the natives now, don't they?" He set down his beer and looked around. "Tourism is down thirty percent according to the paper, isn't it? Ha, that's fine by us!"

"Good," I said. "We just don't want to step into the middle of a family feud here."

We ate and departed the group with their suggestions on how to meet our immediate needs for food and hardware stores.

Outside the club, while we waited for the bus to town, John greeted "Big Mac," the sumo-sized Fijian security guard, who worked seventy hours a week to make ninety dollars for his family of six. He was open and friendly with us; but when asked about the recent coup, Mac shook his head. "The government is way too pro-Indian," he said, "but there'll be some changes next month when the Council of Chiefs meets!" That powerful group of native, regional leaders served to mediate cultural and land disputes.

The low buildings of central Suva (the capital city) reflected an enduring, British-colonial influence. Beyond the port and the dusty open market, we peered through lace curtains in the windows of the Grand Pacific Hotel, a setting where I expected to see envoys dressed in pith helmets and jodhpurs.

Since the first governor decreed in 1875 that plantation owners could not force the natives to work the land, British entrepreneurs began importing indentured laborers from India. John talked with several fourth-generation Indians regarding the recent coup. A cab driver expressed fear and planned to emigrate; but a local retailer just sighed and said, "Native Fijians are like children dressed up in a general's uniform. We wait. It'll pass, and they'll realize they need us to run the businesses."

"Well, that's a bit arrogant," I whispered to John as we walked. "I wonder..."

Other days, when not socializing, shopping, or performing maintenance, we wandered the bustling town and learned to negotiate prices at general stores found on every corner. While John searched for spare parts on back streets, I sat on the sea wall and watched activities at the open market next to King's Wharf. Native families sat patiently behind tables under tattered, blue tarp awnings selling oranges, yams and greens. Friendly, toothless Molly sold her baskets and told me stories of growing up in neighboring Tonga where her father cooked for an English judge.

Most nights we joined yachties at the yacht club to laugh about the common calamities of living aboard boats, such as plugged toilets, faulty fuel filters, and electrical short circuits. I enjoyed the happy-hour banter with less discomfort but returned to the boat as soon as the drunken drivel increased in volume. John still loved to socialize with expats, tell exaggerated stories, and stay until closing; but he now drank no alcohol. When I asked what transpired with Nick in Tutukaka, he just shrugged. I couldn't predict whether he would drink again—that was up to him; but while he abstained, I remained grateful for the closeness we again shared.

In fact, John lived the rest of his life without alcohol and never explained the abrupt change.

A visit to the Ministry of Fijian Affairs in Suva allayed some anxiety I harbored about venturing into remote out-islands among former cannibals. The staff explained traditional customs and provided us letters of introduction for islands we chose to visit. As directed, we purchased two kilograms of dry, spindly, pepper tree roots called *yangona*, the customary gift for a village visit. Eager to learn more about the culture of another group of Pacific Islanders, my excitement built. I wanted to set out immediately.

After three weeks savoring multicultural Suva, we sailed from the main island to explore a few more of Fiji's 321 islands. As John steered out of the broad channel, I read him a few bits from the South Pacific Handbook:

"'Before European contact, native Fijians existed for centuries in a barbaric, feudal aristocracy constantly warring with rival clans, brutalizing their women, and practicing cannibalism.'" I shivered. "It says here they ate human flesh for three reasons: one, as a sacrifice to their gods, two, as a way to honor a brave foe, and…get this…because it tasted good." I looked up to see John reflect my grimace before I continued. "'When the whalers and timber merchants began arriving, they introduced liquor and guns into clashes between native clans. A Swedish adventurer, Charles Savage—' Oh, great name!" I said. "'—took sides in a local dispute and became dinner for the opposition.'"

"Well," John said, "I hear the early Wesleyan missionaries had no better luck. Even thirty years after they arrived, a white minister was killed and eaten by his congregation." He paused, serious. "I guess they didn't like his sermon."

A few hours later, we picked our way through the coral reefs surrounding Mbengga Island. After a refreshing swim on its fringing reef, we met a man in tattered shorts on the beach. He told us to come to the village at 7:00 P.M. for the *sevusevu* (welcoming ceremony).

We ate a quick supper and watched the sky turn orange. I felt nervous, but thrilled, anticipating our first rural encounter. When we landed on the beach with our gift of *yangona* roots in a plastic bag, a host materialized: a trim, young man dressed in a tee shirt and the wraparound skirt Fijians call a *sulu*. When John greeted him with "*Bula,*" he smiled and replied in kind.

"We came to see your village," I said, breathless with anticipation. He beckoned, and John followed him through dense foliage along a narrow, dirt path toward Lalati Village (pop. 100). I trailed along behind, feeling somewhat uneasy and content to appear compliant within the male-dominated, hierarchical society in order to fulfill my curiosity. Then I stopped. *How can we blindly follow this stranger into the overgrown jungle with no way to contact authorities should we encounter trouble?* I ran to catch up to John.

Except for some elders, most of the people spoke very good English, but it seemed odd that they were unable, or maybe unwilling, to convey much of the village's history. I decided they must have been cannibals. *Past tense?* As I stood with John listening to one villager, I noticed an ammunition catalog beside a bench. Recalling Fiji's violent past and the recent *coup d'etat,* I edged closer to John and heard, "Few yachts visit our village anymore." A chill passed through me. *Hmmm. Why was that?*

Inside a cavernous, cement-block structure that they called "cyclone relief," a dozen or more men sat cross-legged on a fine woven mat, socializing. Our legs folded into the unfamiliar pose with much more difficulty. The group hushed as the *Turaga ni-koro,* the appointed village administrator, entered the unfurnished building for the *sevusevu* ceremony. Without any distinctive attire, the *Turaga* engendered obvious respect; he served as Acting Chief because the *Tui* (hereditary chief) was absent. He and other elders settled around a carved, wooden bowl with six short feet. A few women arrived and circled to the back of the group, so I slid back behind John's shoulder.

The *Turanga* motioned toward John, who, with reverence matching the other men, bowed and presented our spindly gift. He delivered a speech he had prepared with the help of the Ministry in Suva, explaining that we were from California, America, and traveled here to learn the customs of the Fijian people. The *Toronga* responded with a brief welcome and directed the ceremony to proceed.

A thin man prepared the *yangona* drink (also called kava or grog) by pounding the pepper roots, rock against rock and adding water. In the old days, he would have chewed the twigs to include some saliva. He mixed and filtered the mix through a cloth. He presented the first cup to Acting Chief, just as a host tastes wine from a new bottle to declare it suitable. Granted acceptance, the preparer ran his hands around the rim of the serving bowl and clapped three times. He presented the next cup to John. One of the elders coached him to clap once, take the cup, drink it down, return it, and clap again three times.

John whispered that the procedure was like his experience with the men in Tonga. Here the women could participate. My first taste of the watery, grey liquid produced a mild, peppery aftertaste; I decided that it took much more tasting to numb the lips and mind as forewarned. The cross-legged sitting, rhythmic clapping, and prayer-like pronouncements that accompanied the kava drinking continued down through the hierarchy of the men and then to the women behind them. Another informal round of the drink was prepared as we talked comfortably with villagers. With an invite to church in the morning, we departed into the dark at 9:30 P.M. with the help of our young guide. Although the interaction seemed formal, it accomplished a respectful means of welcoming and integrating visitors. I returned comfortable with these folks.

A torrent of rain woke us Sunday morning assuring we would be drenched if we tried to go ashore for church as planned. After the sun appeared, a preteen boy floated out to us in the lid of a packing-crate, propelled by a half-coconut bowl in each hand. He brought us papaya and drinking coconuts and said we could still attend the afternoon service.

To show respect, John wore his gabardine *sulu* from Samoa with a sport shirt, and I pulled on my long gauze dress. On the beach, John tied up our dinghy, and again, a guide materialized. During our walk to Lalati, we collected a bevy of six-year-olds, curious about our white skin. The houses were palm-thatched with sides of wooden slats or cinder block; roofs were composed of thatch or corrugated iron. Two paces behind most houses stood a small, thatched cookhouse, barely tall enough to stand in, where women tended the fires—carefully, I suspected.

We located our host, Isaiah, a mature farmer from the chief's family. On his face rode a bushy mustache favored by about half of the men.

He wore a dark-grey *sulu* below the white dress shirt stipulated by missionaries who introduced his forefathers to Christ. The beat of a church drum—a short, dugout log similar to one in Tonga—moved us along. We entered the simple church to find eight rows of benches on each side, but few attendees. The ancient preacher's dark head and hands seemed a part of his black suit and dark necktie, and I wondered at his ability to endure the high heat and humidity there. The local dialect prevailed in the service, but the harmonic voices raised in hymns electrified me as always.

After church, Isaiah brought us into his house of concrete blocks which boasted a fabric couch, a platform bed, and a photo of Queen Elizabeth II in royal robes with crown and scepter. He introduced his shy wife and proudly displayed a picture of his son in uniform with a United Nations Peacekeeping Force in Lebanon. Among Isaiah's extended family, we arranged ourselves around a checkered tablecloth, which lay centered on a 9x12 foot woven pandanus mat. Plates were set out and serving dishes passed. The colorful fare featured wild boar stew glistening with fat-rich gravy framed in broad taro leaves, accompanied by cassava root and greens baked in coconut milk. Metal spoons and fingers made quick work of the feast.

When the meal was finished, women placed a black bowl beside each diner. Believing this to be a finger bowl, I dipped my sticky fingers into near-boiling, lemon-grass tea and squealed with pain. Animated with great concern, Isaiah tenderly touched my forearm, and then coated my burned fingers with salt. My face warmed with embarrassment, but he softly repeated his wisdom, "If you get burned, touch another's skin." *How endearing. How important is the human touch.*

And with that, my fear of Fijians melted like ice chips in the sun.

We departed the next day and explored the Great Astrolabe, a ribbon of reef and sandy motus that meanders for eighteen miles through turquoise waters. We anchored at a few of the palm-covered isles in the area and enjoyed unhurried visits with other affable villagers. As in most of the Pacific Islands, the first question we heard was, "How many children do you have?" (Both were John's, but we let them assume they were ours for simplicity.) At our answer, they responded, "only two?" I knew they were not judging me, only showing sympathy for my assumed infertility, unable to imagine life without six or more children. My mother enjoyed raising the four of us. However, unlike these women, I had a choice, made possible by access to "the pill," which was fortuitous, since a career and travel sounded more interesting to me. In all things, I wanted to explore options and make decisions, rather than float passively and be caught up in a life that may not suit me.

On Dravuni Island, we lazed in clear water over coral gardens and walked white beaches. John tagged along with a young fisherman who speared him a lobster. I watched the women scoop up lunch with nets after immobilizing reef fish with toxic leaves. We spent a week with a village leader and wife and visited their community center where women wove room-size mats from pandanus leaves, and young men cleaned and smoked sea cucumbers for export to Japan. During our month of exploring, we chatted with yachtie friends via our VHF radio and were content to see only two other boats.

West of the Astrolabe Reef, *Renaissance* entered a pristine bay at Ono Island and came to anchor near another sailboat, *Vida Nueva* of Los Angeles. We learned that the retired owners, Bob and Geri, had interacted with natives only when necessary.

"Oh, but in the places we anchor," said Geri, a wide-eyed city woman, "they peek out at us from behind the palm trees. It's frightening."

"Well, of course," I chuckled. "You're in their back yard. They're just curious—and perhaps afraid of you, too. I was concerned too before we began spending time in villages."

We shared what we learned from Fijian Affairs and coached them on what to expect, and they agreed to come ashore with us. On the beach of the four-mile-wide island, a group of women and children, led by a native beauty named Esther, adopted us. As we walked to the village of Vabea, I marveled at the backdrop of green hills split by a waterfall below a volcanic peak. John chattered away with Esther. Bob said little and Geri held herself aloof toward the toiling women we passed in greying tee shirts and smudged *sulus*. At Esther's home (constructed from panels of corrugated iron), she welcomed us with a cool drink of water from the waterfall.

That night the four of us returned with *yangona* for the *sevusevu* ceremony. When prompted by the chief for his reason for the visit, Bob said, "We come on a boat from Los Angeles, a city much bigger than Suva." (*Really? A competition?*) He copied John's clap, drank, then three more claps. Geri waved off the proffered cup and observed the process with strained patience.

When the serving bowl was dry, Esther stood and announced, to my delight, a performance of *mekemeke*, a traditional sitting-dance with song usually arranged for special occasions. Two rows of five handsome women with Afro-style hair sat facing us, dressed in pink polyester tops and black wrap skirts. Swaying bodies and arms with bracelets of fresh flowers and leaves complemented the ballad they sang. A man behind them directed a drummer and a co-ed chorus.

After several songs in pleasing harmony, villagers took a kava break to socialize. Elders engaged John with curiosity about our travels. I congratulated the performers. Adults joked with each other or teased laughing children. I found their joy at an unpretentious social evening infectious. They asked nothing of us. I admired these loving, extended families and felt comfort—no, it was joy—in their midst. In a tenuous balance with nature, with little medicine or technology, life could be short and difficult, but they enjoyed a simple life together and demonstrated a contentment I envied.

With a glance at our stiff, greying compatriots, I hoped they at least socialized with other expats out here. I reflected on my shy teens through age 30 when I stayed on the fringe of gatherings to sustain my safe role as a loner. Many retired people, like Bob and Geri, have fixed their beliefs and attitudes. Thus, opening themselves to new cultures, or any new things, can feel like a major risk not worth chancing. I recognized the importance of being open to and incorporating new information in midlife and beyond. *Was it too late for them to change?*

On Sunday, we looked forward to joining our Vabea friends for church; Bob and Geri offered excuses though religion was not the issue. At Esther's house, we found three women helping her prepare food. Older children amused the younger ones, and I heard no whining. A mallet struck the church "bell"—an iron pipe hanging from a cookhouse roof—to sound the five-minute warning. Everyone dressed up for church, even tolerating neckties and polyester dresses in the steamy, eighty-eight-degree heat.

Inside the concrete building, plain benches sat on a dirt floor. Children filled the first two rows with bare feet stretching toward skinny dogs that lay under their seats. John and I sat beside the *Turaga ni-koro.* Following the first hymn, he went forward to make announcements and welcome us, speaking in Fijian, then English. He apologized for the service being all in Fijian language and offered a prayer for our safe travel home. James, the senior lay pastor, who, like many elders, had few teeth remaining in his mouth, delivered the sermon. He recounted the bible story of how Jesus explained that doing God's work was an exception to the law forbidding work on the Sabbath.

After the service, we joined the *Turaga*, the pastor, and Esther's family for dinner on her floor mat. Esther told us the pastor had used us as an example of the scripture. "...like if John and Judy's boat was damaged, we would come to their aid, today," she said. I was touched, recalling stories of Americans who walk by an injured person, afraid or too busy to get involved. In fact, I recalled doing that myself once as a preteen.

In the morning before departing, we ran ashore to say goodbye and left a donation for the church building fund plus gifts of jam and powdered milk for Esther. As we walked back to the boat, people who knew nothing of the gifts turned with a smile to wish us well.

Happy to separate from the uptight *Vida Nueva* crew, we crossed back to the south coast of Viti Levu (the main island) to explore small bays along its barrier reef. Then we set off toward the western islands. One day, when we attempted to pilot through a narrow maze of coral reef with the sun in our eyes, the grinding of a slipping fan belt added the fear of losing steerage should the engine overheat. Along the tortuous route, we leaned out opposite sides of the boat watching the water for coral heads and yelling conflicting directions at each other, compounding the tension. Hot and frustrated, we finally approached a mass of sailboats anchored in front of the Musket Cove Resort.

Musket Cove aka Dick's Place was (apparently still is) a yachtie favorite in Fiji. Their promotional brochure (1988) forewarned their land-bound guests about us:

> If this is your first encounter with yachties *en mass*, you will find them interesting, engaging and very different to people you have previously met. After all, anyone who by choice takes on the sometimes-mountainous seas of the wide blue yonder, in a craft that is often no more than six times the size of your bathtub back home, has to be different. Yachties are an interesting breed of homosapiens, who can be viewed at close quarters without danger. They have their own language, which to a landlubber is about as enlightening as listening to Esperanto with a Yorkshire accent.

We cooled off mind and body with a swim in the bay and yachties began stopping by the boat. Jim told us about plans for a pig roast on the beach that night after happy hour. Russ brought over our mail from the General Delivery box and pointed out the resort's dinghy landing area. John joined a group to scuba dive the fringing reef, while I enjoyed the luxury of a naked swim off the boat. I baked a quiche for the beach party and wrote post cards to send out on the "commuter" planes that soared over our mast twice a day to deliver tourists to this resort on Malolo Island.

Ashore, I renewed friendships and joined the familiar yachtie banter; but again, found that few yachties had explored the out islands, preferring to remain near expat watering holes running a tab.

After a week of beach parties and book swaps, we were ready to visit more islands. We zigzagged back to the main island for provisions, then turned north for the Yasawa Archipelago—twenty, eroded volcanic islands that stretched northeastward across fifty miles of reef-strewn sea. When we neared the island of Naviti, we had been in the country over two months interacting with the Fijian people, but this location became the most memorable experience for me; not for what I gained there, but for what I was able to give.

We anchored in a deserted bay in front of SoSo village and presented our *yangona* to a stern *Tui Naviti*, a high chief responsible for seven villages on the 13-square-mile island. He spoke openly with John and me for about a half hour. He assigned us a young teen as a guide, and we began a village tour, again attracting a gaggle of kiddies. Chickens pecked along the groomed paths, a couple of cows grazed beyond the scrub brush and a young man herded four goats toward a fenced area. I stopped to admire a pen full of piglets, not because they reflected village wealth, but ever since Mexico, I'd found them as endearing as puppies. We exchanged greetings with families sitting beside typical thatched huts. Near the shore, John stopped to talk with a man beside the village cargo boat. We continued a short way without him to a modern-looking, A-frame house with stone-and-mortar foundation.

"What's this?" I asked Lani, our guide.

She hesitated and looked back, perhaps for John. I decided that this might be a purposeful destination. "There's a man I want you to see. Please come with me."

When she pushed open the door, the curious kids ran away. Lani immediately turned right and waited for me at the base of a wooden staircase. I surveyed the ground-level interior. It was certainly a special place, very Western, and superior to the chief's house. *Who could be hiding here?*

I followed Lani to the top of the stairs and peered into the darkness beyond the landing. She stooped to enter the dark, stifling attic. "Where is he?" I whispered, sensing a need to be respectful.

"Over here" she said, disappearing into the gloom. Tapping ahead with my toes, I followed her across the slatted floor, avoiding solid obstacles like lumber, to the pinched corner where the roof met the floor. A rancid, musky smell reached me.

"Jone?" she called softly, "Jone, I've brought friends to help you."

I frowned. *Me help? Help what?* My heart thumped.

As my eyes adjusted to the din, I stretched to look where she pointed. I took another step, testing the floor. Curled up on a dark blanket, I discerned a human form, perspiration beads outlining black skin. As I approached, he roused himself and slowly turned his head to look at me. He was thin, of indeterminate age. I moved closer. "Hello, Jone," I said.

He lowered his head, said nothing.

My hand covered the forehead over his rheumy eyes and detected intense fever. My mind registered alarm. I stared a question across to Lani. "It's his knee," she said.

I pulled aside the damp blanket twisted around his leg and found the joint swollen to the size and hardness of a coconut shell. I picked up his hand. His entire body was burning up. Even with no medical training, I recognized that a systemic infection was devouring him. He must have crawled up here or been left to die.

I turned back to Lani, whose eyes pleaded for a miracle. "What happened to him?"

She hesitated. "I think he got a cut spearfishing." She dropped her head in despair and then squinted up at me. "And it got worse after rugby."

Perhaps he had contacted the notorious fire coral that could be reproducing inside the wound, but the situation was serious. Soso offered a "nurse," a small dispensary, and "maybe" a doctor in the next village.

"Hang on, friend," I said, gently replacing the man's hand. I turned and stepped back toward the door. "He needs to be cooled off. We need some men to carry him to the beach! Let's go!"

Running back on the path, I yelled for John, "There's a very sick man here. We need to get some medicine!"

John drove me back to our boat, and I explained what I found. While he collected soap, towel and a water bottle, I ransacked our first-aid box. We returned to the beach with antiseptics, aspirin, bandages, and a package of erythromycin. In Mexico I had purchased extra packs of antibiotics, which, having passed their U.S. expiry date, were cheap, though somewhat less potent.

We returned as two husky men helped Jone down the beach. I fed him two each antibiotics and aspirin and helped him drink. We eased him into the eighty-degree, ocean water, and he gasped at the cold.

Because the bacteria in his body had never encountered antibiotics, they were quickly overwhelmed. Within 24 hours he was up and noticeably better; but to insure he took the entire dose pack, we remained in the village for ten days.

I believe we saved this man's life, so I was especially pleased to learn his story. In his late twenties, tall and muscular, Jone played rugby for the Yasawa team. In years past, he served as crew on a kiwi yacht that visited Soso Bay, where he met his future wife. They were custodians of the A-frame house financed by a New Zealand sponsor who rarely visited.

Two days after our arrival, Jone's statuesque wife, Vaki, returned with their two baby boys from a visit with family on another island. We shared several meals with them in the A-frame house, contributing canned beef and strawberry jam.

After my success in doctoring Jone, I came across a shy toddler with a nasty open wound next to her right eye and no one tending her. I applied Neosporin and a bandage that covered most of her cheek, finishing with a long hug to comfort her. In the eyes of many elders, I noticed redness and cloudy cataracts and became very popular dispensing drops of Visine to soothe them. Each day as I approached, several who spoke no English would lie down and point to their eyes. I loved having the simple means to make them smile.

However, I soon got in over my head. Solomoni brought me his teenage daughter who had abdominal pain and a temperature of 101. We had difficulty communicating, but I knew internal injury or illness was beyond me. Fearing doing more harm than good—and perhaps incurring the wrath of former cannibals should she get worse—I gave them a package of erythromycin. However, I insisted, through a translator, that the girl be taken to the main island for treatment immediately or she could die.

With his outgoing personality, my husband made numerous friends in Soso while we stayed and repaired a thru-hull fitting on the village cargo boat. As respect for us increased, the *Tui* invited us to his house again and shared some of his burdens. His radio reported that a yacht at another village had taken videos of naked children intending to depict Fiji in a negative, backward light. John responded with concern and agreed this was unfair.

"In reality," I said, "the islanders demonstrate the true Christian ideals of love and charity. Where we live, many people have forgotten these." Perhaps I was reminding myself.

After some hesitation, a smile cracked the *Tui*'s usual solemn expression, and he shared another concern. "In some villages where tourists visit, our people are begging and pressing foreigners for handouts. I permit no begging in Soso. It only destroys the positive give-and-take that is the 'Fijian way.'"

John complimented his wisdom, and we tried to assure him that most yachties, who also live at the mercy of nature, give back more than they take.

Encouraged, the Tui continued. "At a recent Council of Chiefs, I vetoed a plan to charge visitors for anchoring among the Yasawa Islands." He looked sternly at John. "Don't you pay them, if they ask."

On Sunday, we came ashore to attend the morning service in the white-washed, two-story Methodist Church. After passing through the carved doors, my head fell back to take in the sculpted trim and wooden beams that soared forty feet above us. Carved biblical characters graced the ceiling center and the plastered walls which surrounded hand-carved wooden pews. "Glory to God," I whispered. Again, the clerics spoke little English, but the inspired singing delighted us.

From the church, we walked to the concrete community center where women served us tea with flatbread and cakes on a long cotton cloth atop woven floor mats. The ladies' group organized a contest between two choral groups to raise money, and John had rehearsed with the group that won. I recorded the event on a cassette tape. The Sunday crowd thrilled to hear it replayed, even though it sounded like they sang from inside a tin box.

After my primary patient finished his antibiotics, we said fond goodbyes and sailed north to explore scattered isles, coral gardens, and an underwater cave on our own schedule. Life there was perfect until we ran low on food and water. Two weeks after leaving Soso, we reversed course back to the main island.

In early September with visas soon to expire, we completed paper-work with authorities to depart Fiji. Along our exit route, we stopped again at Musket Cove for a couple of days. John toasted with lemonade, and I with Pepsi, missing none of the expat fun. We said final goodbyes to old friends, including Fred and Rita whose course lay due north to Hawaii. We spent our last Fijian dollars on resort food surrounded by Kiwi, Aussie, and American yachties. I even asserted my desire for a slice of lemon meringue pie. Heavenly!

As evidenced by the widespread biblical names we heard, the dedicated missionaries had succeeded in imparting God's message of peace and love to replace the constant combat and cannibalism of the past.

Filled with warm memories of four months among the Fijians, we plunged into the ocean for a week-long journey to another French island group.

CHAPTER 14

New Caledonia — Another Divided Land

FOUR MONTHS BEFORE OUR ARRIVAL IN NEW CALEDONIA, a socialist coalition of islanders (FLNKS) captured twenty-three *gendarmes* and ignited a bloody civil war. With few details about the outcome, we again worried how such a conflict might impact us. In addition, we expected the same entry frustrations with French authorities that we experienced in the Marquesas. We could have played it safe and bypassed the island state but decided to rest there for a couple days before pressing on to the 1988 centennial celebrations in Australia.

After a six-day sail on a calm sea, we approached the southern tip of Grand Terre, New Caledonia's main island. Peaks of its jagged mountains rose five-thousand feet and formed the spine of this 217-mile-long island. Inside the broad barrier reef, the island's red soil—a stunning contrast with tropical foliage—gave evidence of the wealth of nickel and iron ore it contained.

The modern capital city of Noumea surprised us with friendly French civil servants who issued our visas promptly. They told us that after resolution of the "hostage affair," the rebels retreated into the hills and few clashes had occurred in the past two months. Some locals told us the insurgents wanted independence from France; others called it "political," but when pressed, said, "it's complicated." The rebels consisted of indigenous Kanak people, who constituted the largest portion of the population. They descended from Melanesians who arrived about 1500 BC and assimilated with Polynesian latecomers.

We took a bus downtown and discovered broken windows, smashed vehicles, and debris in the streets. Although the damages appeared to be recent, we noticed that the black, brown and white residents went about their normal business without looking over their shoulders. The Kanaks seemed to keep to themselves, but I never sensed hostility from them or directed toward them. Gathered in the marketplace, the stout and cheerful Kanak women looked festive in colorful cotton "Mother Hubbard" dresses, the style dictated by early missionaries to cover up "too-sensual" skin from neck to ankle. The young men wore sport shirts and red and yellow knitted caps in the style of Jamaica. I watched their cheerful interaction and yearned to know them better, but an inability to speak French hindered me again. On the coast, a remote beach-resort compound segregated flocks of French tourists.

After we fulfilled immediate needs on board, I decided we might find an AA meeting in this cosmopolitan city. John's inquiries, using his improved French, lead us to a modern, two-story building on a hill overlooking Moselle Bay. Inside this auditorium, locals were arranging scenery panels on the stage. A young woman approached us. She was slim with golden brown skin, deep brown eyes, and black hair tied up at the back of her head. We introduced ourselves.

Marie Christine's wide smile faded to a frown when I asked, "Is there an AA meeting here?" She knew nothing of AA, but with a mixture of French and English, we learned that entertainers, including her family members, were staging a play here about their native ancestors, which they recently performed in Australia.

She escorted us outside the building and said, "The music and drama will be presented tomorrow night at eight P.M. I hope you will come!"

"Mais oui, oui!" I said, thrilled to have found this cultural connection.

The next evening, we arrived early to get a seat near the stage. Marie Christine met us and explained that her older half-sister, Marie Pierre, had a leading role in the drama, and that their mother, Anna, would perform in the Lifou Island dance troupe.

The curtain opened to a jungle scene with a young, brown man clad in blue jeans. Beside him stood a weathered black man in a grass skirt, with a woven-leaf headdress and white stripes painted on his face.

"Grandfather. Tell me who I am…where do I come from, who shall I be?" said the young man. Our recent travels had caused me to ponder the same questions, but in middle age.

From there, the stage drama revealed, with great passion and pride, the history and culture of the Kanak islanders. The actors delivered poetic lines in French, but I followed the story via a side-by-side English translation in the printed program. Groups in traditional tribal costumes presented dances and songs from Grand Terre and the three Loyalty Islands. In dresses of bright colors and fresh flower headdresses, the women of *Lifou* sang in the close harmony I loved, and then performed a stomping, shuffling dance accompanied by mouth whistles. We stayed to congratulate the cast, and Marie Christine's sister drove us back to the dinghy dock.

Later, we entertained the three women aboard *Renaissance*—a French word they had no problem comprehending. John and I expressed interest in their lives. With long, wavy hair and big-boned Melanesian stature, Marie Pierre descended from the royal family on Lifou Island. Marie Christine, with a smaller frame and lighter skin, spoke better English than her half-sister, having worked as an *au pair* in New Zealand. I found myself intrigued by the girls' attractive mother,

Anna, who was closer to my age. Because she spoke no English, I struggled to recover a few words from one year of French I studied in high school—a time of misery for the shy girl I was then. With John and the girls as my interpreters, I enjoyed that lovely afternoon showing them the boat and our family album over a jug of iced tea. We agreed to contact them after we explored the west coast.

This family and yachties encouraged us to extend our planned visit. We broke from city life and cruised beside the outer reef past sparkling sandy keys for a rendezvous with a British couple we had met in Fiji. A thirty-year old man with cropped blond hair and the build of a linebacker, Alistair, a former London cop, lived in bikini briefs that he wrapped in a *pareo* (aka *sulu,* aka *lavalava*) when going ashore. His old "cop-per" friends might say he'd "gone troppo" (sun-crazed). Toni, his first mate, kept her sun-streaked hair in a perky ponytail and her petite body in a polka-dot bikini—in a size that might have fit me at age eleven. Shoe-horned into a boat smaller than ours, they brushed off the lifestyle risks and explored with eager enthusiasm.

Fluent in French and a previous visitor to the area, Alistar had *Caldoche* friends along our route. We entered a tranquil bay together unaware he had notified some occupants of our arrival. A yellow speedboat roared toward us with three Europeans holding a pole with a four- by six-foot American flag attached. The merry men yelled in English, "Welcome, Americans!" and "We love you." Their boat turned for another pass. "Come to lunch, *por peche* (for fish)," they yelled, pointing ashore. We laughed, waved, and responded with thumbs up. Their boat raced back toward a row of cabins along the beach.

As distinguished from the "metros" (the military and civil servants who rotate regularly to and from France), *Caldoche* refers to Caucasians born on the island. Their ancestors came from France after 1853 to staff the penal colony and operate the nickel mines. During World War II, they bolstered the allies' fight against the Japanese when Noumea served as a strategic base for crucial operations in the Pacific theater.

Five decades after the war, the gratitude and love for American military personnel burned brightly—to our benefit.

On the beach, a celebratory party unfolded in our honor. I stood apart at first, as their hearty drinking stiffened me. Old Jacques with family and friends nipped on scotch before lunch, slurped wine with lunch, and beer beyond. I feared they might turn belligerent. However, I couldn't resist laughing with John at their antics and affability, and I soon relaxed. The men grilled fish and women tenderized spider conch with pressure cooking.

While we enjoyed the seafood, I picked up enough of the fervent French to understand that these *Caldoche* hated the interloper "metros" who ran the territory. One fellow insisted that New Caledonia should break from France and become our 51st state.

After lunch, we watched men bait traps for sharks, the source of many fin and jaw trophies that decorated the beach houses. As sunlight dimmed, and we prepared to depart, the frivolity waned, and Jacques called everyone close together. "It was an honor to have Americans at our table—only the second time in too many years." He bowed his head. "Thank you." I reflected on our shared history, which I never knew existed, as well as the goodwill left here by U.S. armed forces during desperate times.

For several days we accompanied the Brits to fish and to snorkel among some very large fish. Alistair sectioned an octopus he'd speared for bait and trolled for white fish. He showed us how to find the blood-mouth conch, which tasted like crabmeat. With his encouragement, I became a fishing fool—until I hooked a two-foot long remora that fixed its sucker grid to the bottom of our dinghy. John remained uncomfortable around squirming fish and impatient with my fishing yet tagged along after Alistair like a groupie. Having never traveled outside our country before this trip, my husband relished all our cultural interactions.

After ten days on the coast, we returned to Noumea, and John called Marie Christine; and she invited us for Sunday dinner. I was thrilled, but unsure what to expect. The venue could be a thatched hut with a straw-mat floor or one of many modern houses. I knew one sister had royal blood, and that 90% of residents were Christian churchgoers. I decided we should dress up (cover up) somewhat to be sure not to offend the family. I donned my cotton gauze dress. In the torrid heat, John whined but pulled on long pants.

Marie Christine picked us up at the pier in a car, drove into the hills for twenty minutes, and parked before a two-story, white stucco house with a view of the harbor. At the door, her jovial father, Joel, conveyed a hearty welcome without any English. He had arrived from Normandy four decades back as a soldier and stayed to marry his winsome island girl, Anna, and help raise her young Kanak daughter. Over hors d'oeuvres we met *grandpere* and a third sister, Ann, a high school student.

The group loaded up two cars and drove about fifty miles inland over rolling green foothills to a four-star plantation resort on a riverbank. We dined *al fresco* from china platters of shellfish, tender veal and crepes. John gorged on the feast like a starving vagrant but kept up with Joel and Anna's narrative in French. With the encouragement and patience of the three sisters sitting with me at the other end of the table, I uttered some modest French by the end of the meal. Groups of white folks surrounded us on the broad patio, but I detected no racial animus toward our melded *Kanak*-Caucasian group.

The following weekend the family of five boarded *Renaissance* to explore *Ilot Maitre*, an island-park. We strolled and swam and returned to the boat with an appetite. I couldn't wait to taste the traditional Melanesian picnic lunch that Anna brought. She carefully unwrapped a towel that kept the *itcha* warm and opened dark banana and pandanus leaves to reveal a precious mixture of chicken slow cooked in coconut milk with yams, banana and papaya. I added a carrot cake baked in my propane oven. The men showed their appreciation by comparing distended bellies hanging over their bathing trunks.

We departed the island after 4:00 P.M. for a brisk, downwind sail back to the harbor. Most of the family crammed into the cockpit as John demonstrated how the wind-vane paddle held our course. Anna and I sat down below and made more progress in communicating.

Back in port, Joel and Anna invited us back to the house to shower and use their washing machine. I smiled, said, "*oui*" and demonstrated the "high-5." Because I expressed interest in native customs, Anna played a video of the royal wedding of a *Lifou* nobleman to a Polynesian woman from Wallis Island. Dances at the celebration mirrored those in their theater production, while others looked Tongan. I expressed amazement at how the customs of the early Pacific Islanders had spread and endured across thousands of miles of open ocean without even a compass. John translated for me.

That night, as with subsequent visits, we consumed more gourmet food from the larders of Joel's import business. The girls gave me a traditional Mother-Hubbard dress, a loose colorful cotton dress, similar to a Hawaiian muumuu. I gave them a large puppet to encourage their theatrical interests. The overwhelming generosity of this family defied my understanding. In contrast, the experience left me aware that my typical approach to people had been judgmental, impatient, and stingy. I hoped I could absorb some of the islander humanity.

Four weeks after arrival, we joined other yachts for a nail-biting day-sail through coral reefs from Grand Terre to the Isle of Pines. The natives call this low-lying island *Kunie* for the Melanesian people who populate it. Behind white sands and coconut palms, Araucaria pine trees grow to 200 feet tall, as straight and thin as dark geysers against a soft blue sky. In addition to full-moon beach parties with Aussie yachties, John and I spent a week there exploring inland caves, prison ruins, and a church. In St Joseph's Bay, we watched native artisans craft traditional outrigger canoes, and John plied the carpenters with all the questions his curiosity and language skills could muster.

Upon our return to Grand Terre, I found a nice walu on my forgotten fishing line and invited a Kiwi couple in a nearby boat to share it with us. John noted my growing interest in entertaining. Now, without the worry of his drinking, I felt our relationship rebuild and deepen as we shared our adventures with others.

In the morning we joined the couple for tea. The men departed to inspect a sparkling 48-foot yacht nearby, and I visited with Marge, a New Zealand psychiatrist. Like other women yachties I knew, she had tagged along on this trip to let her partner fulfill a dream of cruising but admitted she missed friends and family and "meaningful work." I confessed that I also missed my career and the recognition it brought me. John was the expert on our boat, and I was secondary. However, I told her, our extended travel had increased trust in our marriage and opened my eyes to how shallow my life had been while I struggled to "get ahead." Then, with no fear of recriminations from her, I shared my struggle with alcoholism. Like our old marriage counselor, she admitted she knew little about the disease, except that her husband had used the principals to quit smoking.

"That's my next challenge," I said. The close connection we made in that brief afternoon surprised me, and I regretted having to leave her. I had never allowed time for friendships, but now I wanted to find friends like Marge.

Back in Noumea, while we began preparations for our next ocean passage, we spent more time with our adoptive family. While we relaxed after dinner one night, John tried to express to Joel and Anna how much we admired the closeness of their family. In French, he said something like, "You remind us of how distant we are from our family members, even when we are in the U.S. The unconditional love demonstrated by all Pacific Islanders embarrasses us."

"Tell them I am learning the language of the heart," I said. "That's how Anna and I have become closer than many English-speakers I know." At times when I felt left out and tended to dip into self-pity, the Serenity Prayer reminded me to accept that I had little talent in languages, so I could feel gratitude that John did.

On November's first Sunday, we were up with the first rays of sun in anticipation of a ten-day passage to the continent of Australia. We pulled the boat alongside the city wharf to winch aboard the rubber dinghy and fold and secure it for transit. Marie Pierre and her boyfriend helped us.

The rest of the family arrived and whisked us to a waterfront café for a simple breakfast of hard rolls and cheese. They presented us a carved mask and a pillow cover decorated with an island map. When asked for a speech, I expressed in English our thanks for their insider tours, generosity, and love. John translated and spoke similarly in French. Marie Christine proclaimed the same feelings in English. And there I sat, a middle-aged woman, who had eschewed friendship for status and material "success," but now aspired to reverse that emphasis.

Back at the wharf, we posed together for a photo, and I promised to write to confirm we were safe in Australia. John climbed behind the wheel, started the engine, and *Renaissance* turned us again toward the open sea. Our dear new friends waived from the pier for as long as we could make them out.

I looked up to John. "Wow. What a great experience. How had we never heard of New Caledonia…and only about hostilities when we did?"

"Yeah," he said. "And ended up staying for six weeks." He stretched to look ahead over the cabin top. "Hey, the reef passage should be dead ahead. Get me the binoculars."

PART IV

Delving Deeper

Highland Dancers, Papua New Guinea

CHAPTER 15

To Australia and Home — Here and Gone

ON OUR SECOND DAY AT SEA, ABOUT EIGHTY MILES WEST of New Caledonia, the sky darkened and formed dense, dark cloud-rolls that flashed with lightning. We found little wind to fill the sails, yet the ocean was chunky and confused. The barometer continued to drop. A ham-radio weatherman warned, "no less than four low-pressure cells" had formed off the Australian coast and violent squalls lay ahead of us. In the damp, eighty-degree heat, I shivered. Turning back meant a dangerous approach to the barrier reef with no sun to show us a path through coral spines. We decided to proceed as planned, hoping the storm front would continue to travel ahead of us.

Three more days passed under the same threatening conditions plus a bouncing barometer with sun and drizzle taking turns. The light wind died at night, so we motored. Six-foot waves from the north clashed with ten-footers from the south, tossing our little boat like a rubber ducky in a toddler's tub. Inside the cabin, unable to anticipate the irregular waves, I suffered hip and shoulder bruises during unexpected lurches.

"Ow, ow, ow!" I yelled to the sky. "Stop this teasing. If you're going to storm, get on with it!" John contributed bolder epithets.

On Day 6, the barometer rose swiftly into the "fair weather" range, but the grey sky delivered cold rain and gale-force winds. On deck in harness, John tied reefs to shorten the main sail. We alternated three-hour watches but made little progress through the jumbled sea.

By afternoon, I'd had enough. "This is insane," I screamed to John over the howl of the wind. "We're getting nowhere. We need to stop. Let's heave-to!"

An hour later, John agreed. We set the rudder to oppose the reefed mainsail, as we had in the unexpected Mexico storm. The boat stopped and the motion quieted. I heated canned stew in a large pot clamped over the burners—a task like tending a stove while riding a rodeo bull. We ate from deep serving bowls with feet braced to keep our seats. As darkness descended, the masthead light spread its beacon across a pitifully short distance. Both exhausted, we slept fitfully through the night, unaware that wind and seas drove *Renaissance* twelve miles off course.

In the grey dawn of our seventh day at sea, I awoke stiff and sore on the wooden cockpit bench and pulled myself up to sit. A fresh gale heaped grey waves in all directions and flung spray from their tips. I looked ahead, gasped, and blinked twice. Off our starboard bow, I saw a ten-story freighter with the letters, H-O-N-D-A, covering its entire side.

"Yow!" I jumped up and tried to guess its course.

I dashed below and keyed the radio transmitter. "Honda transport vessel, Honda transport vessel, near Brisbane. This is sailing vessel, *Renaissance*. Do you read? Over."

"Sailing vessel!" a distressed male voice responded. "Where are you? I can't… I don't see you!"

At this, John popped out of his bunk and peered out a porthole. He did not intercede, but climbed into the cockpit, ready for action. *Wow, he actually trusts me to handle this.*

"Honda vessel, *Renaissance* back," I responded. "We're Here. Hove-to. Off your starboard side... amidships...a couple miles south of you. What is your course? Over."

A long pause followed his order, "Stand by."

When the deck officer located us with binoculars, he expressed great relief. "Found you! Our radar screen gives me a lot of snow from the spray of breaking seas. When your boat settles into a trough between waves, you disappear completely from my view. You're good. We'll pass safely to the east." He confirmed our latitude and longitude, which positioned us about a hundred miles from the Australian shore. However, after consulting our chart, I realized we had camped in the middle of the Sydney shipping channel. Not a safe place for a little boat.

In the morning light, John and I wolfed down some dry cereal, reset the sails, and ran westward at top speed. We yelled to communicate over the din of wind and churning seas. That night, without glimpsing the coast, we stopped again, but kept a stricter watch schedule.

The next day the taxing wind and sea conditions persisted, but when the morning sky brightened, we set off again hoping to cover the last sixty miles into port before sundown. Relying on infrequent fixes from the Sat Nav, *Renaissance* raced on blindly, occasionally surfing down a roller that overtook her. John radioed Bundaberg Air Sea Rescue to report our presence. We continued to search an empty horizon ahead. John tried to refine our position on the chart as the light faded.

"Where is this damned continent?" I said. "Does it really exist?"

At five miles out, channel markers appeared along with the hint of a hillock ashore. Just as the sun hit the horizon, we passed into the mouth of the Burnett River. As directed by the radio, we located the "Sugar Pier" and tied to its oversized fixtures. An eerie sense of unreality overtook me. After eight days of being tossed around the ocean, the boat stood stock still, in silence. Above us, the clouds rolled back to reveal a delicate new moon.

From the darkness above us, an immigration officer called a friendly welcome. He climbed down a ten-foot ladder from the pier and checked our papers for some basic information. After a ten-minute chat, he grabbed the ladder to return to his pregnant wife in a car.

At the top, he peeked over with a grin. "Aye, Mates. Come up to the office tomorrow in 'Bundy,' and we'll finish the paperwork. But mind the tide, she be coming up early."

I turned to John. "Well, that was the easiest country check in…ever."

He smiled. "Yachties are right. Definitely the best place to enter the land of Oz."

That night we slept like corpses. Awakened by the sun, I turned onto my back, conscious. *Something's not right*. Then I chuckled, remembering where we were. Being tossed about was no longer the norm. I shook John's shoulder. "Hey. Get up. Remember, we have to get to town with the tide."

Six miles upriver, we located the marina at Bundaberg, a prosperous farming town, and joined other yachts in transit. The Customs Office there issued a permit for *Renaissance* to remain without import duty, and after we allowed the Immigration "blokes" to chide us with every Yankee joke, they granted us a cheery entry too.

With arrival in Australia, we achieved another major milestone in our journey, but it also meant ending two years of freedom and adventure together. Because we extended our stay in New Caledonia, our schedule and waning funds called for us to pack up and fly to California within two weeks. However, we found the new natives delightful and decided on a few weeks' delay. Our marina berth beside the town was a bargain, as were the pub meals two blocks up the hill. I called a number for Alcoholics Anonymous and within minutes lovable, former boozers adopted us. Reilly, Vern, Tattoo Mick and Trader Ted (and their wives) competed with one another to assist us and get me to meetings. Again, my affliction provided instant local friends.

Our mail package arrived with a letter from John's daughter, Jenn. She was bored with her first job after college and searching for life's meaning. I laughed. "Well, she's ahead of the game. I didn't question that until age forty."

John wrote back to advise her: "The world is out here with lots of options. Find your dream, make a plan, and do what it takes to follow it."

A co-worker at Westinghouse wrote that my old job as Sr. Contract Administrator for the Cruise Missile Program was open, which gave me a lift and sense of happy anticipation. Work promised more legitimacy, predictability, and the security of a paycheck. I organized goods and gear for cleaning, disposal, or storage. John arranged for boat services and located a boatyard to haul "*Rennie*" out of the water and look after her for a year until our return. By then, we expected to earn enough to support two or three more years of cruising.

In the weeks after our arrival, the number of social activities with yachties, alkies and townies escalated. John happily joined every event and pushed me along too. I baked for neighborhood parties, joined the library, and chaired a local AA woman's meeting. New Aussie friends often stopped by the boat for coffee or took us home for dinner. This transition to land with all the spontaneous social situations panicked me. John reveled in the fun and could not understand my unease. I stiffened as the pressure intensified. In this fast lane, sobriety felt unnatural. At AA meetings, members listened sympathetically as I tried to sort out my feelings. Life at the marina was friendly and fun, but parties increased as Christmas neared. Our inevitable departure loomed, and I became impatient to go.

In late December, summer in the Southern Hemisphere, *Renaissance* rose from the water, her barnacles dripping, and settled in a cradle beside other blue-water veterans at the rear of the Burnett Heads Boatyard. A week later with duffle bags packed and Reilly waiting to drive us, I turned for a last look at the vessel that kept us secure for twenty-six months across 12,570 sea miles. "Bye, ole girl," I managed.

At the bus station, we hugged goodbyes to Reilly and family. In Sydney, we boarded a lofty Qantas 747 to recross the Pacific.

At 10:00 A.M. on New Year's Day 1989, we arrived homeless at the San Francisco International Airport in faded clothes, dragging battered bags like poor immigrants. I looked around at the business travelers and young families with a tired smile. *They would not believe what we have been up to for the past two years.*

Within a week, we reconnected with the hectic world of Silicon Valley, leased a junior apartment (to us it felt gigantic), renewed drivers' licenses, and bought a beat-up Toyota hatchback for $700. After he heard our story, the student who sold us the car threw in a couch, mattress, and two folding chairs. We picked up work clothes and shoes we had stored with friends, and they donated bedding and more furniture. We added a twelve-inch TV and portable radio, and I decorated with Australia posters. Nothing matched, the bed lay on the floor, but it mattered little, as we were there to work and save as much as possible to extend our adventure into the Great Barrier Reef. A year of discomfort, in exchange for the freedom of extended travel, I considered an exceptional value.

Within a couple weeks, John found a new job in business-to-business sales. Westinghouse welcomed me back to the Contracts Department. I eased back into familiar work with several familiar people, who had stayed home to raise children, acquire luxury cars, or other priorities. Most greeted me with admiration; some expressed jealousy or shook their heads at the insanity of what we did. Another eyed me with resentment. Someone said, "You're so lucky."

Luck? Ha. It took a major commitment to trade a house for a boat and three years of planning and saving the $20,000 needed to sustain us for two years.

Life in California contrasted sharply with our vagabond life at sea—and not just because the temperature was forty degrees cooler. We were different. The noise inside the office and on the street seemed excessive, as was the speed at which cars and people moved to beat the clock. People even talked fast. John and I focused on work and allowed little time or money for luxuries. We were easily entertained with the simple pleasures, like the startling new graphics used in TV advertising.

I entered Walgreens Drugstore to buy pantyhose (a symbol of freedom lost) but came away thrilled with all manner of treasures, at prices I realized were kept low by the large consumer base, competition, and efficient U.S. transportation. Supermarkets became a curiosity. I marveled at the endless rows of fresh meats, the vast choices of garden produce, a chill case twenty-feet long just for prepackaged cheese. In one aisle, I counted twelve different varieties of tomato sauce and four different brands. Before I lived outside the country for an extended period, I never noticed such abundance here. There were so many options for filling the gigantic refrigerator-freezer in our apartment.

Sunnyvale hosted four AA meetings per day. I couldn't get enough of the fellowship. In discussion groups and often as a featured speaker, I shared my adventures tracking down meetings in Mexico, Tahiti and New Zealand. At work, my cigarette addiction now forced me to descend a flight of stairs and stand out in the cold like a pariah to partake. I tried without success to apply the twelve-step program to the insanity of smoking.

Personal computers with thick paper manuals began appearing in businesses that year. In our office, twelve administrators shared one chunky unit. I, like most others there, resisted the new technology as too cumbersome. Fifteen years later, I read of a thirty-something couple who expressed horror at being without internet access for four weeks during two years of travel. Technological advances aside, the personal benefits of extended travel in the future will correlate with our ability to break the glue between eye and screen long enough for meaningful interactions.

John and I flew back to Massachusetts for my brother's wedding and a reunion with my family, which included my father, stepmother, older sister, and both brothers. I had not seen them for over five years. We frolicked in autumn leaves of red and gold and recalled a happy childhood. Always conservative in most things, my father showed unexpected enthusiasm about our midlife travels, perhaps because my new stepmother had introduced him to exotic travel. I reconnected with family on a deeper level because of my experiences with families across the Pacific during the prior two years.

While there, we drove around our small hometown chasing memories and sat down at a deli for lunch. “Order up, Jack,” said the counter clerk. I turned to recognize a high-school classmate, a football hero I had adored at age seventeen but was too shy to approach back then. Dirt and oil covered his face and his Shell Oil jacket. His linebacker muscle had turned into flab. He collected his order and slouched to the door. I guessed he had never experienced life outside our town. *How sad.* I felt a flash of appreciation for the parental support and encouragement.

In September, the TV showed Category 4, Hurricane Hugo make landfall in South Carolina causing billions of dollars in damages to the southeastern coast. Nature, our antagonist, tormented folks on land, as well as the sea, and reminded us again that humans are not in control.

After 5:00 P.M. on October 17, most co-workers had deserted the open maze of cubicles in my second-floor office area. I had remained to strategize with my manager about a pending negotiation, when the floor began to shake under our feet. I steadied myself on the doorframe of his office and turned to face a clanging noise behind me. The central columns supporting the roof of the building were banging against the decorative boxes that enclosed them. Outside a window, a sturdy oak tree twirled in the air as if swung by Paul Bunyan. I dove under a desk. The lights flickered. My stomach turned over. The 1989 San Francisco earthquake registered 7.2 on the Richter scale.

Although it seemed an eternity, it was over in fifteen seconds. With remaining staff, I ran to exit the building and drove home. On detours around fallen power cables, I spotted dazed people standing in front of houses, their predictable world upended.

Our apartment defined chaos. The TV had fallen face down on the carpet beside a lamp with its shade askew. Shattered mugs and glasses disgorged from kitchen cabinets lay on the slate floor with maple syrup and catsup mixed with their glass shards. An eerie fear engulfed me, as if victimized by a vandal. A half hour after the big quake, a 5.2 aftershock hit, and I dove again for cover. I switched on the portable radio and changed out of my business suit, hosiery, and heels.

John called from work in Palo Alto. "Hi. I'm in an old building, on the third floor. The damn ceiling fixtures were crashing around my head! Must have been a bad one."

"I'm OK," I said, "but the radio's reporting a major quake that ran up the San Andreas Fault from here. Fires, major damage in San Fran. They say to avoid the freeway ramps. Take the frontage roads."

"OK, I'm out-a here. See you soon."

In the past, both independent and trusting, we had never called to check on each other; but after two years of 24/7 togetherness, we'd become accustomed to facing trouble standing together. He hadn't asked if I were OK, but his call felt like he had.

John's arrival comforted me, as it did during chaos at sea. That evening several more aftershocks occurred. We ate canned chili and stared at our tiny TV screen. A terrifying film clip showed a car disappearing when a flap of the upper ramp on the Bay Bridge broke away like a trap door. An elevated freeway ramp collapsed onto a lower section crushing many cars. My office building closed for structural assessment. For weeks, aftershocks kept everyone on edge. The media reported damage costs equal to the $7 billion caused by Hurricane Hugo and a final death toll of sixty-three (most from the ramp collapse). It occurred to me that staying home could be more hazardous than crossing an ocean.

In our first nine months back in California, John and I saved 60% of our gross incomes, enough to cover living expenses for many years of cruising. However, other stress arose at the end of our stay that made me short-tempered. John began to spend vast amounts on boat gear. We argued over priorities and saving cash for emergencies. The government began to phase out cold-war production contracts, and Westinghouse began layoffs. I could see that staying home with an employer was no guarantee of keeping a job.

In November, I drove home listening to the car radio describe the jubilation as the Berlin Wall came down reuniting East and West Germany. I marveled at the human drive for freedom that so many Americans take for granted. Suddenly, a heavy van overtook me and passed on the right—its tailwind shaking my little car. I had yet to become accustomed to speeds much faster than the five MPH that we traveled by boat. A red traffic light stopped me. I revolved my shoulders to shake off the tension. I looked past the fast food joints, the knots of cars, and tangles of power lines to glimpse a maturing, red-orange sunset upon a distant hill.

Yes, I could stay in California, as I could have stayed in Massachusetts, but having traveled some, I saw more options—choices I could make now with midlife gusto and maturity. *There's so much to take in, and now is the best time.* I smiled. In a few weeks, we'd be free again and back home on *Renaissance* in Australia. The light turned green.

On December 1, we gave a month's notice at the apartment and at work. Time accelerated as departure day approached. Last chance. Go or stay? My mood cycled from elation to uncertainty, panic to impatience. I was keen to travel but would miss the project team interaction and intellectual challenges.

The shadow of mortality, the impetus for our journey, had appeared again with the quake. Also, that year, a dear coworker died suddenly, and a car crash severely injured a girlfriend. *Poof. Life can take you out so quickly.* I had used up forty-seven of the fifty-two years my mother had. *Maybe I don't have long to live either.* If we don't make choices, we drift, experience only what happens to float by, and are left with regrets.

Once again, while able, I chose freedom to explore new vistas where challenges only intensify the hues.

CHAPTER 16

Inside the Great Barrier Reef — Aussie Escapades

ON JANUARY 3, 1990, WE EMBARKED ON A DIRECT FLIGHT of 7,500 miles across the Pacific from Los Angeles to Sydney, Australia, to return to a life of discovery. In our coach seats, I hugged John's arm and chattered about freedom and future expectations. He matched my excitement.

Eight hours into the flight and beyond the point of no return, the pilot of the newly-instituted, long-haul Boeing 747 announced engine trouble. The dozing passengers, doing their best to endure the fourteen-hour flight, squirmed and sat up straight to listen. The plane held five hundred of us captive forty-thousand feet over the mid-Pacific, where I knew only tiny islands lay. I raised the window shade, saw nothing but clouds, and thought of Amelia Earhart.

The amplified pilot's voice continued, "In about an hour, we will be landing in Nadi, Fiji, the nearest Pacific airport with a runway long enough for us. I'll keep you updated on our progress."

After a startled silence, groans and pips of concern surrounded us: "Oh, no!" and "What the hell?!" and "No runway?"

I turned to John. "Well! What a great way to re-enter our midlife journey."

"Yeah, if we make it down alive," he said with a thin grin. His arm hugged me close with assurance we'd see it through. "If not, we've had a great adventure."

My lack of worry surprised me. *Where did I get this positive outlook?* No longer was I drunk, depressed, or easily crushed. Perhaps I was beginning to just "accept the things I cannot change"—the essence of the Serenity Prayer. Buoyed by career confidence, an optimistic mate, support of family, and armed with growing patience and flexibility, I faced the future with a new sense of promise.

In Fiji, we deplaned among businessmen, tourists, and Australians returning home—all jet-lagged and disgruntled by the anxiety and delay. After being told of a twelve-hour layover for repairs, most passengers went to bed in the hotel provided by the airline. John and I decided to make hay in the sunshine. Thrilled at the opportunity to revisit Fiji, we hopped an open-air bus to Lautoka. We walked through town to the market place and talked to natives with a familiarity that might amaze a short-time vacationer. I no longer hung back but felt comfortable engaging with the interesting Fijians that John uncovered.

Our broken flight finally arrived in Sydney shortly before midnight—again fortuitous for us. A customs officer, eager to get off work, profiled us as vacationing tourists and waved our checked luggage through his lane without inspection. John shot me a sly smile. Those bags contained mounds of boat gear and electronics, probably subject to significant import duty.

At a city auction, we bought a station wagon with a severe case of hail-stone acne for a few hundred Aussie dollars, claimed a pod of pre-shipped cargo, and began a six-week tour. We circled south from Sydney Harbor to the Canberra capital, then back along the Snowy Mountains through rural towns, weaving our way north to Bundaberg.

Along the way we contacted friends and relatives of AA members we had met the prior year. When Australians say stop by anytime, they really mean it, even though we had never met the folks who took us in.

For example, Greg West and family, who were finishing a new home out "in the bush," welcomed us heartily. During our two-day stay, their three kids (ages eight to fifteen) introduced us to the lore of the bush country, from poems to spiders. While Lorraine and I baked a birthday cake, John joined the kids with battered clubs for "bush golf" in local sand and dry scrub.

"Let Mr. McCan have his go!" yelled Graham, the eldest.

"Oh. Sorry," peeped the youngest with the inflection of a British gentleman.

At dinner Michael told us that his dog, Snuggles, had fleas and that he planned to "give him a wash in kero."

"Ugg," I said, picturing a tub of sugary Karo syrup. "Will that work?"

Greg picked up my confusion and explained the boy meant diluted kerosene.

The Aussies kept us guessing as they love to cut off words and often add -ie; for example, "mossie" for mosquito, "relies" for relatives, or "Brizzie" for the city of Brisbane.

As we crossed into Queensland and approached Bundaberg, our excitement grew to reunite with our boat and Bundy friends. The Reilly family, who supported us before, piled out to greet us when we arrived that February (summer) afternoon. George Reilly, a local AA ambassador, was a jolly, barrel-chested Scotsman-turned-Aussie, who everyone just called "Reilly." His wife, Jan, a hardworking, petite blond welcomed us like lost cousins. Their active daughters, ten-year-old Anita and almost-teen Becky enthralled us with their school projects.

John and I stayed with the family for four weeks while preparing the boat for launch, happy to share a mattress on their living room floor. Each day we awoke to the bubbly kids and a kiss from Cinderella, a mongrel dog that wagged its whole body. Each evening, we dragged ourselves back from the hot, dusty boatyard for a shower and some tasty Aussie "tucker" cooked up by Jan. Their thoughtfulness embarrassed me with gifts when John forgot my birthday. On weekends, we joined the couple for AA meetings and picnics, and John admired the heroic stories told by the men. AA members introduced us to an intimate level of cultural interaction not available to other visitors—such as their peculiar sports and political system.

On the morning of our scheduled boat launch, we arrived early at the boatyard with an incoming tide. With John and a friend aboard, *Renaissance* tentatively wet her smooth, blue bottom in the salty sea and seemed to shiver with excitement—or perhaps it was just the jerking of the cable lowering her cradle down the launch ramp. Dusted off and freed from bondage, she floated, gingerly drawing away from the land where she languished for fifteen months, while we worked to reclaim her. Her engine fired. Released into her natural element, she seemed to taste the wind like a thoroughbred tensing for a good run. She turned toward the sea, but John coaxed her back along the shallows to be sure her systems were ready. A surge of joy arose inside me and a tear tumbled from my eye. More work remained, but soon we would be voyaging free again.

Satisfied with her, John waved, and they headed for the river to return to town. I drove the car back past acres of sugar cane that had surrounded the area since indentured islanders worked these fields a century ago.

At the Bundy marina, we moved aboard and stayed five weeks to complete preparations. As before, social activities abounded among ubiquitous yachties, the Reillys, and other reformed alkies; and I felt comfort within this realm. Sometimes I grumbled about the drudgery jobs like mildew control and hauling dirty duds to the Laundromat; but free now from my job, I had the time, met interesting people, and benefited from the exercise. John also had dirty jobs like engine oil changes and caulking against leaks. Such chores constituted a part of our simple lifestyle.

A bon voyage party in May with local friends sent us out to sea with *Renaissance* dressed in a ragtag of collected flags. Our hosts, Reilly and Jan, accompanied us for a two-week holiday, which eased our separation from merry Bundaberg. A brisk wind took us fifty miles to Lady Musgrave Island, the southern-most part of the Great Barrier Reef. We anchored as the sky turned pink and watched graceful shearwaters fly low across the two-mile-wide lagoon, the aqua water reflected on their white bellies.

Each morning, our friends scurried onto the foredeck to throw out fishing lines. Still not comfortable around squirmy fish, John was content to banter with them at arm's length. Reilly lectured on bait and sinkers, but Jan landed the largest fish. I watched and baited hooks, hoping to become more successful at catching free food. Throughout a week of beachcombing, we feasted on coral trout, trevally, and an aqua parrotfish, played rummy, and sang along with John Denver on tape.

We snorkeled at two other reef islands before sailing seventy miles back to the mainland to say fond goodbyes to them on a windy pier.

The Great Barrier Reef is a broad, aquamarine ribbon that parallels the coast of Queensland for 1400 miles, encompassing 900 islands. We traveled north and the distance between the continent and the reef increased to over a hundred miles. At our slow pace, we could not reach the Reef during the daylight, which we needed to navigate the coral mazes. However, the wide channel inside the Reef offered hundreds of high continental islands to explore at our own pace. Heading toward the Equator in autumn, we entered the subtropical region where winter temperatures remained above sixty-six degrees. Vacationers disappeared during these cooler months, so we met few other vessels along the way.

From the green coast of Queensland, we sailed toward rock islands that rose sharply out of the sea like giant stepping stones. Flocks of butterflies, black velvet with china blue spots, fluttered up and down over the water as if in a garden. On another day, a herd of dolphins joined up, racing and leaping across our bow wave. I felt thrilled to be cruising again with my best friend and lover, sharing adventures under sun and random rain. Weeks passed in honeymoon happiness as we sailed, explored, cuddled, and made memories together. Our responsible, productive life in the U.S. faded. During the next weeks of directional meandering, this workaholic accomplished nothing but fixing simple meals. John puttered and tinkered with all the boat's moving parts.

On the unoccupied Percy Islands, we discovered memorabilia from past travelers: poems, pictures, tattered flags and boat names painted on canvas scraps. When we climbed for a long view, wild cockatoos crowed complaints at our presence. Near the top, a hawk with golden wings soared above the trail. Back on the beach, overheated with the exercise, we stripped and dove into the emerald water—until cold undercurrents drove us back into our clothes.

After six weeks in our floating hermitage, even I missed human contact, and we returned to the mainland for supplies. As we approached Mackay harbor, the affable Pier Master assigned us via radio to pole berth C4—whereupon we faced a new challenge.

Queenslanders found pole moorings more secure than floating docks in areas subject to strong currents or surging seas. We had noticed boats moored to poles in the river at Bundaburg, but never tangled with them. Once inside the stone breakwater, we halted before two parallel rows of pilings, each about fifty feet apart. The goal was to tie lines at our bow and stern to center the boat between two poles. Our stern pole became another boat's bow pole. A long metal handle ran vertically on each pole with a two-inch steel ring attached. We had to attach our lines to the rings, which slid up and down with the tide.

With a crosswind, John made two unsuccessful passes at the front pole, hoping I could thread the rings, but two men in a dory appeared to help set our lines. On ten-foot, nylon leashes, fore and aft, our boat jerked over sea swells that slipped into the harbor. That night I awoke with a start several times, certain we had broken away. I much preferred swinging free at anchor, although that held other uncertainties.

Ashore the next day, we located groceries and shared an AA meeting. The Cruising Yacht Club of Mackay welcomed us to join members for a friendly barbeque under darkening skies. Back on the boat before sunset, we made popcorn and played cards, listening with growing concern to hourly forecasts of approaching gales.

"Bang, Ba-bang!" At 4:00 A.M. I started up from a deep sleep in our forward cabin. Through the porthole on my side, I saw shore lights in streaks of rain. The view had changed, meaning we were loose. Closest to the door, John leaped down from our platform bunk and scrambled for his rain gear. I grabbed at a sweatshirt, pictured the stone breakwater, and hit the floor with a strangled feeling in my chest.

John turned from the driving rain in the cockpit and yelled, "We're holding only by the stern line!" He threw open the cockpit locker and yanked out a heavy coil of anchor line. I arrived in the cockpit zipping up my slicker, as he turned to our dinghy tied alongside. I blinked into the darkness and confirmed that *Renaissance* faced south instead of north. Her forward line had broken, she'd pivoted on the aft piling, and resided in the open space behind us.

John slung the rope coil over the rail and slid into our dinghy tied alongside. The outboard started with roar, he waved an OK, and I cast him off across the choppy water. Then I stiffened with angst, leaned out and yelled, "Your life jacket!"

He crouched low against the gusty wind and drove the rubber boat forward. The blowing rain stung my eyes. I watched him grip the pole slide with one arm and force the new line into the ring with the other. He dragged thirty feet of line through the ring and back into the dinghy. When he returned alongside, I retied the dinghy and helped him haul both ends of the rope to the foredeck. He winched up the rope to bring the bow back in line and tied a second line into the rings on both ends. While the boat continued to buck against the wet gusts, we added chafeguards made of hose to the straining nylon lines.

With nothing further to be done, I looked down and realized my bare feet were wet and very cold. John's sweat pants were drenched. We returned to bed at 6:15 A.M. with socks and an extra blanket. Although the wind roared and the boat continued to surge and jerk, I slept.

Two hours later, we woke to shouts nearby and dashed out again. From its berth in the row beside us, a powerboat named *Outsider* performed the same trick as *Rennie*; except when it pivoted into the space behind, it slammed into the broad catamaran that occupied it. In the powerboat, a grey-haired woman made futile attempts to keep the two vessels from banging together.

"Look!" I pointed. A small man with thin, white hair rowed an inflatable dinghy (difficult under the best conditions) against the wind and rain attempting to replace *Outsider*'s broken line. At his feet lay a coil of rope attached to the bow of cruiser. Short of the pole, the elderly man held up the end of his line in surprise—and when he stopped rowing, the wind blew his dinghy aside. I radioed the Pier Master for help.

John never hesitated in going to their aid. I noted with pride that he had gained much confidence since our trial cruise when he froze after the tornadic gust knocked over our boat near Baja. In our dinghy, he caught up with the older man and towed him back to his boat. His petite wife must have been frantic. The gale winds shrieked. A seaman appeared in a sturdy launch with cordage to reconnect the errant boat to its forward pole. After a struggle, he and John maneuvered *Outsider* back into her proper position.

Without help the couple could have lost their boat and their lives. I recalled a similar situation with an older American couple on a yacht anchored in Tonga where two native fishermen swam out to save them during a squall. I recognized that active travel was best enjoyed well before retirement age.

When the wind eased, the elderly captain rowed over with a bottle of wine to thank John. Although neither of us was drinking, we accepted it to pay it forward. We stayed on board that day waiting for the storm to pass. Trussed to poles beside the sugar wharf, *Renaissance* had little room to maneuver should we break away. Frustrated and inconsolable, John paced like a trapped tiger, desperate to get away. I stayed clear of him, but his fright increased my anxiety. The storm moved south, and the next day we escaped the harbor early, surfing down the resolving waves.

During June, we traveled another 265 miles up the central section of the Great Barrier Reef Marine Park, encountering few humans. As we hiked among pine and palm trees on Brampton Island, we discovered an interior lake. Beside the picnic area, a wild kangaroo lounged. I laughed at his bravado. "Looks like he's waiting to collect a park entrance fee," I said to John. "This is what it's all about, memories like this to sustain us for whatever the future brings."

We navigated through the Whitsunday Islands, named by our old friend, Captain Cook, which now boasted pricy resorts within national park land. The superfine sand of Whitehaven Beach squeaked as I shuffled my feet along part of its three-mile length. The place reminded me of carefree days at the beach as a child. According to my journal, I "wasted" most of two whole days prancing, clowning, taking photos and drawing stick figures in wet sand.

At a rustic resort further north, we sat around a bonfire with fellow travelers listening to stories about another native—the saltwater crocodile. Neville, a slim, self-described bushman with a cultured Aussie drawl was also the chief of police in the sugar town of Giru.

"Making lots of noise will usually scare away a croc," he said. "But, then's the time I took some tourists into the bush to see one. We came upon a big one so intent on stalking a pelican, that me banging on a metal pan did not move 'im." Neville ran his weathered hands down his pant legs before he continued. "Northern crocs are lazy, but smart. They'll hang out under boats waiting for scraps. Oh, and never, never swim or throw food scraps off the boat at the same time each day. They remember! And they've gotten real cheeky now that they are protected." A grim silence followed.

"Ya know how to separate two crocs?" A long pause as he pulled at his boot top. "Give 'em a Yank!"

As we cruised, boat projects usually consumed one day out of each week. John now served as an able mechanic, electrician and plumber. I did appreciate his keeping all systems operational and believed that getting dirty was his favorite part. While he worked, I cleaned; and local radio stations provided a depth of cultural and practical information, as well as a breadth of global prospective I never heard in the States.

After six months in Australia, we arrived at Townsville in Northern Queensland, which became a base for our final two months in the country. We pampered ourselves for a week with plug-in power, washer-dryers, and hot showers at the modern Breakwater Marina before we explored further north. A local couple in the adjoining berth had recently returned from a cruise to Papua New Guinea (PNG) and the Solomon Islands—our planned route. Based on rumors, they had outfitted their boat with electrified lifelines and a six-shot flare gun near the door to deter unwanted visitors. However, they experienced no conflicts with people there.

One day, John and I peddled our folding bikes around the massive rock hill that dominates the area to fulfill some provisioning needs. After a few stops, I consulted my AA directory and said, "There's a meeting at noon a few blocks from here. Let's go." He hesitated, and I continued. "and then I'll buy lunch." At that, he agreed.

In front of a tatty wooden building with no signage beyond an address number, we locked our bikes to a utility pole. John opened the door, and I passed inside the low building. After two steps, I stopped as the closing door extinguished the sun, leaving me in darkness. A fan whirred disbursing a musky smell. A throat cleared. White pinprick eyes appeared. I sensed John close behind me. My eyes became accustomed to the dim light, and I stiffened as blue-black skin of the occupants slowly differentiated from the shadows. Eight Aboriginal men sat around a table staring at us. Behind them, wide-eyed women and children shifted in creaky chairs. *What is this?* I took a step back. *Oh, oh, oh. I don't think we belong here.*

"Sorry," I said. "Sorry. Is this...we were looking for the AA meeting." The silence continued, and I tensed to bolt from the room.

One of the black men recovered from his surprise and rose slowly from behind the table. "Mmm. Yes. This is an AA meeting. This is the Aboriginal Recovery House. I am Kenny. You are welcome." He motioned us to sit.

"Thank you. I am grateful you are all here…to help me," I said. With a tense smile, I turned, scanned the faces of the men and nodded my head. "I am Judy, a recovering alcoholic, and this is my husband, John. We come from America."

I sat down near the table. John perched on a chair at my side. The leader rustled in a notebook and began reading the preamble of Alcoholics Anonymous, which is the same worldwide. I sighed, comforted and looked at John. He sat on the edge of his chair, arms stiff, jaw clenched. I reached to pat his knee and offered a smile of reassurance.

As the familiar words comforted my mind, I took a deep breath and relaxed. I listened, and my thoughts drifted. I marveled at how this program could unite such divergent cultures to help us fight alcohol addiction together. I could imagine no greater cultural difference from my background than that of the thin black man sitting next to me.

I knew little about these Aboriginals, except that they shared a painful history here. Their ancestors lived in Australia about 50,000 years before the country was "discovered" by Europeans in 1788. After decimating the native population with the virulent diseases that they introduced, the invaders hunted down, raped and massacred the surviving natives for almost two centuries. Their incidence of alcoholism was twice that of the white Australians who introduced them to liquor.

These Aboriginals believed in the spirits of ancestors and benevolent connections of all living things. I liked that idea; it made sense to me.

"We admitted we were p-power...less over alcohol..." A new man, gaunt and battered by the disease, stumbled over unfamiliar words in the "Twelve Steps of Recovery." I smiled recalling my stuttering start in AA. Empathy filled me and I breathed: *God, help him.* I had heard these words read at perhaps five hundred meetings I had attended in the past four years. As I listened, I recalled my struggle and felt strength and gratitude build inside me.

Another man began struggling with the words on his page. "Made a…decision to turn…our will and …our lives over to…" He looked up at the group leader who nodded encouragement. "To the care of God."

Just as the United States almost extinguished Native Americans and exploited African slaves, Australia abused their Aboriginals. This included a misguided policy in 1930 that removed black or mixed-race children from mothers "for their own good." A national referendum in 1967 overturned their status as "non-persons," but with that, made it legal for them to drink alcohol. The modern, and I believe misguided, government solution consisted primarily of blocking their access to alcohol. *That won't stop addicts like us!*

Kenny introduced the discussion meeting. In a familiar format, he told his story of what it was like while he drank—the violence, jail, attempted suicide—what happened in AA to change that, and what his life was like now as a counselor. I noted vast differences in my experiences compared with prisons and the extreme battering the disease had inflicted upon him. However, as he described his journey of recovery, my heart melted as I recognized our similarities.

I decided that these new members might be suspicious of us and hesitant to join the discussion, so I raised my hand to share my story. I confessed my fear as I had entered their meeting. "I am white and a woman. I am as different from you as night and day. But my focus on being different almost killed me. I thought only men or fools were drunks, but I drank every day to pass out. Only when I accepted that I was powerless over alcohol could I see the similarities that all alcoholics share. And then I joined you in this fellowship to change my life."

I paused and watched understanding dawn on these men. I expanded on my struggle to get sober and the serenity and blessings I have by staying sober.

Three other men shared their despair and broken lives and the suffering that they caused their families. I admired them. Their courage was greater than mine. It had allowed them to rise from a place more hellish than mine. A rush of gratitude filled me, and I rededicated myself to my recovery and helping others. After Kenny closed the meeting, several men and their families surrounded us with their earnest curiosity and love. We hugged, and they thanked us for our visit.

"Well. That was pleasant surprise," I said after we settled in a booth for lunch. "The program works everywhere. It makes me appreciate what AA members have given me...including the opportunity for such an encounter! I hope those guys all make it."

John took my hand across the table. "It was a shock, at first, going in there," he said. "But you were great. . .for what you shared with them. AA is amazing."

I marveled at how far I had come in my recovery—not just in losing the compulsion to drink, but also in my ability to feel compassion for others, any others. And now, I wanted to learn more about the Aboriginals.

A few days later, we anchored beside Great Palm Island, one of many Aboriginal Reserves established by the government. About seven miles wide and shaped like a boot, the island included eroded mountains and rain forests, surrounded by a coral reef. At the end of its eight-hundred-foot pier we tied the dinghy, and John met two teen fishermen clad in football jerseys.

"How long did it take you to get here on that boat?" said one whose curiosity overrode his shyness.

People often asked us this, perhaps thinking in terms of nonstop travel. When John answered truthfully, "two years," they shook their heads.

These young men obviously had both black and white ancestors, which earned them the pejorative, "creamies". However, I found them bright and handsome. It remains a mystery from whence these aboriginals originated, but their appearance could place them anywhere in the Pacific islands among racial mixes of Melanesians and Polynesians.

I had anticipated a dismal community there, perhaps like some American Indian reservations. As we stepped from pier to land, I pointed out a two-story cinderblock building covered with dramatic Aboriginal art which depicted "dreamtime:" crocodiles, snakes, turtles, kangaroo, manta rays, fish, crabs and crayfish, all filled with jagged patterns and dotted lines. The sacred creatures soared in arcs over my head. The artist had rendered them in traditional colors of red ochre, sun yellow, white, and black. Curious, we entered the building to find, not just a gallery, but a dark saloon with regulars slumped over their midday liquor. Some seemed keen to talk with us, but after a quick photo of me next to a wall painted with a ghostly human figure, I led a quick exit.

Behind the building, we found the artist: a shy 30-year-old, clad in ball cap and a striped sport shirt. I complemented his work, and John tried to draw him out with questions. He told us little and focused on completing the fine graphics on a long crocodile tail with dips of a tiny brush into a half-pint can of paint to make the white dots characteristic of this art. A simpler mural fronted the Palm Island State School, which let out just as we walked past. People we met here and later at the Kuranda Reserve surprised us with their healthy, happy outlook.

After exploring other islands to the north, we returned to Townsville and began preparations in earnest for our next ocean passage and to meet all our needs for several months in the Third World. We spent days inspecting all operating systems on the boat. We borrowed a car for provisioning. Yachties told us the islanders were ardent traders and wanted white rice, sugar, towels, tools and fine sandpaper. "And the kids go crazy for balloons and hard candy."

I spent a day storing away $1,000 worth of fresh drugs, first-aid supplies and groceries. A local dentist cemented a loose crown and provided fluoride tablets. Anticipating flare ups of my skin again in the equatorial climate, I obtained steroid tablets. Because malaria remained a threat at our destinations, we began prophylactic Chloroquine tablets two weeks before departure. We awaited a final mail package from home.

John's pre-departure anxiety returned. He nursed a severe cut on his heel and worried about an old stomach "ulcer." He kept finding new boat projects to delay us. Finally, I faced him, asked him to sit, and took his hand. "You always feel this resistance before setting out on a long passage," I said. "From Mexico, Bora Bora, Tonga, N-Zed… It's normal. Sure, staying put is easier than hurtling into the unknown again. But we always discover amazing places. You love sailing…and we are prepared. Right?" He nodded in agreement.

In early September, we departed the mainland and anchored again at Great Palm Island to get a head start on crossing the Great Reef. The next morning, the oceanic weather forecast allowed at least three days of clear weather ahead in the Coral Sea.

"We are ready," I said after breakfast. I latched the interior locker doors. "Nothing to hold us back now."

John climbed on deck with little enthusiasm. He hauled up the mainsail, then the anchor, then both jibs. We raced to cover sixty-five miles to cross The Great Barrier Reef in daylight. The sailing was grand, and the transit took several hours. I lifted my face to the sun and savored the salty air. I gawked at the coral gems below the crystal aqua water that reached to the horizon. John paced on and off the deck again inspecting every piece of gear for potential problems.

At 4:30 P.M. I spotted the buoy marking the edge of the Reef. Suddenly the water turned from turquoise to navy blue. I felt like we floated off the edge of the planet.

Beyond that sea boundary we relaxed and switched to ocean-transit mode. John zipped his safety harness to take the first watch (and settle his nerves). I lay down on the bunk for a nap before supper. I smiled inside and out, excited to be traveling again, and drifted off to sleep.

CHAPTER 17

Papua New Guinea — A Primeval Land

UNDER AN OMINOUS, GREY SKY THAT COMPRESSED THE humidity and swelled the heat index, we trolled toward a mounded, green island called Samarai. From modern Australia to Papua New Guinea (PNG), we had logged about five hundred miles—only the distance from San Francisco to San Diego—but soon felt like we had traveled back a hundred years to a steamy jungle land of primitive native cultures and colonial traders.

In a cove beside this government outpost sat *Mystic Muse*, the sailboat home of Dave and Sue Muse, whom we had met in Townsville. Dave, a lanky American and confident seaman, and Sue, his Australian wife, had visited the area in a previous year. The opportunity to travel with this congenial couple provided reassurance against our natural fears of this alien world.

After John dropped anchor beside the *Muse*, a heavy launch sped toward us driven by a very black man. It banked a tight turn around our boat, and Dave's head popped out. He shouted a hearty, "G'day! Glad you could make it out," mocking our apparent reluctance to leave the western world. "We'll be over later to get you checked into the country."

The Independent State of Papua New Guinea occupies the eastern half of the island of New Guinea, as well as numerous islands to the south and east. Mainland PNG total area approximates that of California. After seventy years of Australian governance, PNG gained independence in 1975—about the time reports declared that its residents no longer practiced headhunting or cannibalism—only a half-generation of time had passed when we arrived. We knew little about this isolated land, except that it played a strategic role in the Pacific War. There could be physical danger and/or danger in misunderstandings. Apprehension again tempered my explorer eagerness.

Ashore I found myself staring at the purple-black skin of the Papuan natives—just as they stared at my white skin and straw-colored hair. Their Melanesian features matched those of the Australian Aborigines. Caucasians represented a tiny minority in the area, which humbled me. Samarai and adjacent islands hosted an interesting mix of expats. Australians would say these white men had "gone troppo" for choosing such isolation in the torrid land, but most of them seemed quite sane and content with life apart from cutting-edge modernism. I could relate to such outliers.

Dave introduced us to Joe. Short and stocky, this gentle Aussie had lived in Samarai for ten years with a native wife and showed us his boat repair yard. Joe introduced us to another Caucasian, Ernie, a thirty-year resident with an enlarged spleen from bouts of malaria, who owned a small island nearby. German residents, Rolf and wife Kate, had arrived two years before us.

Ian, another Aussie, first arrived as a contract geologist and had stayed for over fifteen years with his wife Julie (their two teenagers attended boarding school overseas). He invited six yachties to Pearl Bay for a barbeque on his dock—a recycled WWII landing barge. He leased the property for his house from villagers who fished from dugout canoes. Ian was preparing a history of Samarai that spanned a century.

"Before the Pacific War, Caucasian, Japanese, Filipino, and native traders co-existed in this booming, frontier town. So prosperous, it supported three pubs," he pointed to a faded photo on his wall. "In 1942 as Japanese troops approached, local Aussies torched the buildings and wharves to avoid having these properties fall under enemy control."

His sepia photographs showed Japanese gun emplacements on the southern coast of the PNG mainland and muddy Aussie soldiers emerging from its jungle. He described the malaria, dysentery, foot rot, and venomous serpents endured by those who fought in the area's stifling swamps and spoke of the characters who remained after the war. Ian had become part of that history.

Dave and Sue pressed us to attend the Milne Bay Provincial Show, scheduled to coincide with the fifteenth anniversary of PNG's independence. Along with games and agricultural exhibits, this rare event would include reclusive tribes from the Highlands performing *singsings*. I needed little encouragement.

"Lead on, Dr. Livingston," I chided Dave, referring to an ancient Scottish explorer.

Renaissance raced *Mystic Muse* across the narrow China Strait to the eastern end of New Guinea. We approached a verdant coastal plain behind which a chain of mountains rose out of thick rainforest up to 13,000 feet and ran inland for 750 miles. Because of its treacherous terrain and dense jungle, PNG remains one of the world's most diverse and least explored countries—geographically and culturally.

In ten-mile-wide Milne Bay, about sixty miles below the Equator, the air felt like a blast from a pizza oven, and the humidity seem to blur the edges of branching rivers and sheer mountains. Clouds covered the peaks and cascaded into deep valleys, perhaps explaining why hundreds of aircraft were lost there during WWII. Sunbeams pierced holes in the overcast sky spotlighting coconut trees along the overgrown shore that hid vestiges of battles. I tried to imagine this paradise as the site of the

1942 Battle of Milne Bay, when battered and desperate soldiers helped arrest Japanese plans to invade Australia.

As advised, we tied our boats to coconut palms ashore, and Dave engaged a guard. Down below I prepared a backpack with water and wallets to go ashore, but drums and cheers drew me back on deck. An open boat with furled sails festooned in bright red and yellow streamers approached. Majestic native men, clad only in scarlet loincloths and headbands, crowded that vessel and sang in close harmony to a quick drum rhythm. I blinked in awe at the spectacle.

In the open market, we exchanged welcoming smiles as we walked with Dave and Sue into the main town of Alotau, accompanied by a cacophony of traffic, chants, and cheers of escalating independence celebrations. I was delighted at the variety of shops, and we stocked up on inexpensive anti-malaria pills to extend the prophylaxis we initiated before arrival.

On a flat rugby field within sight of the sea, we joined crowds of Melanesians, dressed in everything from sport shirts to loincloths to leaves. On stage in suit and tie, Deputy Prime Minister Diro opened the Provincial Show with a hope that such events would provide education for the people and encourage future tourism. He spoke in English, a nod to decades of British and Australian governance. However, the official language of PNG is *tok pisin*, (talk pidgin), derived from English to overcome hundreds of area dialects and facilitate trade. PNG government parliamentarians still conduct debates in this ubiquitous language.

Show activities commenced with contests I recalled from county fairs of my childhood: three-legged races, greased pig chase, and tug of war. Stages featured boxing, string bands, even rock music. As we stood in the heat among hundreds of black visitors and participants, I smelled the musk of the close crowd and felt a chill of fear at being such a tiny racial minority. I counted only eight or ten white faces including ours. When the term headhunter came to mind, I stiffened, assessed the crowd, and moved closer to John. However, curiosity again overcame my trepidation. As I relaxed and listened to the surrounding Papuans, I recognized some of the common words in phonetic pidgin. My linguist husband tried it: "*Me John bilong Amerika*."

The plain paper program, prepared on a manual typewriter with a faded ink ribbon, listed the exhibits, events and their locations. I found what I sought. "It says the 'traditional dancing, drama, and legends' are over on the soccer field. Let's go see that."

The four of us strode to a roped-off area and stood transfixed before an assemblage of dance groups from the Highlands Region. Smudged dirt and glistening sweat covered their compact, muscular bodies. They wore sparse costumes woven from leaves, flowering stalks, and the feathers of rare birds-of-paradise. White feathers dangled from a lattice of branches that sprang from one man's back twelve feet into the air. I spotted feather headdresses with colorful headbands, very similar to those of American Indian chiefs. Thick paint in reds and ochre covered all or half the dancers' faces; others displayed skin painted black topped with white dots, creating a fearsome appearance. Groups of hunched men whirled about the field pounding on long, narrow drums, yelping and stamping broad feet. The monotonous beat accompanied chanting performers who hopped and turned independently. On the sidelines, tribal women and girls wore only coarse grass skirts, some decorated with red painted fronds.

"This is very unusual," said Dave. "The Highland tribes rarely venture out of isolation in the mountains. They communicate in very primitive dialects and still hunt with arrows like stone-agers. See the long bow in that guy's hand?"

"Oh, yeah," said John. "I certainly wouldn't challenge any of them."

"This is an amazing display," I said. "It's like witnessing our own human evolution!"

Even with an overcast sky, the heat drained away my energy, and I walked as in a time-warp dream. I could smell the decomposition and touch this place as it existed in ages past. Beyond the field, ten-man canoes raced up the bay with a mystical backdrop of hazy, blue mountains.

In one area of the sports field, rows of booths displayed health and agricultural exhibits and items for sale. Pamphlets warned against HIV, alcoholism, and wife-beating. Missionaries sought converts. My favorite was the tobacco counter to feed my remaining addiction. Men rolled dark tobacco leaves in newsprint to fashion foot-long cigarettes called "big pella stix." I purchased a stack of them, which I cut into thirds to smoke. They delivered a fresh, mild taste without a filter.

On the ground everywhere, I noticed red splotches, betraying the popularity of chewing betel (areca) nut. A user mixed the nut in his mouth with bites of a green stick and caustic lime powder. Chewing turned the combination red and apparently induced a feeling of euphoria. Some women held big wads inside their cheeks. The red juice escaped down their chins when they smiled, revealing teeth eroded down to black nubs. Long-term devotees might have trouble eating more than gruel.

John stopped to talk to a young man, who I noticed held betel nut "fixin" in his hand. "What happens when you chew that?

The native gave him a scarlet smile. "Feel good! Fee-eel good!"

"What if you don't have it? Do you feel sad?" I said.

"No, but then I want more. Quick."

I smiled with recognition. I could certainly relate to such an obsession. I started to explain the danger of addiction to him, but he just shrugged. Not a problem for him.

The next day at the fair, a small native man with a bright red mouth collapsed to the ground near us. Although conscious, his limbs convulsed. A uniformed policeman appeared and dragged him away. Drugs are drugs. I thanked God again for my deliverance. We ate lunch from booths and stayed to watch some of the finalists in the dance-dramas, which reenacted hunting scenes and legendary battles. Before the fair closed, the cumulative heat drove us back to the boats.

I cooked supper for our friends, and we replayed our recollections of a rare and amazing day. After I cleared away dishes, John spread out a nautical chart across the table. Dave traced a chain of islands with his finger, and I realized our route in the coming months would take us even further from any security of the life we had known.

From the mainland, *Mystic Muse* led us into the 250-mile-long Louisiade Archipelago, which divides the Coral Sea from the Solomon Sea to the north. For four weeks, our boats wandered among ten volcanic islands and ninety coral motus. Clearing skies allowed the sun to highlight shimmering underwater reefs. The glowing aqua lagoons reminded me of French Polynesia without the tourist hotels. We had our pick of idyllic anchorages with short day trips between them. A warm breeze ruffled the dark sea as we sailed past two large islands and headed for a third called Basilaki. As we entered the bay, Dave landed a tasty wahoo. This stirred John's competitive nature, and he now had more patience with my fishing efforts.

Trim, thatched huts lined the shore with a backdrop of jungle and volcanic cones. Curious women with babies paddled canoes out to us. Sue procured lemons from one for the fish she served us that night. However, after learning that the village tolerated a resident crocodile ("don't worry he only eats dogs and piglets"), we departed in the morning.

As we pulled our dinghies onto the beach at Slade Island, we encountered several children, including a four-year-old pixie who pointed at us and bawled, "*Dimdim*," the pidgin word for Caucasian. I had never been called 'dim' before, at least not to my face; but from their perspective, I supposed we appeared double dim, as we couldn't even climb a coconut palm.

Several kids ran ahead, but a demure boy of twelve walked beside us to translate for the elders who we stopped to greet. A large village known in the past for its fierce, sadistic warriors, Tubetube contained a church established by a missionary buried there, and a resident *dimdim* who hadlabored for two years translating three books of the bible into the local dialect. Tidy dwellings with walls of split bamboo slats and roofs of thatch stood on stilts four feet above the sand. Interlaced branches formed pens for prized pigs, and outhouses stood on piers above the water.

Our young guide told us that the men were away working in community gardens on a neighboring island. He introduced us to Elizabeth, one of three teachers at his school who rotated every two years. The stout, native woman showed us a closet library and her classroom decorated with samples of student weaving. On the wall in block letters, the classroom rules reminded students:

I WILL IN SCHOOL BE CLEAN,
SPEAK ENGLISH SO TO UNDERSTAND SIGNS AND STORIES,
NO SWEARING.

Two days later, we picked our way carefully through a sunken coral garden and reef to anchor beside an island reminiscent of the emerald lagoons in the Tuamotus. As the light faded, Romulus, a wizened old man in tattered shorts, paddled out to greet us. He stood in his hand-hewn canoe holding onto our boat. In English and *tok pisin,* he told the story of how he slayed with his spear a 14-foot-long "*puckpuck*" (salt-water crocodile) that had surprised him as he gathered coconuts on the beach.

"I have the teeth, the jaw," he said trying to describe the size by circling his arms overhead. "Must come to my house and see 'im!"

The next morning the sun bored into my back like a hot poker as the four of us walked to the village as promised. Smiling residents pointed out the church under construction and a village cargo boat that lay tipped on the beach awaiting repairs. Like any of us, they wanted the best for their families, but life must have been more difficult here because they had known some prosperity in the past. In prior years they dried coconut meat and sold it as copra—until the world price collapsed. With the support of extended families and Christianity, they farmed and fished to meet their needs. These people were poor, but this was not like the poverty of our inner cities. They accepted and made the best of their situation—the difference between happiness and bitterness. Especially in need of clothes and medicine, they also valued pencils and notebooks, but they neither expected nor requested handouts from us.

We stayed in this lovely setting for a week, dividing our time between village visits and watching the antics of reef occupants through our swim masks. We inspected the enormous, dried jaw of Romulus' *puckpuck*. Life became a simple affair: swim, eat, visit, read; repeat. Fresh water arrived with afternoon showers. This place seemed to represent the paradise I thought I sought from the outset. These islanders had freedom, little stress, and a meaningful existence working together in a caring community.

However, to achieve this serenity, I might need to regress to a traditional role where "a woman knew her place." *No thanks*. After a taste of education, freedom and a career, I couldn't go there. Papuans in paradise have sparse intellectual stimulation, no medicine, and die at about age 62. My problem was cultural. Back home, I had countless options and opportunities, but those did seem to complicate everything. Did I really need a high-stress job? *Could I find a compromise?*

One day John and Dave departed for spear fishing, and a native lady appeared in a mini-canoe alongside our boat at anchor. Without a word, Betty passed me her infant son followed by a coconut and a papaya. I felt uncomfortable without knowing the intent of her visit, but it became her simple attempt to connect, woman to woman. We sat in the cockpit, baby Mathew gurgled, and she said little—until a sizable outrigger canoe set forth nearby with four men aboard. She hailed them with a shrill, wavering call that startled me. We watched the men rig a short, triangular sail and run off with the breeze. Before Betty departed with baby, I pressed upon her a bag of powdered milk for him. She may not have understood much English—no matter.

An hour later, a native paddled close with his son and held up two gigantic lobsters. The local variety without claws are called painted crayfish. They display shells of mottled green with black and white spots and pink antennae. I offered a length of cotton fabric for trade and held out a bucket.

A short time later, a gleeful John returned from his adventures. He stood in the dinghy to report: "The three of us snorkeled along the reef for four hours. Awesome place! Caught four fish and five crayfish. Here's my share," he said, holding up two small crays.

"That's wonderful," I smiled and pulled the dishtowel off my bucket. "And here's what I caught…er, traded for."

"Whoa ho." He thumped the boat deck with a drum rhythm. "We eat good tonight."

When two other cruising boats arrived the next day, Betty, her mate, Apetay, and neighbors hosted a barbeque for us. They brought baskets of fresh fish and six crayfish that weighed about four pounds each. Although aware that *dimdim* fancy crayfish, the natives seemed to care little for crays and tossed them casually into a flaming bonfire. Seeing this, John decided to demonstrate the preferred New England method of preparing lobster by steaming. A large kettle appeared at his request, and he filled it with two inches of water from the beach. He entered Betty's cookhouse, next to the family's thatched hut, and stoked the fire.

Within minutes, he dashed out the door coughing, followed by a cloud of smoke. Others dashed in to control the fire. Since he had nearly burned down the house of our hosts, John capitulated, apologized, and placed the "bugs" back on the bonfire.

Under trees of fragrant frangipani and red fuchsia, we sat on woven mats in the sand and filled our bellies with seafood, yachtie side dishes, and Betty's coconut pumpkin. Sixteen adults, black skin and white, sat in a close circle exchanging stories as the orange sky darkened.

Later, as we walked down the beach to our dinghy in the dark, I recalled a story and scanned both sides of the sandy path. I turned to old Romulus and asked, "Where do the crocks…er…*puckpuck*…stay at night?"

He shrugged.

Further down the archipelago, we entered Deboyne Lagoon, which enclosed two high islands. During the war, the Japanese established a seaplane base there and flew recon missions to plan the capture of Port Moresby, only a hundred miles north of Australia. During the Battle of the Coral Sea in 1942, American bombers drove them out of this base, at great cost to both sides. On a post-war copra plantation, where villagers tended rows of vegetables, we unearthed a U.S. flamethrower backpack.

Outside the lagoon, we raised sail and set course directly for a volcanic peak on Misima Island, the site of a gold mine that shipped out two dozen bars a day through the 1980's. We approached through a haze of heat, and again I imagined time travel to an early South Pacific crossroads. Near the bustling port, we anchored close to mangrove fingers that emerged from dense jungle. Excited shouts and laughter echoed from the jetty where merchants loaded supplies to trade in outer islands. Three well-stocked general stores manned by Chinese and British expats served the animated crowd.

Dave and Sue provisioned with a plan to island-hop from Misima due north 1200 miles to meet their daughter in Guam for Christmas. The night before they departed, we regifted them the bottle of wine from the couple that we helped in Mackay.

A week of antibiotics to resolve my chest cold had probably increased my sun sensitivity. Without the benefit of cooling swim, the relentless heat in the crowded harbor caused my eczema to flare up again. The bites of sand gnats ashore compounded the misery, driving me mad with itching and grumpy with interrupted sleep. I began another course of steroid tablets, sought a breeze under the boat's awning, and smoked *big pella stix*. Ashore, John chatted with expat frontiersmen and watched the islanders barter.

Within two days, I felt better and eager to experience the chaos of the open market. All space adjacent to the wharf teemed with natives arriving from all points of the compass with needs to fill or crops to trade. Their meet-and-greet carnival atmosphere was infectious, and the mixed-race crowd was friendly and curious about us. John talked while I haggled for fresh vegetables. We approached a group gathered around a commotion and peeked over black heads to see a snarling, stamping, wild boar with circular horns and a bloody mouth. The terrified hog screeched and thrashed against the frayed ropes that restrained it. Someone speculated about how old it was, although few natives knew how old they were.

John turned to me. "The man wants 400 *kinas* for that pig," he said. "Sorry, Love, that's beyond our budget."

"Oh, and you would kill and dress that beast?" Together we laughed.

Instead we spent our last *kinas* on a frozen chicken. At this, our last government outpost, we officially checked out of the country, but explored for another two weeks.

Alone again, we sailed southeast for the Calvados Chain of coral islands. At one of them, Maurice paddled out with his shy wife to welcome us. We invited them aboard and plied them with tea and cookies to hear stories about their life. In accordance with customs of the matrilineal society, he lived alternate years at the villages of his in-laws and was accumulating wealth in pigs and yams to provide a feast to honor his wife's family.

A week later we met him again at the village of his wife's family. Maurice took John and an Aussie yachtie spearfishing and returned with ten painted crayfish to share with everyone. Kids and loose piglets, a dozen each, frolicked alongside us as we explored the seaside village. Beyond flowering trees that held chattering red parrots, statuesque women walked a path from their garden bearing bundles on their heads. Most wore only a short length of cotton around their waist.

Near the water, John and I settled on a grassy patch beside a man mending an outrigger sail with a needle made from bone. Curious children plunked down beyond our reach. I asked them for a song, but they turned away with shy giggles. John and I began singing "Waltzing Matilda" guessing they had heard it from Aussie visitors, but we forgot the words. More giggling. We smiled, then ignored them for a moment and talked together. Two girls' voices rose, soon joined by the boys in harmony, singing. "We are one, big, happy family; God's children are we." I flushed with delight. The song, I surmised, may have arrived with missionaries decades ago.

After we finished our seafood picnic, I noticed a handsome young man smiling from a platform on stilts. He petted his pigs like family dogs and chopped coconut into pieces with a machete to feed them. Fascinated by pigs since Mexico, I approached him and sat admiring the piglets, trying to pat them too. As I lingered with them, the native put aside his shyness and told me he hoped to become a pig breeder—an important position in any village. He told me he fattened neutered males for funeral feasts when people came from many islands. Funerals held great significance due to an enduring custom to keep departed ancestors happy.

In those days, I felt ever so content. Anchored above our own aquarium, we floated with snorkel, mask and fins over delicate coral gardens. The inhabitants below seemed to reflect life back home. Giant clams, two feet across, their wavy lips dotted with neon blue spots, conjured up a childhood horror movie. Clown fish flitted with false starts but feared leaving their anemone homes. Stern Napoleon wrasse and shark detectives with black-tip badges patrolled the sandy shallows. In the deep-blue distance, iridescent blue fish moved in unison like dancers.

The more John and I confronted novel situations, the closer we became, and the more confident I felt interacting with the world. John still departed often to confer or explore with others, and I enjoyed my alone time. But now, when he returned glowing with stories of what he'd seen and learned, I experienced immense joy watching him expound—while we sat together drinking lemonade.

For our last stop in PNG, we motor-sailed to the Catholic Mission at Nimoa Island. An acolyte showed us the century-old church, small hospital, dwellings and classrooms arranged around a trim, grassy quadrangle. The rector of seven years, Father Joe, invited us to his study for tea. A cheerful fellow of forty-eight years with thin blond hair, his lean body tanned like leather, he was dressed in stained shorts and a faded tee shirt. He admitted to receiving little financial help from the Church, saying that most of his support came from operating the mission store, which I guessed included bartering. He told us he spent a week at a time on various islands spreading God's word, and we knew many of the same characters there.

Before our goodbyes, the native schoolchildren serenaded us: "Friends are like flowers, beautiful flowers. Friends are like flowers in the garden of love..." The song tripped an emotion switch inside, and a tear of joy ran from my eye. In contrast with our tentative entry into the country, the song summed up a memorable and eye-opening, eight-week visit in Papua New Guinea. Travel always carries a risk, but this path opened my heart.

On the first day of November, we pushed *Renaissance* from the protection of the Archipelago lagoons and splashed into the blue Solomon Sea toward another little-known nation.

CHAPTER 18

The Solomon Islands — Wounded in War

AFTER A WINDY, THREE-DAY OCEAN CROSSING, WE approached the small island of Ghizo, named for the notorious leader of a tribe of headhunters who inhabited it—until a rare amalgamation of neighboring clans massacred them. The independent nation of the Solomon Islands consists of six long islands and hundreds of smaller islands and coral atolls, all sitting in a diagonal line about 930 miles long.

We slowed to avoid trailing mangrove roots and entered the narrow harbor at Gizo, the capital of the western islands. The hot air dripped with humidity and smelled of low tide and sour musk. After a month in PNG with few fresh vegetables, I squealed and pointed as we passed an open market near the town landing. John dropped the anchor inside a semi-circle of thatched huts built on stilts along the shore. We scampered about the boat cleaning up, eager to get ashore to check in at the government center and look for our mail at general delivery.

For two days, I endured extreme heat while we explored and exchanged stories with local expats and yachties. By the third day, the skin covering most of my arms and legs had flared again into the same raised heat rash I had controlled in PNG with steroid pills and cooling swims. The dirty harbor at Gizo deterred me. My eczema blisters spread and tormented me with intense itching. I cursed my skin and this affliction I had borne to varying degrees since childhood. Stoic and hoping to quell it by avoiding exertion, I lay on the boat under a small fan, dozing in a Benedryl fog, while John joined new friends for scuba diving.

One afternoon he returned excited as he described the glories of an underwater wall of corals. His voice trailed off as he observed my wounds and shook his head. "Let's get you some more steroid pills… they always work," he said. "You're missing a great experience." I refused, fearful of side effects, like bone loss, from overuse.

Two days later, when eczema covered my entire torso, I hobbled on swollen feet beside John to a clinic he had located in town. We waited two hours for a brisk, young British doctor, who commanded me to stop using cortisone ointment and antibiotics.

"Those just desensitize you and make your skin even thinner." He handed me a six-day, dose-pack of stronger steroids.

Then, he turned on John. "And forget about your stomach upset from the malaria meds! The local variety of malaria can kill you in three days. Both of you! Get back on the chloroquine and add Mefloquine," he said and scribbled on a prescription pad. Sufficiently chastised, we followed his directions.

Armed with a 90-day visa, a full diesel tank, fresh veggies and pills, we set off to investigate the Western Province. The first islanders who arrived here from New Guinea practiced cannibalism and black magic for centuries. Decades after Europeans decimated the population with diseases and kidnapping for indentured services, Britain, as a protectorate, took over the islands in 1893 to establish law and order. This prepared the way for waves of ardent missionaries. Catholics, the first to arrive, bore the brunt of native reprisals against abuses of the white traders.

No one can visit the Solomon Islands without an awareness of the extreme loss of life, ships, and planes that occurred here during World War II. After the Japanese lost five aircraft carriers in the battles of Coral Sea and Midway, they invaded the Solomon Islands to establish an air base from which to occupy New Guinea and invade Australia. The fierce battles of 1942-43 in these waters changed the course of the Pacific War.

We made several stops along New Georgia, a forty-five-mile-long island that Japanese forces had occupied. In a mangrove-lined harbor that served as their supply depot, we swam over an 80-foot Japanese freighter that lay frozen in the act of landing a truck; an aerial bomb sank her in water so shallow her two masts stuck up above the water.

Further along that coast, we found a settlement called Munda, where the United Church (Methodist) administered area trade, schools, and a clinic. Now only ten days from Gizo, my eczema had taken control again, but a kind Kiwi doctor replenished my steroid supply.

Miserable and sidelined again with this debility, I thought: *why not abort this whole, damn trip?* The answer always came back, from the other side of my brain, a resounding, *NO*! I couldn't abandon my mate or my boat—to return, to what? Fluorescent lights? Stressful, ten-hour workdays? No, the opportunity to experience this amazing geography, history and culture made me resolve to endure the discomfort. I kept repeating, "this too shall pass." And it did, when the pills kicked in three days later. In the cool morning light, we stood beside the Munda airstrip where the Japanese built a camouflaged runway by interweaving fronds from tall coconut palms and then cutting away the internal trees. It took them only nine days to complete it. I imagined their Zeros taking off to join a dogfight over the channel. Even after the runway was discovered and bombarded by the Allies, the dogged Japanese held that base for eight months.

Further afield, John and I sat with an ancient islander who vividly recalled the war as a twelve-year-old. He shivered in eighty-degree heat as he described the ear-shattering noise of bursting bombs that fell from the sky in those days. Terrified and uncomprehending, he ran with his family under screaming airplanes and booming cannons to hide in the hills of this island.

"When the Japs ran away, the GI's were good to the people," he said. "They brought us back to our village and helped us." My eyes filled. I took the hand he had raised and squeezed it in mine.

From Munda, we crossed the channel to Rendova Island, where Americans established a base for PT patrol boats in June 1943. As we neared the green, overgrown shore looking for an inlet, a boy in a miniature canoe suddenly appeared, paddling hard to intercept us. We followed him to a hidden entrance behind a barrier island into a narrow lagoon. Other canoe-kids engulfed us, and the dinghy we towed was soon full of splashing, chirping, local cherubs. After anchoring, we jumped into the water with them. John teased and tickled them and unsuccessfully tried to climb into a canoe. Back under our awning, I launched air-filled balloons and took photos of the clamor.

That night John and I sat close together in the cooling cockpit watching a full moon rise over the palms. Children's songs wafted across the water.

"It's so peaceful here," said John. "But the war in the Solomons went on for a couple of years. In school I learned a little about these battles… but being here gives me chills when I consider the devastation these innocents endured."

The next day, accompanied by a string of curious kids, we visited three villages packed closely around the lagoon. The SDA (Seventh Day Adventist) Church supported the grade school we visited. John stopped to watch a man carve out a canoe; other men carved bowls and walking sticks. Everyone smiled. I thought about my family and wished we could all be as content.

Back across the sea channel, we located the narrow entrance to Viru Harbor, which hid a war-time Japanese garrison. As we followed the narrow inlet, its steep, vertical sides closed in on us blocking the morning sun. I felt a ghostly chill. Ahead on the cliff, hundreds of feet high, John spotted the long barrel of a leftover Japanese cannon aimed down at us. We could not have dodged its shell. After a dogleg right, the waterway widened where cliffs eroded and three rivers met. I exhaled a sigh of relief to discover a settlement in this tropical oasis.

Soon after we anchored beside the village of Itemi, three men arrived with their carvings to sell and spent the afternoon in our cockpit. They unwrapped pieces of black ebony and rich kerosene wood intricately carved, inlaid with shell, and stained with *tita* nut and charcoal. The large pieces included a storyboard, carved with dolphins, turtles, crocodiles, and the sacred shark. Sculpted "noosa" heads with dog-like snouts represented figureheads from traditional war canoes.

John cajoled and chatted with the men, and they all tried to judge which pieces of art that I liked the best. To mark our fourteenth wedding anniversary, John picked out a carved group of eight dolphins set into a base suggesting a rolling sea. I agreed that these playful travelers suited us. Then the bartering began. The carvers suggested trade items, and I dragged out excess possessions without which I had thought we could never live. In the end, we cheerfully gave up a sleeping bag, tools, clothes, towels, knives, canned beef, and Solomon cash.

After they departed, a solitary black man paddled up seeking to improve his English. "I learned English working in a restaurant, but now I work here in the sawmill." Two words he wished to understand were 'compromise' and 'condolence.' I listened closely as John defined them and thought about the word 'humanitarian' too.

We moved to Seghe Point to mail a letter home and met "*pella blong Seghe*" (fella from Seghe) named Darryl, who directed us to a snorkeling spot. A perfectly preserved PBY Catalina aircraft lay in twenty feet of water so clear that the plane seemed just beyond my fingertips as I floated above it. The broad wings and triple fuselages of this nimble bomber flashed silver-white in sunbeams that shot through the water. Then I noticed its mangled propeller and grieved another gravesite.

In December, we entered Marovo, the world's largest lagoon at 270 square miles. It incorporates a volcano island. The area reminded me of Tahiti, but without the tourists. As soon as we settled in front of a small dive resort, I jumped over the side to cool my torrid skin. With a big sigh, I floated like a lit match snuffed out in the water. John departed to join scuba divers on a reef wall full of fish and corals. Under our awning, I opened a new novel and my last packet of steroids pills.

Across the lagoon we spent an afternoon on the beach with a talented, young woodcarver called John Wayne. He shared with us the politics of his remote village of 200 souls. "Several months ago, the village chief took money from the Japanese for bait fishing rights in our lagoon—then he left here to become the Minister of Natural Resources in Honiara (the capital)." I guessed that a modern seiner net could scoop up more fish in a day than this village subsisted on for a year.

"And now, two brothers claim the role of chief, but spend all their time bickering." He sifted sand through his fingers. "A reorganized form of local government is proposed. Perhaps that will resolve it."

I nodded. "It's crazy, but we suffer the same things in our country." All humans have a propensity for greed as well as goodwill.

As we lingered beside the lagoon, it occurred to me that before this trip I had never allowed myself the luxury of sitting for hours talking with anyone, let alone a stranger. I had always pushed myself to accomplish more and have more. Now I understood the value of social interaction where people could connect, enjoy and appreciate each other without an agenda.

We sailed overnight across a wide channel to the Eastern Solomon Islands. On our morning approach, the flat sea reflected a dark sky, heavy with humidity and foreboding. To our right the 8,000-foot peaks of Guadalcanal Island rose from below the horizon. In this area, Japanese and Allied (Australian, New Zealand and US) forces fought six major battles in a four-month period.

Our diesel engine throbbed, and John held the wheel. I sat in the cockpit across from him with a guidebook and area map. "We're following the same route the Allied fleet took to deliver the first U.S. Marines to Guadalcanal," I said. I leaned over the rail to see ahead and pointed to the left. "There's Savo Island, where the first naval battle occurred on the night after the Marines landed." That night, Japanese battleships surprised and sank four U.S. supply vessels before dashing away, leaving our untested troops without support.

The prow of our boat knifed into the oily waters of Iron Bottom Sound, named for this graveyard of sixty-seven warships and hundreds of aircraft from both adversaries. Sweat stood out on John's tanned back as he gripped the wheel and stared ahead. "So sad," he said. "They only had rudimentary radar then. It must have been a horrendous night terror."

In 1942, about 38,000 young men died in this pivotal area fighting for control of the airfield on Guadalcanal. We stood together with reverence as we motored along part of the island's ninety-mile length. Its wooded hills lumped up like a pile of dark corpses. Ahead of us, distant heat lightning cracked through the sky like an echo of the thunderous air-sea battles. The somber mood continued after we arrived in the rain at the nation's capital of Honiara three days before Christmas. We sought shelter behind Point Cruz, where the retreating Japanese suffered a bloody defeat. I spent a sleepless night on a restless sea caused by a distant tempest.

Unlike that of the Marines, our landing on Guadalcanal the next day was a joy. In Honiara, the capital city, the locals waved hello, the open market displayed colorful mounds of produce, and various shops beckoned me. In an open-air museum outside of town, we inspected cannons and warplanes, which again touched my heart at the tragic losses.

With a renewed supply of Solomon dollars from a New Zealand bank, John and I separated for shopping in the dusty town center. I entered a well-stocked chemist shop seeking more supplies to sooth my itchy skin. After locating medicated shampoo and antihistamines,

I boldly asked the clerk for prednisone tablets. An Aussie pharmacist appeared like a genie. I explained my recurring problem in the heat, and to forestall a lecture, assured him I knew the risks of side effects. He beckoned me closer and told me of a time he took "heaps" of steroids, stopped them abruptly, and went into a coma. He laughed at the memory, and I joined him with a guarded chuckle. After I swore to stick to the proper dosage and to taper off slowly, he dispensed one hundred tablets. *Wow. I'm saved.* Next door, I added some groceries and two cartons of manufactured cigarettes to my backpack. I bought John a gift and skipped back to the beach.

On Christmas Eve, we shared a turkey dinner with yachties at Hotel Mendana and stayed to watch kids from three local churches perform a familiar pageant. In burlap costumes, they dramatized the birth of Christ, although an enthusiastic "King Herod" stole the show. One cherub troop sang a carol in *tok pigin* that ended with "white *pella*, black *pella*, all happy too." The evening was an unexpected delight and recalled the harmony of simple childhood Christmases with my family.

After ten days exploring "Guadl," we headed for the open market. John photographed the scene but made no effort to help select produce. He flirted with the local women in their bright cotton dresses. The shy girls giggled and hid behind their hands.

"Hey," I yelled to him. "How about some help over here?" Sweat ran down my face. We loaded a big backpack with gorgeous green beans, cucumbers, yams, bell peppers, bok choy, and cabbages. I vowed never again to take such beautiful produce for granted.

From Honiara we crossed the sound to the Florida Group where two high islands tower over Tulagi Island, the prewar capital. U.S. Marines overcame stiff resistance to capture the Japanese seaplane base there and endured repeated attacks from air and sea that attempted to dislodge them.

We tied *Renaissance* to a rusty landing barge in Tulagi to explore an area littered with battle relics both above and below the water. Several boys from Mbola Village appeared alongside the boat in canoes.

Adorned with necklaces of dolphin teeth and seed pods, they offered exotic fruits to trade: pineapple, pawpaw, star fruit, bush limes, white apples and green bananas. For these treasures, I gave up two faded t-shirts, a lipstick and my last *big pella stix* tobacco. Later, I dug out a spare piece of rope and tied up the hand-me-down shorts of little Robert, who giggled and glowed at the attention. John decided to clean the growth and stains from our boat's waterline and attracted two boys in a Tom Sawyer maneuver, demonstrating how much fun he was having splashing and singing. More kids appeared and everybody wanted a brush. I adored their natural joy.

At sunset ten boys returned under the stewardship of a lanky teen named Kingsley. They assembled in our cockpit and began to harmonize in a local dialect, although I discerned an occasional "Jesus" and "hosanna."

In the following days, Kingsley showed us wreckage of American and Japanese ships and took us to meet a special man. Wrinkled, grey-bearded Titus, surrounded by several topless, pipe-smoking lady admirers, held court. He welcomed us with great sincerity and smoked the cigarette I gave him. With rheumy eyes he stared across the water to Guadalcanal and recalled the war he had experienced. The love he expressed for compassionate American GI's again filled me with pride. I wondered, too, how many innocent natives died during the battles over their homeland.

One day as we lay at anchor between islands, two elders approached in a dugout canoe. Pointing at our flag, they said, "American welcome!" We all talked about our lives, but soon their demeanor turned solemn and serious. One man expressed fear that another big war was coming to the Solomon Islands. "The radio said the 'Gulf War' is approaching. What will we do?"

John leaned closer to them from our cockpit and explained. "A country named Iraq sent soldiers to invade another one called Kuwait—just like the Japanese invaded the Solomons. Like they did here, Americans will fight Iraq, to help the people in Kuwait." The weathered faces of the men relaxed, and John continued. "Don't worry; they are a very, long way from here. You will be safe." We respected their fears and felt glad we could reassure them.

We crossed thirty miles of ocean to Malaita, a narrow tropical island 100 miles long with an interior spine of mountains that rose to 4,700 feet. For centuries prior to WWII, the Solomon Islanders subsisted in clans, divided into the inland "bush people" and the coastal "salt-water" people, who raided and killed each other regularly. Malaitian men had a reputation for being the most brutal.

We approached a thirteen-mile-long coral reef that enclosed the aqua waters of *Langa Langa* Lagoon. Using a hand-drawn map from a yachtie friend, we angled for anchorage in a mangrove-lined cove facing the renowned village of Firifau, built on an artificial island. Six small canoes followed us propelled by brown boys; some with straight black hair and some with curly, blond hair. When we beckoned, they remained at a distance, until I threw inflated balloons out on the water. Traffic dispersed. The kids yelped, paddled hard, and jumped into the water to catch "baa-loon."

One naked five-year-old was a practiced boatman. With the canoe's gunnel only two inches above the water, he jumped in and out of the canoe without swamping it. To remove any water he brought in, he swept the rounded bottom of his boat with the side of his foot. As the kids splashed and giggled around us, we joined them in the water. When dismissed, they promptly disappeared.

A man named Peter came alongside in his canoe to welcome us. A stocky boat builder of perhaps forty years, he described construction of the solid-looking, artificial islands, built with bricks cut from calcified coral. This unique solution, begun about seven generations in the past, protected the lagoon people from savage headhunters in the hills. After we dealt again with the rumor about a new war returning to these islands, I encouraged him with questions about local life. As in Morovo and Tulagi, leaders on Malaita took money from the Japanese for bait fishing rights to the detriment of the villagers.

In Boat Builder's Village, Peter showed us a three-story boathouse covering an eighty-foot cargo boat—a project that would take thirty months to complete. Peter introduced his wife and three young daughters with faint circular tattoos on their cheeks. As we walked through the village, I marveled at how well the children shared and played together. Near a small stream, a child dumped a pail of water over his head to finish his bath. "That boy is six and just started school where he'll begin learning English," said Peter. "The elders understand the value of education, but it seems not a priority for our government. Few can go on to high school."

Inside the lagoon, we journeyed north in emerald waters beside a lush green shore. At the north end of the long island, we anchored near the administrative center of Auki. A fine rain fell on that muggy afternoon but did not deter the curious canoe kids who again surrounded us. I watched Augustine, a boy of six or seven, paddle and swat flies over an infant, who lay in front of him waving her arms as if to imitate his strokes. *What American mother would allow her baby 300 yards from shore in a tippy canoe? How many American brothers his age would be so responsible?*

Ashore, we mailed letters home, surrendered visas, and provisioned for a two-week transit north across the Equator. Accompanied by leaping dolphins, we motored a short distance to a placid, tropical bay. While we rested and made final preparations to leave these islands for a long, ocean passage, we listened to ham radio reports describing the U.S. tomahawk missiles—ones for which my Westinghouse-team built interfaces—falling over Baghdad, Iraq, at the start of Operation Desert Storm. In a pastoral setting on this side of the world, these reports felt surreal.

That afternoon, a handsome native named Gideon approached our boat with some carvings. We traded a bath towel for an inlaid Malaita war club, one-third the size of the original article. The talkative fellow enthralled me with cultural stories. He said the land behind us was taboo, a burial ground of ancestors they still worship. Wives were still purchased with red shell money and dolphin teeth.

"There are still naked, warlike people in the hills. We fear them and try to avoid them. They don't come here now, but just fight with other bush tribes."

"My grandfather came from Santa Isabel Island on headhunting trips to this bay and settled here. My uncle worshiped sharks. He believed they helped and guided our fishermen back from the sea. Just before he died, he told us boys not to be like him—to worship God!"

Gideon worshiped with the local Seventh Day Adventists. However, the SDA now forbid killing and eating of dolphin. The Catholics said natives who do this must confess to the sin of murder.

"Honiara has a lot of crime," he said. "I know a man from here who went to jail over there. He stayed in a dark stone room with dirty water and a waste pail. When he returned, he warned all the boys here not to do crimes. Is there crime in America?"

As the sun sank behind the canyon walls, we finished preparations for a morning departure on the next leg of our journey, about a thousand miles from Melanesia to Micronesia. I precooked rice and reorganized canned foods for easy access while underway. John packed away excess gear and set up the evening bug netting.

Too hot to sleep together, we settled down that night in separate bunks. I heard a slap and a drowsy voice say, "Damn mosquitos."

PART V

Challenges Back North

Typhoon Omar in Micronesia

CHAPTER 19

The Federated States of Micronesia — Pohnpei, Chuuk and Puluwat

IN THE MID-PACIFIC, A MERCILESS SUN BEAT DOWN ON THE cockpit awning, and the droning engine added heat to the cabin. The air moved only because our boat passed through it at four mph. Day after day, we plodded through the torrid doldrums and crossed the Equator without sighting a single vessel. With great stealth, I attached a rope to a bucket and dropped it over the side for water. I dumped the contents all over John and his book in the cockpit, which started a refreshing water fight.

After seven days at sea, the 2,595-foot volcanic peak of Pohnpei Island broke the horizon. With little wind, it took us another day-and-a-half to reach the iridescent, coral-strewn waters of its outer lagoon.

Pohnpei is one of four island-states of the Federated States of Micronesia (FSM), that spread east-west covering the same distance as Washington, DC to Denver. For thirty years before it bombed Pearl Harbor, Japan ruled this island group with strict programs for trade, agriculture, and commercial fishing which relegated the natives to slavery. At that time, Japanese colonialists outnumbered Micronesians on Pohnpei by nearly three to one. After WWII, the FSM islands became a trust territory of the USA.

In the port of Kolonia, while we waited for immigration officials, John set about cleaning the three-foot *mahimahi* I had hooked outside the barrier reef. I set down a container for the fillets beside him and smiled, recalling how squeamish he had been about handling fish well into our travels. I had changed too: more tolerant, more confident.

Once cleared by authorities, we motored deep into an inlet, its steep sides thick with tropical rain forest. The five-star anchorage held eighteen yachts. After four months of isolation in primitive countries, I didn't hold back on socializing with the yachties. Every morning for a week, we hiked to town along a paved road where giant hibiscus and broad-leafed breadfruit trees shaded shacks kludged together from woven mats, wood scraps and squares of corrugated iron. In Kolonia, nine-blocks long, we discovered general stores, rustic restaurants, a post office, and a treasured Laundromat. The Bank of Hawaii issued us local currency—the U.S. dollar. American products had replaced the Australian goods of the South Seas. I was amazed to find the kava ceremony, here under the name *sakai*, transported two thousand miles from Fiji.

Re-oriented, re-provisioned, and partied out, we motored around the eastern side of the island and anchored in a protected bay. A striking volcanic plug rose from the shallows and dense jungle climbed from the shore toward jagged peaks. After lunch, we set off to locate the legendary Kepirohi waterfall and found it only with the help of two native boys. From seventy feet above us, a thick veil of fresh water spread across a black rock face and splashed down a chunky cliff into a deep pool that covered a half acre. With sweat dripping from my brow and my arms outstretched for balance, I picked my way across the broken rocks of a creek bed. I slid into the cool water with a gasp. John dove in beside me.

A yachtie family swam across the pool to join us. Danny, a robust American in his late thirties, and Louisa, a slim Australian of similar age, were completing a global circumnavigation with their precocious daughters: Mia, 6, and Lydia, 4. We sat and shared cruising experiences and together planned an expedition to explore the mysterious Nan Madol archeological site.

The next morning, we climbed aboard their stalwart, wooden sailboat, *Cytheria*. The couple had completed much of the woodworking and rigging themselves on the 40-footer which allowed them to getaway while young enough to gain the most from their travels. Danny impressed John with his carpentry. The blond girls sought my attention. Having grown up on the boat, home-schooled, and assigned important responsibilities at sea, they chirped and bubbled with personal questions for me. Most of their contacts were with yachtie adults, so they readily chimed into our conversation with astute observations. I feared they would have little patience with spoiled or over-protected children of their own age when they resettled in Australia. This bright six-year-old would "not suffer fools."

On an incoming tide, we set off to survey Nan Madol, the settlement of an ancient society that carbon dating places in the 13th century. Since the family had no outboard motor, we towed their wooden longboat behind our rubber dinghy. We picked our way seaward through spotty coral reefs to the 220-acre site, which includes ninety, man-made islets separated by canoe canals. The chatter and singing of the girls added to our happy anticipation of the adventure.

From the outer lagoon, we spied a corner of the ancient city—thirty-foot-high walls that were built log-cabin style using logs of basaltic rock. As we drew closer, we confirmed that the hexagonal logs measured up to twenty-feet long and could certainly weigh 15 tons each. Local legend said that black magic caused these massive columns to fly from the volcanic peak into position in these walls, yet modern investigators cannot explain how the ancients could transport even one such log using natural materials. Composed of 250 million tons of rock, Nan Madol's construction is a feat that rivals that of the Easter Island monoliths, yet I had never heard of its existence before our arrival.

We turned into a canal about twenty-feet wide and trolled alongside the dark walls, staring in silent awe at the somber scene. The kids quieted. The soft thrumming of our outboard motor provided the only sound. An occasional palm tree raked the sky and resolute scrub sometimes softened the scene. I felt a chill as my mind flashed, for some reason, on a movie reenactment of Aztec human sacrifices. At a break in the wall, we tied up the boats and mounted chiseled steps into a vast, stone-covered courtyard. When the kids ran ahead, Louisa barked at them to stay close.

Investigators seem to agree that Nan Madol originated as the ceremonial and political seat of the Polynesian Saudeleur Dynasty. The site we visited had housed the nobility and the priests, who presided over worship of their gods and elaborate processes for burial of the chiefs in a fortified corner of the site. For two hours, we wandered among walls of stone, ceremonial platforms, and crypts. Danny and the girls climbed down into a dim chamber below the plaza. In the stillness of the hot afternoon, I sensed the presence of ghosts. *What, me, the ever-analyst contingent? Umm, yes.*

I moved closer to John and whispered, "This place is giving me the creeps. There are some kind of evil vibrations."

"Yeah. I feel it too. A sense of dread," he said close to my ear.

I grabbed his hand to my side and lifted my head like a spooked deer to focus my senses. A breeze lifted fronds on a lone coconut palm. I shivered. *What was it about this place?* John waved at Dan, and we began a slow retreat.

The Pohnpeians abruptly abandoned the stone city in the mid-1800s, around the time an American whaler brought smallpox; and some tell of the mysterious death of a German governor circa 1900, after he disturbed the remains of nine-foot giants in the main temple. Native clans still consider the site taboo and believe that those who even speak of its history will die. Even in recent years, stories persisted of strange lights and fireballs over Nan Madol, which they connect with death.

We cruised down another channel and had explored but a small part of the complex when John noticed the tide receding. To avoid grounding the boats (a welcome excuse), we retraced our wake back to our anchorage.

Frequent tropical downpours kept our water tanks full and pressed me to rinse out sweaty clothes. One morning, I was on deck with a mouthful of clothespins to hang two tee shirts to dry. Hearing a splash behind me, I turned to see the towheads, Mia and Lydia, alone in their twelve-foot, wooden skiff, each pulling on a heavy, eight-foot-long oar. They had come to deliver Valentine's Day cards they made for us. My heart melted at their thoughtfulness and efforts.

We completed our eighty-mile circumnavigation of Pohnpei Island with two more stops and then one in Kolonia for provisions. Exiting the barrier reef, we sailed to nearby Ant Atoll. The water in the lagoon lay still and as clear as gin. Inside, *Renaissance* followed a winding "road" of deep blue water bordered by shallows of light aqua. We pulled up before a half-mile-long motu, complete with sandy beach, arching palms, and a mini-jungle. On the windward side of the reef, the surf rumbled like a distant highway. The physical beauty of this atoll within sight of Pohnpei's volcano ranked high among the scenic places we had visited, so sharing it with new friends made it most memorable.

Cytherea had arrived ahead of us, so we rowed across for a visit. John inspected the traditional, gaff-rigged vessel again, not missing a detail. Below his bushy mustache, Danny wore the smile of a perpetual optimist, expecting excitement and ready for anything. Louisa and the girls showed me their lessons from correspondence school. Mia and Lydia were confident swimmers and fearless about confronting a new challenge. They were considerate and accepted direction without the whining I despised in so many American kids. As we departed, Louise slipped me a pan wrapped in a towel—for Mia's birthday cake, which I had agreed to bake as a surprise.

Two days later, *Akvavit*, a sixty-foot, steel ketch pulled in to share our Eden. Her captain, erstwhile poet and storyteller, Harrison Smith, and first mate, Lorrie, had modified their boat for sail and abandoned Alaska fishing to wander the lower latitudes. We had followed them via ham radio since Mexico and heard about their rescues of shipwrecked yachties near Australia and some islanders south of Pohnpei. Although we had never met, Harrison chided us for stalking them since Tonga.

One night I invited crews of both boats aboard to share some fish chowder. While we ate and chatted, Danny rallied enthusiasm for a safari to bag some coconut crabs, which he described as "elusive, ugly, and delicious."

The next night, before the moon rose, six adults carrying buckets and work gloves made a stealthy landing on the beach impersonating Navy Seals. We assembled with whispers and indecipherable hand signals. I shook with excitement for my first hunt. Using his machete, Danny whacked open some coconuts for bait. As I slung a camera around my neck, my too-big work gloves fell off, and I groped the ground to retrieve them. Holding a rubber mallet ahead of his waist, big John hung back, afraid of snakes and unsure what he would have to confront.

Lorrie brandished an ice pick. "I'm going to de-leg 'em at the joints so they can't run away," she said.

Harrison, tall and distinguished in flowing white hair and beard, laughed and shook his head at this rag-tag bunch of bogus big-game hunters.

With a pail over one arm and my camera in the other, I pushed close behind Danny, who set out the bait in three spots along the jungle path. Louisa held the flashlight for him. I felt a tickle on my leg and looked down with my light, suddenly afraid a crab had grabbed me. Nothing.

Ahead, I heard rustling. Up a tree, I saw Danny's faded red tee shirt. Down he jumped yelling for a pail. The diameter of the man's curved arm, the rangy, wriggling monster was dark green-gray with two claws, four long legs and a fat sack under its lobster-like tail. Louisa caught another and Danny the rest, filling three buckets.

Back on *Renaissance* the crabs took turns steaming in my spaghetti pot. The meat tasted very rich, and John ate so much his stomach rebelled for the next three days.

Yachtie gatherings always included talk of weather. In Micronesia, tropical storms typically form near Pohnpei and grow as they track westward between June and November. On March 1, the ham radio advised that our fair weather would hold. However, lying snug inside Ant Atoll, we were unaware that the typhoon season had already begun. We toasted news that Desert Storm had ended with the withdrawal of Iraqi troops. It was time for us to push off as well. Having shared such fun and (almost) fearless adventures with friends here, I found good-bye extra difficult, especially when the little girls blew kisses from their passing deck.

Cytheria sailed away East, *Akvavit* South, and *Renaissance* West.

In rising winds and churning seas, we covered 380 miles in three days. John slept little and dreamed about sea disasters. I started antibiotics for an ear infection and dreamed of living in a beach house. Finally, dark clouds broke up, and we spied the 1200-foot peak of Moen Island in Chuuk State, the largest and most populous of the federated states.

Moen is one of eleven, high islands inside Chuuk Lagoon. Shaped like a melted triangle, the lagoon is circumscribed by 140 miles of coral reef. Once inside, we satisfied government officials and anchored near the Continental Hotel beside a yacht we knew from the Solomon Islands.

During WWII, this lagoon served as the primary anchorage, supply, and maintenance base for the Japanese Imperial Navy. In February 1944, five American aircraft carriers surrounded the atoll and sank in place the Japanese fleet: twelve warships, thirty-two supply ships and

249 aircraft. Their existence explains the attraction of scuba divers from around the world who visit the state.

Over the next few days, we slept and snorkeled, explored Moen by moped, and enjoyed restaurant food. One morning John took our dinghy to another boat to join a group for a scuba dive. I stayed behind, planning to relax and snorkel over the coral near our boat. As I rearranged some food storage inside the cabin, my muscles began to ache. I also felt feverish, far beyond the rising air temperature. Was it the flu or a flare up of the past week's ear infection? Soon I was burning up with a body temperature at 102 degrees.

A severe pain exploded in my skull, as if someone had clobbered me with a lead pipe. I screamed. My hands flew up to hold my head from breaking apart. As I sat down, severe cramps seized my calf muscles. The sudden attack left me panting with fear and shock. *What is happening to me?* My mind raced. I could think of no explanation for such an extreme attack. *I could die here alone. What can I do? How to get help?* By now John and the other divers would be underwater. Crippled with pain, I couldn't swim ashore. Desperate, I grabbed painkillers from our first aid kit, chugged them down with water, and laid down in a sweat-soaked tee shirt, groaning and suffering.

By the time John returned in midafternoon, my pain and fever had receded. He climbed into the cockpit animated with excitement of the diving experience. He looked down into the cabin for me.

"It was awesome," he said. "We went down about a hundred feet. Inside the ship, there were cups and forks set out, like they just had dinner."

I dragged to my feet, turned toward the cockpit door, and stared up at him. "Something horrible happened to me today," I said. As I explained the pain symptoms, a powerful chill shook me. I grabbed for my beach-towel shawl. "I took some codeine. Didn't help."

Concerned, but puzzled by my symptoms, he had no answer either.

The next day I felt better, though achy and weak, so John joined the divers again. I swallowed antibiotics and rested all day. Far out in the lagoon, he experienced cramps and fever like I described, though not the splitting headache. He aborted his dive and curled up in the boat to wait for the others to surface. Back home, he went to bed believing he had the flu.

The third day he felt fine and set out again with the divers. After he left, a hammer cracked my skull again and symptoms seized me with even greater force. The pain tore into my head and legs like a cleaver. Again, I burned with fever.

The fourth day I was fine, but John began writhing and crying out with the extreme pain and dangerous fever I had experienced. He endured several hours of misery before the pain left him exhausted. We were mystified, at a loss for an explanation.

On Day 5, it was my turn again. For a third time, I endured terrible pain and the fever increased to 104 degrees. Yachtie friends suggested we could have dengue fever or another tropical disease; they pushed us to abandon the first aid kit and find a doctor.

"We have to go," I said. "I can't endure this screaming headache. Something horrible is happening."

John nodded and retrieved his wallet. We dragged across the hotel grounds and climbed two blocks to the island hospital. Holding onto John's arm, I stared at my feet, summoning strength for each step. My jaw clenched with the muscle pain, the burning fever, and the fear of what I might face.

At the clinic, I slumped into the nearest chair, and John checked in with an island girl. My mind registered dust and disinfectant. I stared at the concrete block walls. As we waited our turn, my hands held my bowed head in a futile attempt to confine the agony. John frowned his concern. After forever, a nurse confirmed my fever and ushered us into a grey room with two chairs and a long metal table. A giant, Fijian doctor with compassionate eyes approached me. While I answered his questions, he turned to watch John spasm with sudden chills. He considered my symptoms and ascertained our travel route. "You came up from the Solomon Islands? Sounds like malaria. When did you stop taking the prophylactic tablets?"

"The day after we departed," I said and lowered my head with dawning guilt. The doctor in Gizo had warned us to continue chloroquine for two weeks after leaving the country. However, on the second day at sea, John stopped taking the pills, blaming them for a stomach upset, even though he may have been seasick. *And I had followed his lead. Dummy! Idiot!*

Bites from an infected mosquito, perhaps on our last night in the Solomons, introduced the malarial parasite into our blood. The alternating pattern of the symptoms reflected the life cycle of the parasites as they developed, multiplied, and entered my blood stream. The previous prophylactic tablets we took served to delay onset of symptoms for two months—the reason we had not suspected malaria.

"Only a special blood test during the parasite's active cycle can confirm the diagnosis," the doctor said, "So, assuming I'm right, I'm giving you both heavy doses of chloroquine."

The drug dulled our next attacks and proved him right. He then arranged for the military hospital in Guam to fly down a stronger drug. At our final clinic visit, the doctor mused, "Lucky you missed the drug-resistant strain—that can prove deadly." I began to cry as I considered our close call. I didn't want to die. I recalled the Baja storm, when I really didn't care if I did. But now, I loved the life I had that held such joy and promise.

We remained in Chuuk Lagoon for over two weeks, fighting malaria and slowly regaining our strength. After an early cyclone passed to the north, we set out at dawn to get across the coral lagoon safely during daylight. As the sun neared the horizon, we slipped through the reef pass for an overnight, moonlight cruise to the minor atoll of Puluwat.

In the short entry passage, the boat grounded twice, but we anchored in the aqua lagoon that could hold no more than six boats our size. The overhead sun illuminated colorful coral gardens in the crystal water below, and a brilliant white beach surrounded us. Again, I marveled that such beautiful places existed. With mask and fins, John inspected our hull and checked for any damage to the keel during our entry.

As we cleaned up the boat, a brown-skinned man of impressive size, dressed only in a scarlet loincloth, approached in an outrigger canoe, paddled by another man.

"Welcome. I am Ermit, Hereditary Chief of the villages," he said, refolding his legs in the canoe floor. "My brother just died. The stakes you see with orange leaves near the pass indicate a mourning period here."

I leaned closer and smiled my sympathy; John added his concern and our wish not to intrude on their customs.

The Chief nodded. "Normally the mourning period is three months, when no work or fishing is allowed in the lagoon." His face relaxed. "But I have shortened it to three weeks. It is finished this weekend." He smiled and confessed a desire to work on his sailing canoe.

"We have read about the legendary navigators of Puluwat and their ocean canoes." said John. "I hope we can meet them."

"Oh, yes. You must come in to visit," said Ermit.

I shared John's enthusiasm for meeting the residents of the pear-shaped atoll, about 2.5 miles long, which encompassed the lagoon and two primary islands. From the beach that afternoon, we followed a tidy trail past thatched huts. In the interior jungle, the heat became oppressive and my weak knees wobbled, but friendly folks guided us to Ermit's concrete abode. We joined him in the shade on a woven mat.

The chief talked about life in the atoll. He told us he was thirty-six, and conveyed, with good humor, the universal laments of a politician trying to please all his constituents in three villages within the cultural tenets. All eight hundred inhabitants lived on the eastern island called Puluwat, which included a few brick and concrete buildings such as meetinghouses, a grade school, a middle school, and two churches: Catholic and Lutheran.

"What do you do when someone gets sick out here?" I asked Ermit.

"We have no doctor. For very sick ones, the government will send a boat to take them to hospital in Chuuk. It's a rough trip into the wind and often they die on the sea."

A chartered boat costs $1500. He had argued with officials that it is cheaper and better for the people to train a nurse for each village, who could give treatment authorized by a doctor via the marine radio. "The government agreed, but I see no action yet." His tight lips betrayed little hope on that front.

"So, I have a book..." In a native dialect, he called to a girl who brought him a dog-eared paperback titled, *Where There is No Doctor*, published in California. I was skeptical, but noticed the pages held simple English text with basic illustrations that covered common illnesses, injury, and childbirth.

John changed the subject to his own burning interest. "The Puluwat navigators are considered the best at reading the ocean currents, the stars and other signs of nature and have crossed the open sea without a compass. Are they here now? Are the ocean sailing canoes here?" he asked. I had pondered the lengthy migrations of the Pacific Islanders and was also curious.

Ermit smiled with pride and called for a young man to take us to them. In a clearing near the lagoon, we joined a group of men also in loincloths. I approached them as if in the company of wizards or at least the most learned of men.

After pleasantries, a guide took us into a traditional canoe house to inspect the boats. Each long-distance canoe was not a dugout log but constructed in two parts and then lashed to a short, stout outrigger pontoon. Like elders of both sexes, the two lead navigators were slim. One of the elders explained their unique observation methods of navigating long distances without instruments. Nearby, a muscular young man sat rubbing coconut fiber on ample thighs to form the braided twine used to rig the sail. Beside him sat a three-year-old boy who mimicked his every movement but produced no twine. I witnessed knowledge being passed to the next generation by word and deed, like it had been for centuries.

Talk then turned to the Pacific War. With great sorrow and anger, the elders expressed deep hatred of the Japanese. They described the cruelty of their captors, who forced the people to build a sizable base camp and lighthouse on the western island of *Alet.* Infirm elders or those who refused to work had hands chopped off or were beaten to death. One man said that toward the end when their food ran out, soldiers resorted to eating some natives.

Back on our boat, I turned to John. "I can't believe that brutality—and cannibalism! And I don't think these people would lie about it, either. How could men be driven to such hostility, inhumanity?"

"Well, you know," he said, "terrible things happen in war, and much of what occurs is never spoken of again. Perhaps it should be."

The next morning, I called John on deck to watch three, loaded, outrigger canoes ghost across the lagoon under triangular sails. The hulls and outrigger pontoons were painted red and decorated with black symbols. A platform connecting the pontoon to the canoe provided a seat and a means of balancing the vessel in strong winds. The crew returned my hearty wave.

The family in another visiting yacht showed little interest in the local people and spent most of the week following fish around the outer reef. We joined them one day for a trek on the unoccupied island of *Alet.* It was hot-and-heavy going in the dense jungle before we reached the overgrown Japanese compound that had supported thirty thousand troops during the war. We entered a roofless, two-story house with Roman columns, cove moldings around the ceilings, and sculptured circular staircases. Strafing allied aircraft had added bullet-hole deco to the thick walls. I trudged up the stairs of the lighthouse to find solar panels operating a prism lamp and a magnificent view of the entire atoll.

Snorkeling and village visits occupied a part of every day. The local men were of medium height and bulky like Tongans. Some men, like Ermit, were rotund, but others exhibited well-muscled chests and arms.

All except tikes wore loincloths folded with a sash in front; from behind, only a g-string separated the cheeks of muscular gluts. The women were smaller, but wiry strong. Older women were comfortable topless, but young women covered up with T-shirts. Beyond their teens, most were plump and shy, covering their mouth with a hand, when I focused attention upon them. All except the elders spoke English.

On Easter Sunday, John succumbed to the flu, but I felt comfortable ashore and followed villagers to a two-story Lutheran Church that appeared like a white apparition out of the jungle. Men in loincloths stepped off the path and pulled on long pants and white shirts from bundles they carried. Inside the white concrete walls, I saw an altar decorated in red, green, and yellow flowers behind which a young pastor conducted the service in the local dialect. Parishioners sat on tan linoleum flooring: men to the left and ladies in dresses to the right. Women in the front rows belted out hymns, and men across the aisle harmonized in rumbling bass tones. The harmonics of their passionate voices covered my skin with goosebumps.

After the service, Ermit invited me to stay for their picnic. When he moved away, several women, deferential around men, came forward to greet me and offer me food. One explained how they prepared breadfruit and buried it for up to two years to preserve it without refrigeration. They offered me a vintage piece. The unappetizing, greenish brown, doughy mass tasted of vinegar; however, it would provide sustenance beyond the growing season when needed.

A white-haired woman, bent with osteoporosis, understood only our body language. She laughed at my amazement and cradled my arm. I smiled up at her and felt an emotional bond. A nearby woman evidenced a struggle with asthma; I returned later to give her my emergency inhaler, demonstrate the dose process, and experience her grateful relief. As I walked back to the beach, a shy teen named Rejoice beckoned me to her thatched hut, saying she had a gift for me. She opened a cloth containing ten, tiger-cowrie shells. Each polished beauty covered her hand. I selected one, and her smile lit up my life.

No material goods could provide the warmth and joy I felt among these women. I had spent most of my time building a lucrative career, but never stopped to experience, or even consider, human connections such as these. In early sobriety, I learned that helping others was an anecdote to self-pity, and these travel experiences exemplified another tenant promised in the AA literature: that God works through people. My happiness was proof.

The night before our departure for Guam, where our sailing days might end, John and I sat close together in the cockpit trying to sum up this journey together. The orange sky turned black, thousands of stars came into sharp focus, and we fell silent. A full moon rose over Puluwat palms, whose silhouettes lined the lagoon.

I felt a deep sense of peace and harmony and mouthed a prayer. "Let us remember to live a life of simple virtues and to pass on the love we have found in these islands."

CHAPTER 20

The U.S. Territory of Guam — Work and Other Natural Disasters

DAWN REMAINED MY FAVORITE TIME TO BE ALONE AT SEA to witness the birth of a new day, a blank page, opportunity unfolding.

After our second night at sea, I picked out tiny lights dancing on the horizon ahead. Above them, a mountain shadow emerged from the predawn mist. I stared, fascinated. I realized that this could be my last discovery of land while coming in from the sea, and I wanted to remember it. As the sky lightened to a pink hue, a tiny airliner with a flashing light rose from a high plateau and arched southward.

We're home. At least for a couple of years. Like a kid nearing Disneyland, my excitement grew. My head filled with all the amenities the U.S. Territory promised: endless electricity, marina convenience, varieties of fresh food, a dentist, television news, and jobs to rebuild our savings. This island, 780 miles north of the Equator, also offered swaying palms and coral lagoons. I anticipated an ultimate paradise. A goal fulfilled.

For forty years, Guam existed as a peaceful protectorate of the U.S. (Navy), until Japan seized the island on the same day it attacked Pearl Harbor. The Japanese enslaved and brutalized Guamanians for thirty months before Americans recaptured the island in 1944. Now, forty-six years later, Japanese tourist dollars there exceeded contributions of the U.S. government.

I woke John by shaking his shoulder. "I found Guam. It's floating out here, right where it should be." I turned to the stove for another cup of coffee.

Later, we sat in the cockpit eating cinnamon oatmeal and watching the thirty-mile-long island take shape against a lighter sky. Harnessed to a warm trade wind, *Renaissance* carved through blue-grey water toward land. John looked pensive. "Did you know that Magellan discovered Guam? Up here in the western Pacific, it was only the first island he hit after four months at sea." He stretched his arms over his head. "He was the first white guy to cross the Pacific…started out from the bottom of South America totally blind as to the size of this ocean."

"Well, we've covered a lot of it on our journey too," I said, squinting up at the full mainsail. "It's been a great ride. Glad I came along."

"Oh, we're not done yet," he said. I did not encourage him to elaborate.

On April 6, 1991, four-and-a-half years after we sailed from San Francisco, we lowered sails before the dark bluff outside Apra Harbor. Inside, the smell of diesel fuel assailed us from the commercial port. Yachtie friends monitored our radio call to the harbormaster and called back to welcome us. We cleared with U.S. Customs, and reunions began next to the steel shipping container they called a yacht club. We lazed for hours on that warm beach and shared travel experiences. I felt none of my former impatience with people; now I truly cared about them. Yes, I noticed the drinkers, but they provoked none of the anxiety I felt among them in Mexico. A couple from our California marina drove us around town and left us excited at the prospect of living in Guam.

The next day, our bubble burst. A mail package from home contained an IRS demand for delinquent taxes and penalties in excess of $29,000. Phone calls confirmed that our taxman had ignored our account for years while he sank into dementia. With depleted savings and desire to avoid further penalties, finding jobs became urgent. We parked the boat in a new marina some distance from the port, purchased a beat-up Toyota, and offloaded excess gear into a storage unit.

John endured a short, but dangerous expedition with FEMA, then became a salesman for Guam Freight Forwarding. After three frantic months of job searches, I signed on as a project administrator at Concrete Constructions-Guam, an Australian company with a contract to build an addition onto the Guam Hilton Hotel. The CCG General Manager, a tall, loose-jointed sort, possessed a ready smile, but expected productivity and a fifty-five-hour week. As the only female on the professional team, I accepted lots of good-natured ribbing but was delighted to be able to pick up computer skills I had missed as Microsoft Windows was evolving.

For a stalwart blue-water sailing vessel with over 20,000 miles under her keel, poor *Renaissance* had to be embarrassed at her situation. She sat trussed up in a sissy marina, no longer able to even swing with the breeze at anchor. Offending her sleek lines, an air conditioner jammed her forward hatch, a TV antenna tangled her rigging, and panty hose hung drying in the head. The crew she protected for years abandoned her for the sunny part of each day.

Living on the boat allowed us to save most of our income, as well as the luxury of swimming in the clear water that flowed over the reef and through the marina. However, this environment came with a risk. Guam resides in "Typhoon Alley," and storms began forming east of Guam in March. By September, three of them had built to typhoon strength (over 75 mph) but passed north of us. The following month, Typhoons Orchid, Pat, Ruth and Seth threatened, but passed to our south. Quite accustomed to such storms, Guam maintained the Harbor of Refuge in a dredged delta behind the commercial port. Its fixed moorings could shelter about a hundred small boats. We traveled to the Refuge during some storm threats and became familiar with its layout and procedures.

In November, Typhoon Yuri concentrated its power around a distinct eye and targeted us with gusts up to 100 mph. As it approached, we unplugged from the marina and sailed north ten miles to Apra Harbor. Inside the Refuge, the harbormaster assigned us a rectangular space on an underwater grid of concrete moorings. There we secured *Renaissance* among other boats aligned in columns and rows. Anxious about the storm danger, we huddled inside our boat to wait, hopping this ogre would also draw away from the island. As night descended, fierce winds and tension rose. At 9:00 P.M., local radio reported the fast-moving typhoon had passed fifty miles south of us. We escaped without loss or injury. However, many island structures sustained extensive damage, and power outages lasted for days.

With the repeated stress of warnings and the destruction caused by Yuri, my ultimate paradise began to tarnish with risk. Back at the marina, I insisted we discuss our situation. "We're here to pay off our debt, but we are facing these storms with no insurance on the boat. She's our primary asset! Besides, *Rennie*'s overdue for maintenance and could break down. She'd be hobbled, subject to further injury, and we'd be homeless."

"Yeah, I checked. Without a military connection, there's no place here to haul out the boat to work on her," he said.

"We can't leave Guam during typhoon season. So, what are our options?"

"Sailing *Renaissance* back via Seattle after the season would be a real bitch of a trip…and the cost to ship her to California is twenty-five grand. Not good." He squirmed in his seat and looked down at his hands. "After we finish work here, we can sail west to Manila for haul-out services and continue cruising." He paused, anticipating me. "Guam might not be the right place for us to settle, but I won't leave the cruising lifestyle."

"Never say never," I said, also dissatisfied with these choices. "I guess we can decide next year…if we survive this one."

The storm season faded, Christmas decorations went up, and island life returned to the hum of a frontier town. Even without storms, the Government of Guam ("GovGuam"), by far the largest employer, seemed unable to keep electric power flowing with its poorly maintained generators.

Besides complaints about unreliable power and water, John began to carp about local politics and the lack of professional sales opportunities. Retail sales bored him. Since our arrival, he had been making long-distance efforts to reconcile with his mother, now that his father was gone. I thought this might reflect the same yearning I felt for the family warmth we had experienced throughout the Pacific. In December, his mother loaned him funds to purchase (with a partner) a small mini-storage business. He loved working outside and rented new units as fast as they built them. He auctioned off abandoned goods himself and made a success of the business.

The dawn of 1992 provided endless balmy days that lulled us back into paradise mode. As I returned home from work one day, a charter boat captain at the marina handed me a fresh *mahimahi* abandoned by a vacationer rushing to catch a plane. I completed my scuba diver certification. On the weekends, we snorkeled among the corals with yachtie friends and enjoyed frequent potluck socials at the marina. We spent Sundays learning more about the island. The indigenous Chamorro people, descended from early Polynesian wanderers, represented 40% of the 135,000 population and most were employed by GovGuam. Anderson Airforce Base covered a large section of the island, yet few of their residents attended traditional festivals in outlying villages like we did. One day on his sales route, John happily accepted an invitation to lunch with some locals—until he discovered they were grilling fruit bats, a Pacific island delicacy. He had conquered his queasiness with fish; but bats, never.

The AA fraternity supported many meetings around Guam. Now with seven years of sobriety, I chaired a culturally-diverse AA meeting. Being a leader and spending time with newcomers gave me the satisfaction of helping others to recover and served as a constant reminder that I remained only one drink away from a drunk.

My position at CCG became the most exciting, most challenging—and most fun—of any I ever held. Keeping up with the Aussie guys ten hours a day and five on Saturday was tiring, but I loved being part of the team. By summer, herds of shipping containers filled with heavy equipment arrived, along with more Australian men and a few wives. They set up a 3,000-square-foot office at the hotel site, where I monitored subcontractor progress and OSHA safety compliance. Led by animated Eddie, the freewheeling general foreman, the site office reverberated like the Tower of Babel with a crazy mix of Chamorro, Korean, Tagalog, Chinese and English corrupted by Aussie slang, Tennessee twang, and Dutch profanity. To encourage the team spirit, the company hosted lavish holiday and lively beach parties, which John and I appreciated even without the boozy content.

After a year on the job, I earned paid vacation time and chanced a solo journey back to Boston to join a profound reunion with my father, super stepmom, three siblings, and their spouses. The ribbing and recollections among us recalled a happy childhood. I realized how much I missed family and appreciated the stable life I had known growing up there. My Puritan ethic of hard work and addiction to travel would remain, but oh how my world had expanded.

Unlike the previous year's typhoon season, the worst storm arrived first. Forecasters underestimated tropical storm Omar as it approached from Chuuk in August, 1992. From the space photos published in the daily paper, it looked enormous. When it stalled and intensified, we took no chances. John topped up fuel and carried our air con unit with excess gear to the mini storage. I filled water tanks and prepared the boat for sea.

Outside the breakwater, we motored north toward Apra Harbor. A brisk wind disturbed the sea and fueled my anxiety. We discussed plans and prospects with this tempest which looked much stronger than Yuri. I tried to expel some fear as I yammered away about saving our boat. John stood stiff behind the wheel.

Inside the Refuge, the harbormaster assigned us to a central position in the underwater grid of moorings, and we began work to secure *Renaissance* among the other boats. The 300-foot bluff of Nimitz Hill behind us provided shelter from the wind, but it also trapped the heat and humidity. My sensitive skin flushed red in protest as we assembled our mooring materials under a hot sun. In snorkel, mask and fins, John thrashed about in the shallow water to connect metal shackles to rebar loops ten feet below the surface, bow and stern, on each side. I fed double anchor lines out to him. Back on deck, we pulled the lines taut to hold the boat in equal, four-point restraints. Late that afternoon, Omar attained typhoon status.

The next morning more boats arrived to fill slots on the grid. While John cut lengths of hose for chafe guards, I organized rain gear, food, pillows, and tools to be handy. The Coast Guard predicted a direct hit with gusts over 150 mph. We met with our neighbors on each side to discuss tactics.

After lunch, the sky darkened, and the wind increased to a shrill whistle in the rigging. At 4:00 P.M. Omar waged a full-on attack. The heavy air tasted of salt and soot. With a last look at the vessels that surrounded us, we hunkered down inside the cabin. The rigging rattled and the mast transferred wind vibrations to us via the cabin floor. Waves of rain came in with the gusts, pounding the deck as though we sat under Niagara Falls. The roaring deluge greyed out the groan of our straining lines.

The wind exceeded 60 mph, wailed for three hours, and then increased. Silhouetted in a yellow glow from the port, a sailboat behind us heeled over and stayed at a forty-degree angle. Higher gusts knocked us over; I sat down hard and braced with my arms to stay upright. I peered up at our arched ceiling for some assurance it would protect us should a mast (maybe ours) crash down on our deck.

"Sustained wind must be over a hundred now," John yelled over the din.

"I hope no one breaks loose," I called. "Even if we hold, those bigger guys beside us could smash us to bits."

We tried to play cards but lost our place with each gusty blast. I picked up a novel and read the same paragraph four times. We listened and waited.

The VHF distress channel squawked with reports of roofs flying off and an untended yacht loose in Apra Harbor. Our AM radio, its antenna gone, crackled with static. The barometer plummeted and bounced on the bottom of its gauge. Suddenly the wind dropped, and the rain subsided, which signaled the arrival of the eye of the storm. The sky lightened to grey. Like us, boat crews dashed on deck to replace chafe guards and into the water to inspect shackle-mooring connections.

After an hour's peace, Omar's wind wound up like a siren. We ducked below as gusts attacked from the opposite direction. Darkness deepened. Our home heeled over to the gunnel for the interminable duration of an explosive gust. I smoked and watched through a porthole for trouble. I played solitaire at the table, holding cards under my forearm to keep them from sliding off the table when we lurched.

Refusing a sandwich, John started a crossword puzzle. The Coast Guard channel confirmed 120 mph sustained winds and reported two Navy ships had dragged anchors and grounded in Apra Harbor.

The awning on a nearby boat ripped loose with a loud crack. Instinctively, I threw my arms over my head for protection. My playing cards flew to the floor. I looked toward John for comfort but saw him huddled against the hull.

He looked up at me, sat up, and revisited his crossword puzzle. "Five spaces, Utah's neighbor," he yelled.

"Who cares?" I yelled back with my arms flailing. "This paradise came with a giant string attached. It's too damn dangerous. We gotta get out of here!"

I pressed against the main bulkhead with a pillow around my head, praying we could survive without a collision or crash of heavy debris. After midnight, we slept fitfully in separate corners, while irregular gusts roared and torrents washed the decks.

At dawn, the wind had subsided to a mere 50 mph. We slid open the aft hatch to peek out. *Amazing.* No boats had broken loose, although two sustained broken masts. In time, the radio reported a major disaster in Guam: widespread destruction from waves and flying debris, a thousand roofs torn off and three-thousand people homeless. With estimates of $450 million in damage, FEMA and the Red Cross promised to fly in relief supplies.

Following Typhoon Omar, island power and water did not flow for four weeks. Most businesses remained closed, many never recovered. Quite shaken like other yachtie survivors, we remained for two weeks in the refuge, even though it became a torrid sauna. No one had air conditioning, but, at least on board, we were self-sufficient with water, power and stove.

I had endured enough risk and discomfort. It was time for a decision.

After dinner one night, we sat in the cockpit hoping for a breeze as the sun hit the horizon. "It's miserable here," I said. "And not worth the risk to lose this boat or sustain injury in these storms." I pulled at my sweaty tee shirt. "We are recovering financially, but Guam has limitations like any remote place. I want to be closer to my family and find an enduring community. When my job ends, I want to go home."

John turned away, thoughtful or petulant, I couldn't tell which, so I continued. "We have to begin saving for retirement. You've only a dozen years to work before you are sixty-five—"

"We continue cruising!" he said. "After CCG, you can get another good job here, and I'll get crew to help deliver the boat to the Philippines—"

"What? Me work, to pay for you to cruise? And let you and *Rennie* get in trouble without me? She's my baby too. No way, Jose!" I said.

"Wait!" he said. "You can meet me there, then we can cruise Thailand and Malaysia."

I shook my head. "Oh no, dear dreamer. No more split ups. We go on together."

With the CCG Hilton project fully-staffed, I moved back to the town office to become the Human Resources Department. The General Manager chided me, "You're our 'token Yank.' I need you to make certain we comply with all the U.S. labor laws here. Oh, and get H-2 work visas for a load of laborers we're bring in from Korea, China and the Philippines."

I accepted the challenge. John, an HR Manager before we met, helped me climb a steep learning curve. I convinced management to accept some operational restraints. I wrote a personnel manual and set up medical and 401(k) plans equal to the benefits of the Australian staff. I put in long hours, but now I did it for the intellectual workout that tropical lolling lacked, as well as the human interaction I now sought and enjoyed.

During the remainder of 1992, typhoon warnings came almost weekly, and our dash to The Refuge became a tedious routine.

In the spring of 1993, John left me on board to spend three weeks on the mainland reconnecting with his family. He attended his son's wedding with his daughter and accompanied his mother back to her Florida retirement village. He returned grateful to be back in the fold, at least tentatively, but admitted it would take more effort to maintain their trust.

The next time I brought up our future, he listened to my proposal to return home. "Beyond midlife, we face greater risk of illness or injury," I said. "Back there, you can find a more interesting job than here—with benefits to protect our assets. We can live simply and save for retirement and more travel later."

"I know," he allowed. "And it's best I get back into the job market before I'm fifty-five." He sighed and looked up the mast. "Keeping the boat involves a sizable, upfront investment, whether we continue cruising or not."

I suspected he had been thinking about our last discussion in light of his trip home, and I was pleased. "I hate leaving the cruising lifestyle, too, but we'll find another boat to cruise the Caribbean, I promise."

"OK," he said. We smiled at each other with relief of a decision made, together. I grabbed his hands in mine, pulled him close, and kissed him.

At age fifty-one I wanted less heat and more reliable electricity; a little stability and some cerebral opportunities to evolve further. We decided to stay in Guam through the summer until CCG completed the hotel project, so I could receive severance pay, while John enhanced the ministorage business. We talked about a road trip through western national parks to settle in Florida for some quality time with aging parents.

Yachtie friends began leaving in their boats. Sharing perils and epiphanies with them over the years created a closeness I had never-before experienced with people; yet we were, by definition, destined to separate. But worse, how could we leave our *Renaissance?* She had carried us a long way, taught and protected us, and showed us an amazing world. Our parting was painful, but necessary. Perhaps she would facilitate the rebirth of another couple. We advertised her in the local paper, and three people responded with offers.

We signed her bill of sale and turned away from her. From the roadbed above the marina, we watched her move beyond the breakwater. I sniffled and turned to find tears in John's eyes too. We shared a long, wordless hug.

John found a buyer for his share of the ministorage business. I said a fond goodbye to the Aussie blokes at CCG, as they wrapped up at the Guam Hilton. In an apartment, we sorted tokens of our transformational journey and packed them for shipment to California. And then, we dove deep into the aqua island waters for a last visit with Pacific sea life.

As departure day neared, I reflected on how this journey began. With a vague goal of seeking a more meaningful life, I had left behind a specialized career that evaporated anyway. I had been an aloof workaholic, a hapless alcoholic, in a marriage I had bruised. Then, I discarded trappings of success as defined by others.

The seven-year journey from our trial cruise awakened and transformed me. I thrived in a sparse but adventurous lifestyle in magnificent settings with my best friend and lover. My attitude and priorities changed. I opened myself to a fascinating world, tested myself, and gained confidence in overcoming obstacles. I discovered acceptance, compassion and unconditional love. This journey represented my greatest success and a source of strength I often drew upon later.

In Guam, my last hope of finding paradise, I embraced a new goal: a balanced life with John to include less work, less material excess, and more time for family, friends, and helping others.

Like success, paradise is an illusion, something we must define for ourselves.

EPILOGUE

An Unexpected Retirement

"HELP! HELP! JU-DEEE! AHHHHH AH."

I jerk out of a dream of being lost in a maze. *What?* It's dark. *Where am I?*

"Help meeee!"

A searing nerve shoots down my leg, and I jerk it up. I'm in our guest room.

He screams out again in pain and anxiety. "Help, help, help!" My gut cramps with panic, or is it fear? It seems I just got to sleep.

Another scream knifes through my brain. *OK! I'm awake.* I'm up. I'm running across the house to the master bedroom where John lays thrashing in sweaty sheets. He looks up with rheumy, pleading eyes. "I can't stand it! Ow, ow, oowwww."

The clock glows 1:35 A.M. "I'm here." I grip his hand. "Do you want another Dilaudid, you can have another one now." I lie—it's really not due until two o'clock.

Oh God. I'm frantic for a solution, some way to help him—and I know this pill could trigger another terrifying narcotic hallucination. *Do something,* my brain commands.

For the past five years, life has delivered variations of this heartache during which my husband has suffered with severe backpain, the source of which doctors could never explain. He was bedridden two of those years. Helpless, I have stood by him through agonizing recoveries after each of five failed spinal surgeries and a morphine-pump implant. Together, we had traveled through diagnostic detours and dead ends, anxiety attacks that mimicked heart attacks, and interminable emergency room visits. Every two weeks we endured an hour-long drive each way to his pain management specialist to adjust the dosages in the pain pump, change meds, and add narcotic patches.

John has given up trying to read and stares at the TV, uncomprehending. His only relief comes with unconsciousness. *This is insanity. There has to be an answer!*

After leaving Guam, we drove an old Dodge van from San Francisco to the east coast to spend time with our families. In Florida, we settled in a small apartment near elderly parents and looked for work. I wasn't concerned—we'd done this before. However, this transition was more difficult than the previous one. We were both over fifty, without current computer skills or local job references. Initially we accepted what jobs we could find. Within a year, my father and stepmother passed away. We bought an old house and spent weekends together renovating 1400 square feet—endless space with limitless water, hot water, plastic chairs, and fresh vegetables—even ice cream-on-demand. At the end of ten years, we sold that house for a nice profit.

We moved north to a home with a dock in South Carolina and bought a forty-foot sailboat to fulfill our retirement dream of sailing the Caribbean Sea. One night as we fitted her out, John swung aboard from the dock and felt a twinge in his lower back; the next morning three burly firemen lifted him from the boat to the dock on a stretcher. Thus, began his ordeal—and mine.

The year the pain began, he was sixty-four with no health insurance coverage. While we sought a remedy for his escalating pain, the medical bills consumed our retirement savings at an alarming rate. His health came first. To recover our down payment and stop loan payments on the boat, we returned it to the dealer. When strangers drove it away, John said nothing, but I knew he was heartbroken to let it go. I was too. My eyes burned with tears, and I hugged him close. I used the cash to negotiate discounts on bills for his subsequent surgeries.

Later I sat struggling with a new computer application he had set up to pay bills. He called out in that unremitting pain and interrupted my tenuous concentration. Further frustrated, I exhaled with the growl of an angry bear, but I rushed to attend him.

Most nights, I doze until dawn. I arise restless with a mind that runs like a treadmill. A dropped spoon starts a crying jag. Sometimes I wake to a dream scream and rush across the house to find him sleeping. I read the same paragraph in a magazine three times before I throw it down. I wallow helpless, hopeless until jerked into the next crisis.

My symptoms typified Post Traumatic Stress Disorder. People recommend physical activity to relieve my stress, and sometimes I swim. From our boat dock, I yell my frustrations across the rippled river. Then, I leap high, hands at my sides, and smash my head into the water. I swim head down with closed fists punching the water to release the anger I cannot show in the sickroom. It helps. I return to the house flaccid, until another anguished cry cramps my muscles for fight or flight.

After the second year of this chaos, stress hospitalized *me* with a bleeding ulcer. Without hesitation, my brother and his wife arrived from Florida to care for us both. Antidepressant drugs stabilized me, but for John, the hell continued: more diagnostics, more surgery, and more hopes dashed. Between his hospitalizations, he tried so hard to rehabilitate, but the pain continued unrelenting. The stress of watching his suffering cramped my neck. While he lay drugged and bedridden, his mother died alone in Florida.

Emergency room doctors warned against the high levels of narcotics prescribed by his pain specialist. One afternoon John awoke yelling and repeating, "A 'copter landed! Marines in the backyard. They're attacking us!" He thrashed, screamed craziness, and shook a fist at me as I tried to calm him. I backed away, fearful. After one of my many 911 calls, police and ambulance staff stood in our bedroom arguing over jurisdiction. I turned and left the room; my hands covered my ears, my eyes squeezed shut.

After three years of this, an emergency appendectomy hospitalized me again for ten days, and my brother arrived again to help us. I promised I would take better care of myself. A church friend, aware of my suffering, asked if I would leave my husband. I stared at her, having never considered that.

I found a psychologist who understood a caregiver's reality: "You can't help him, if you are sick." She increased my antidepressant dosage, ordered me to employ a nurse's aide for a few hours a week, and insisted I get away for at least a week's respite. I booked a five-day cruise for myself, and John's daughter arrived from the west coast to relieve me.

On that cruise liner, it took me two days to decompress and sit still. The crew and vacationers offered ready smiles that lifted me. The ship offered me great luxury—I could sleep, eat, and participate when I wanted. My mind cleared, and I regained some hope. From the observation deck, I gazed across the ocean to the horizon; a tear fell on my shirt as I recalled our journey together. I grieved for him, for myself, and for the life we had together. It was all gone.

We don't discuss the future anymore. John may remain homebound, but I will continue to comfort and encourage him. Today, my dreams are smaller, expectations blurred, and choices limited. I pray only that he is released from pain.

We could have put off our dreams until retirement—but ours arrived with no options. I suffer no regrets. I am grateful for memories of what we shared together. We chose travel in midlife equipped with work experience, still-supple minds, and the physical ability to embrace the world fully. The adventure deepened our marriage, changed my priorities, and fortified me for future change and challenges.

I still try to accept the things I cannot change and live one day at a time; but whatever comes now, I am sober, and we are still together.

Go or stay? I say Go. Follow a dream. Try something different, in depth, in a different culture. Breakaway—at least for a few months.

ACKNOWLEDGMENTS

I am most grateful for the optimism and determination of my husband, John McCandless, who engineered this amazing journey and supported my struggles to become a sober and empathetic woman. I wrote much of this memoir over the twelve years I was his caregiver, but he read only a few drafty chapters before he died in 2016.

The book began after I transcribed journals which covered eight years of our adventures, but the story took shape after I joined the Lowcountry Women Writers in Beaufort, South Carolina. I remain most grateful for this patient, inciteful, and clever critique group, especially the founding members: Stephanie Edwards, Martha Weeks, Katherine Brown and Joan Harris. I also appreciated the literary expertise and insights of my editors, John Reed and Cherri Randall as well as several beta readers who helped me stay focused on my theme.

For my personal evolution described herein, I am indebted to the Pacific Islanders, the yachties, expats, and recovering alcoholics we met who opened my eyes, in addition to my family, for their love and assistance during our travels.

Judy McCandless 2019

BIBLIOGRAPHY

Carroll, Rick, and Yosihiko H. Sinoto. Huahine: Island of the Lost Canoe. Honolulu: Bishop Museum Press, 2005

Melville, Herman. Typee: A Peep at Polynesian Life. London: Penguin Classics, 1996

Hinz, Earl R. Landfalls of Paradise: Cruising Guide to the Pacific Islands (5th edition). Honolulu: University of Hawaii press, 2006. *We used the first edition, published by Western Marine 1981) It is an informative history and overview of Oceania excellent for planning.*

Lucas, Alan. Cruising New Caledonia and Vanuatu. Melbourne: Castle Books, 1981. *Alan published several other cruising books covering Australia, PNG and the Solomon Islands all with helpful diagrams and photos of anchorage approaches, but many are now out of print.*

Stanley, David. South Pacific Handbook, 3rd ed. Chico: Moon Publications, 1986. *This practical guide, part of a series, was extremely helpful to us in all territories of Oceania where we traveled. A more recent update (2004) is available.*

Werner, David, Carol Thuman, and Jane Maxwell. Where There is No Doctor, A Village Health Care Handbook Berkeley: Hesperian Foundation, 2017 *This classic public health text, first published in 1970, is still used in all remote areas of the world and recommended for travelers to those areas.*

Wood, Charles E. Charlie's Charts of Polynesia. Surrey (Canada): C.E. Wood, 1983. *Another very informative reference book with detailed charts of small harbors, but it may be out of print.*

ABOUT THE AUTHOR

Judy McCandless grew up four blocks from the sea in Marblehead, Mass. with a passion for travel. At age 24 she drove to California for adventure and stayed to marry, complete a B.S. in business and advance to corporate positions in contract negotiation, the last one with Westinghouse in Sunnyvale, CA. She lived aboard a sailboat with her husband for seven years, traversed 20,000 miles of open ocean and has achieved over thirty years of sobriety. She can be reached at WorkaholicsAdrift@gmail.com